T0047474

ACT® READING
PREP

The Staff of The Princeton Review

PrincetonReview.com

Penguin
Random
House

The Princeton Review
110 E. 42nd Street, 7th Floor
New York, NY 10017
Email: editorialsupport@review.com

Published in the United States by Penguin Random House LLC,
New York.

Some of the content in ACT Reading Prep has previously
appeared in English & Reading Workout for the ACT, published
as a trade paperback by Random House, an imprint and division
of Penguin Random House LLC, in 2019.

ISBN: 978-0-525-57034-9
eBook ISBN: 978-0-525-57038-7
ISSN: 2691-7165

The Princeton Review Publishing Team
Rob Franek, Editor-in-Chief
David Soto, Senior Director, Data Operations
Stephen Koch, Senior Manager, Data Operations
Deborah Weber, Director of Production
Jason Ullmeyer, Production Design Manager
Jennifer Chapman, Senior Production Artist
Selena Coppock, Director of Editorial
Orion McBean, Senior Editor
Aaron Riccio, Senior Editor
Meave Shelton, Senior Editor
Chris Chimera, Editor
Patricia Murphy, Editor
Laura Rose, Editor
Alexa Schmitt Bugler, Editorial Assistant

Penguin Random House Publishing Team
Tom Russell, VP, Publisher
Alison Stoltzfus, Senior Director, Publishing
Brett Wright, Senior Editor
Emily Hoffman, Assistant Managing Editor
Ellen Reed, Production Manager
Suzanne Lee, Designer
Eugenia Lo, Publishing Assistant

Editor: Eleanor Green and Patricia Murphy
Production Editor: Emma Parker and Liz Dacey
Production Artist: Gabriel Berlin and Jason Ullmeyer

Printed in the United States of America.

10 9 8 7 6 5 4 3 2 1

Acknowledgments

The Princeton Review would like to thank Cynthia Ward for her leadership on this book, as well as the following individuals:

Anne Bader, Kevin Baldwin, Nicole Cosme, Anne Goldberg-Baldwin, Bradley Kelly, David Mackenzie, Danielle Perrini, and Jess Thomas.

Additionally, thank you to Gabriel Berlin, Emma Parker, and Liz Dacey for their time and attention to each page.

Special thanks to Adam Robinson, who conceived of and perfected the Joe Bloggs approach to standardized tests, and many of the other successful techniques used by The Princeton Review.

—Amy Minster
Content Director, High School Programs

Contents

Get More (Free) Content vi

Part I: Orientation 1

1   Introduction to the Reading Test 3

    Welcome 4

    Fun Facts About the ACT 4

    Strategies 7

2   How to Approach the ACT Online Test 11

Part II: Reading 27

3   The ACT Reading Test 29

    Fun Facts About the Reading Test 30

    Personal Order of Difficulty (POOD) 30

    Pacing 32

    Process of Elimination (POE) 32

    The Basic Approach 32

4   Working with the Answer Choices 39

5   Dual Passages 51

6   Additional Reading Strategies 63

    Work Just the First Sentences 64

    Work the Passage "As You Go" 67

    Find the Golden Thread 76

7   Advanced Reading Strategies 81

8   Reading Practice Drills 97

Part III: Practice Reading Tests 111

9   Reading Practice Test 1 113

10 Reading Practice Test 1 Answers and Explanations 123

11 Reading Practice Test 2 137

12 Reading Practice Test 2 Answers and Explanations 147

13 Reading Practice Test 3 159

14 Reading Practice Test 3 Answers and Explanations 169

15 Reading Practice Test 4 181

16 Reading Practice Test 4 Answers and Explanations 191

Part IV: College Admissions Insider 203

Get More (Free) Content
at PrincetonReview.com/prep

As easy as 1•2•3

1 Go to PrincetonReview.com/prep or scan the **QR code** and enter the following ISBN for your book:

9780525570349

2 Answer a few simple questions to set up an exclusive Princeton Review account. *(If you already have one, you can just log in.)*

3 Enjoy access to your **FREE** content!

Once you've registered, you can...

- Get our take on any recent or pending updates to the ACT

- Take a full-length practice ACT

- Get valuable advice about the college application process, including tips for writing a great essay and where to apply for financial aid

- If you're still choosing between colleges, use our searchable rankings of *The Best 388 Colleges* to find out more information about your dream school.

- Check to see if there have been any corrections or updates to this edition

Need to report a potential **content** issue?

Contact **EditorialSupport@review.com** and include:

- full title of the book
- ISBN
- page number

Need to report a **technical** issue?

Contact **TPRStudentTech@review.com** and provide:

- your full name
- email address used to register the book
- full book title and ISBN
- Operating system (Mac/PC) and browser (Chrome, Firefox, Safari, etc.)

Look For These Icons Throughout The Book

PROVEN TECHNIQUES

APPLIED STRATEGIES

MORE GREAT BOOKS

STUDY BREAK

CONSIDERING AN ACT® PREP COURSE?

Pick the Option That's Right For You

ACT COURSE

 OUR MOST POPULAR!

- 24/7 on-demand tutoring
- 36+ hours of classroom instruction
- Review and practice books

ACT TUTORING

- 18-hours of customized tutoring package
- Expert tutors matched to your goals
- Interactive score reports to track progress

ACT SELF-PACED

- 1-year access to online materials
- Practice drills for self studying

www.PrincetonReview.com | 1-800-2-REVIEW

Part I
Orientation

Chapter 1
Introduction to
the Reading Test

WELCOME

The ACT can be an important part of college admissions. Many schools require or recommend their applicants submit either SAT or ACT scores. It's worth keeping in mind, though, that the importance of these tests will vary among the many colleges and universities in the United States. If you haven't already, make sure to research whether the ACT is required or recommended for admission to the schools you plan to apply to.

During the COVID-19 pandemic, many schools went test-optional to account for the numerous students whose SAT and ACT tests were canceled. Some of those schools have returned to requiring test scores, while others have not yet but still may. For the most up-to-date information on the schools you are interested in, check out their admissions websites.

Even if ACT scores are optional, you may still want to submit them if you think your great ACT scores will boost your chances of acceptance. Furthermore, ACT scores are often used for scholarships, so it can be worth putting time into preparing for the test if you can save a good amount on your college education in return.

When colleges require standardized test scores, they will accept either SAT or ACT scores. The expert advice of The Princeton Review is to take whichever test you do better on and focus your efforts on preparing for that one.

Since you bought this book, we assume you've already made the decision to boost your ACT score. This book provides a strategic and efficient way to improve your scores, specifically for the Reading test. For a more thorough review of content and exhaustive practice, we recommend *ACT Prep* and our *ACT Practice Questions* book.

For more on admissions, see The Princeton Review's *The Best 388 Colleges* or visit our website, PrincetonReview.com.

FUN FACTS ABOUT THE ACT

The ACT is nothing like the tests you take in school. For example, you may read a lot for school, but do you take speed tests on comprehension?

All of the content review and strategies we teach in the following lessons are based on the specific structure and format of the ACT. Before you can beat a test, you have to know how it's built.

See The Princeton Review's companion books, *ACT English Prep*, *ACT Math Prep*, and *ACT Science Prep*.

Structure

The ACT is made up of four multiple-choice tests and an optional Writing test.

The five tests are always given in the same order.

English	Math	Reading	Science	Writing
45 minutes	60 minutes	35 minutes	35 minutes	40 minutes
75 questions	60 questions	40 questions	40 questions	1 Essay

Scoring

When students and schools talk about ACT scores, they mean the composite score, a range of 1–36. The composite is an average of the four multiple-choice tests, each scored on the same 1–36 scale. If you take the Writing test, you'll also receive an additional Writing score on a scale of 2–12. The Writing score is an average of four 2–12 subscores: Ideas and Analysis, Development and Support, Organization, and Language Use and Conventions. Neither the Writing test score nor the combined English plus Writing English Language Arts score affects the composite. Be sure to check ACT's website to determine whether your target schools want you to take the ACT Writing test.

Students also receive subscores in addition to their (1–36) composite ACT score. These indicators are designed to measure student performance and predict career readiness, as well as competency in STEM (Science, Technology, Engineering, Mathematics) and English Language Arts. ACT believes that these additional scores will give students better insight into their strengths and how those strengths can be harnessed for success in college and beyond. In addition to the 1–36 score for each of the tests and their composite score, students now see score breakdowns in the following categories:

- **STEM score:** This score represents students' overall performance on the math and science sections of the ACT. The goal of this score is to help students better understand their strengths in math and science and how they might use those strengths to guide their academic and career goals.

- **Progress Toward Career Readiness Indicator:** This is meant to help students understand the extent to which they are prepared for a future career. It can also help teachers guide their students toward numerous career pathways.

- **English Language Arts score:** This score measures achievement in the English, Reading, and Writing portions of the exam (for students who take all three of those sections), and it allows students to see how their performance compares with others.

- **Text Complexity Progress Indicator:** This is intended to help students determine how well they understand the kinds of complex texts they might encounter in college and whether they need to improve. This score is based on a student's performance on all of the reading passages.

There is also a section on the score report that breaks down each section into categories and tells you both how many questions there were in each category and how many of them you answered correctly. Some of these categories can be useful in helping you know what you need to study: for example, if you missed a lot of questions in the "Geometry" category, you should brush up your geometry skills. But if you did poorly in the "Integration of Knowledge and Ideas" category, it's not quite as obvious what you need to study. Don't worry about these scores, though—they're there because they align with federal academic standards, and school districts that use the ACT for standardized testing for all juniors want those scores, but colleges don't typically look at them for admissions purposes.

It's All About the Composite

Whether you look at your score online or wait to get it in the mail, the biggest number on the page is always the composite. While admissions offices will certainly see the individual scores of all five tests (and their sub-scores), schools will use the composite to evaluate your application, and that's why it's the only one that matters in the end.

The composite is an average: let the full weight of that sink in. Do you need to bring up all four scores equally to raise your composite? Do you need to be a superstar on all four tests? Should you focus more on your weaknesses than your strengths? No, no, and absolutely not. The best way to improve your composite is not to shore up your weaknesses but exploit your strengths as much as possible.

> To improve your ACT score, use your strengths to lift the composite score as high as possible.

You don't need to be a rock star on all four tests. Identify two, maybe three tests, and focus on raising those scores as much as you can to raise your composite. Work on your weakest scores to keep them from pulling you down. Think of it this way: if you have only one hour to devote to practice the week before the ACT, put that hour toward your best subjects.

Single-Section Tests and Superscoring

ACT has said that they will eventually allow students to take one, two, or three individual sections in a day, as opposed to needing to take the entire test. You will need to have taken a full ACT before using this option, and single-section tests will only be offered on the computer.

One piece of good news is that ACT has begun Superscoring. If you take the ACT more than once, ACT will automatically take your highest English, Math, Reading, and Science scores and average them together to calculate a new "Superscore" composite.

Sounds great, right? We think it is—this gives you the opportunity to show your best ACT score to schools. Colleges and universities still have the option whether or not to accept the Superscore, but for the schools that let you Superscore, this is all positive for you.

> Single-section testing is great, but research your goal schools' testing policies before relying on it!

Of course, you might have grabbed this book because you've already decided to take a single-section test. So let's move on so we can dive in to the good stuff!

Reading Score

There is no content to review for Reading. Instead, it's entirely skill-based. However, that does not mean that you cannot increase your Reading score. Quite the contrary! Learning the strategies necessary for answering Reading questions quickly and correctly and improving test-appropriate reading skills will lead to a higher score.

Time

Time is your enemy on the ACT. You have less than a minute per question on the Reading test, and there's no extra time for reading the passages. The Princeton Review's strategies are all based on this time-crunch. You can think of the Reading as an open-book test: you can neither waste all your time reading the whole book nor skip it all together.

STRATEGIES

You will raise your ACT score not by working harder but by working *smarter*, and a smart test-taker is a strategic test-taker. You will apply an effective and efficient approach and you will employ the common sense that frequently deserts us when we pick up a #2 pencil.

Check out these helpful Princeton Review signature strategies.

Each test on the ACT demands a different approach, and even the most universal strategies vary in their applications. In the chapters that follow, we'll discuss these terms in greater detail, customized for Reading.

Personal Order of Difficulty (POOD)

If time is going to run out, would you rather it run out on the hardest Reading passage or on the easiest? Of course, you want it to run out on the questions you are less likely to get right. The trick is to know how to pick your order of passages and questions.

Taking the ACT on the computer? Check out Chapter 2, our guide to the Computer-Based Test!

We'll discuss in greater detail what POOD means in Chapter 3, but for now, understand that you have to make smart decisions for good reasons quickly as you move through each test.

The Best Way to Bubble In

Work a page at a time, circling your answers right on the booklet. Transfer a page's worth of answers to the answer sheet at one time. It's better to stay focused on working questions rather than disrupt your concentration to find where you left off on the answer sheet. You'll be more accurate at both tasks. Do not wait until the end, however, to transfer all the answers from that test onto your answer sheet. Go a page at a time.

Now

Does a question look okay? Do you know how to do it? Do it *Now*.

Later

Will this question take a long time to work? Leave it and come back to it *Later*. Circle the question number for easy reference to return.

Never

Test-taker, know thyself. Know the topics that are your worst and learn the signs that flash danger. Don't waste time on questions you should *Never* do. Instead, use more time to answer the Now and Later questions accurately.

Letter of the Day (LOTD)

Just because you don't *work* a question doesn't mean you shouldn't answer it. There is no penalty for wrong answers on the ACT, so you should never leave any blanks on your answer sheet. When you guess on Never questions, pick your favorite two-letter combo of answers and stick with it. For example, always choose A/F or C/H. If you're consistent, you're statistically more likely to pick up more points.

Note: if you are taking the ACT on a computer, all of the questions will have answer choices A, B, C, D (or A, B, C, D, E on the Math test). On the paper-and-pencil ACT, every other question will have answer choices F, G, H, J (or F, G, H, J, K on the Math test).

Process of Elimination (POE)

On Reading, it's more important, and often easier, to know what's wrong and eliminate it rather than to try to find out what's right. You may have absolutely no idea what you have read, but you'll likely know what you haven't and be able to eliminate a few wrong answers. Using POE to eliminate at least one or two wrong answers will substantially increase your odds of getting a question right.

Proven Techniques

Familiarize yourself with these Princeton Review techniques before you dive into the practice drills.

Pacing

The ACT may be designed for you to run out of time, but you shouldn't rush through it as fast as possible. All you'll do is make careless errors on easy questions you should get right and spend way too much time on difficult ones you're unlikely to get right. To hit your target score, you have to know how many raw points you need. Your goals and strategies depend on the test and your own individual strengths.

On each test of the ACT, the number of correct answers converts to a scaled score of 1–36. ACT works hard to adjust the scale of each test at each administration as necessary to make all scaled scores comparable, smoothing out any differences in level of difficulty across test dates. There is thus no truth to the notion that any one test date is "easier" than the others, but you can expect to see slight variations in the scale from test to test.

This is the scale from the 2021-2022 free test ACT makes available at www.act.org. We're going to use it to explain how to pick a target score and pace yourself.

Reading Pacing

Scale Score	Raw Score	Scale Score	Raw Score	Scale Score	Raw Score
36	39-40	24	27	12	9-10
35	38	23	26	11	7-8
34	37	22	24-25	10	6
33	35-36	21	23	9	5
32	34	20	21-22	8	–
31	33	19	20	7	4
30	–	18	19	6	3
29	32	17	17-18	5	–
28	31	16	16	4	2
27	30	15	14-15	3	–
26	29	14	12-13	2	1
25	28	13	11	1	0

When it comes to picking a pacing strategy for Reading, you have to practice extensively and figure out what works best for you.

Some students are slow but good readers. If you take 35 minutes to do fewer passages, you could get all of the questions right for each passage you do. Use your LOTD for the passages you don't work, and you should pick up a few additional points.

Other students could take hours to work each passage and never get all the questions right. But if you find all the questions you can do on many passages, using your LOTD on all those Never questions, you could hit your target score.

Which is better? There is no single right answer to that. True ACT score improvement will come with a willingness to experiment and analyze what works best for you.

Be Flexible

The worst mistake a test-taker can make is to waste good time on bad questions. You read a question, don't understand it, so you read it again. And again. If you stare at it really hard, you know you're going to just *see* it. And you can't move on, because really, after spending all that time, it would be a waste not to keep at it, right? Actually, that way of thinking couldn't be more wrong.

You can't let one tough question drag you down. Instead, the best way to improve your ACT score is to follow our advice.

1. Use the techniques and strategies in the lessons to work efficiently and accurately through all your Now and Later questions.
2. Know your Never questions, and use your LOTD.
3. Know when to move on. Use POE, and guess from what's left.

Now move on to the lessons and learn the best way to approach the content.

Chapter 2
How to Approach the ACT Online Test

In this chapter, you'll learn what to expect on the ACT Online Test, including how to apply its computer-based features and our strategies to the question types in each section—English, Math, Reading, Science, and Writing.

If your ACT will be pencil-and-paper, skip this chapter.

At the time of this book's printing, the option to take the ACT online at a testing center was postponed. ACT also plans to offer at-home online testing, although an exact rollout date has not yet been announced. For up-to-date news on both options, check the ACT website.

WHAT IS THE ACT ONLINE TEST?

The ACT Online Test is the ACT that you take on a computer, rather than with a pencil and paper. Despite the name, you can't take the ACT from the comfort of your own home; instead, you'll have to go to a testing center (possibly your high school) and take the test on one of the center's computers.

The ACT Online Test has the same overall structure, timing, and number of questions as the pencil-and-paper ACT. The scoring, score range, and scoring method are also the same. If the ACT Online Test is basically the same as the pencil-and-paper ACT, who would take the ACT Online Test?

WHO TAKES THE ACT ONLINE TEST?

ACT has been offering versions of the ACT on computer since about 2016. The first students to take the ACT on the computer were students taking the test at school. Schools and school districts decided whether to give the test on the computer.

As of September 2018, all students taking the ACT outside of the United States take the test on a computer (except for those students with accommodations requiring the use of a traditional pencil-and-paper test).

ACT has indicated that eventually students in the United States will have the option of taking the ACT Online Test instead of the traditional pencil-and-paper version. Students choosing this option will get their scores in about two to three business days (e.g., take the test on Saturday, have your score the next Wednesday). However, at the time of this printing, no specific timeline was available.

Single-Section Retesting is an incredible option for students. However, colleges still have the option to accept or not accept these new scores. Research your target schools early so you know your options!

Single-Section Retesting

If you are happy with the score you receive from a single test administration, you will still have the option to send just that score to colleges. If your score in one section is not as high as you'd like, you will eventually have a chance to correct that. Students who have already taken the full ACT may choose to take one, two, or three sections again using Single-Section Retesting. ACT will then produce a "superscore" consisting of your best results in all tests (English, Math, Reading, Science, and Writing (if you took it)). Note that not all colleges accept a superscored ACT, so do your research before taking advantage of this option.

ACT ONLINE TEST FEATURES

So, besides the obvious fact that it's taken on a computer, what are the differences between taking the ACT on the computer and taking it on paper? Let's start with what you can't do on the ACT Online Test. You can't "write" on the screen in a freehand way. You're limited in how you're able to mark the answer choices, and each question appears on its own screen (so you can't see multiple questions at one glance). You will also be given a small "whiteboard" and dry erase pen with which to make notes and do work.

So, what features does the ACT Online Test have?

- Timer
  - o You can hide the timer by clicking on it.
  - o There is a 5-minute warning toward the end of each test. There is no audible signal at the 5-minute warning, only a small indicator in the upper-right corner of the screen.
- Nav tool
  - o You can use this tool to navigate directly to any question in the section.
  - o The Nav tool blocks the current question when opened.
  - o It also shows what questions you have flagged and/or left blank.
  - o You can flag questions in this menu.
- Question numbers at the bottom of the screen
  - o You can click on these numbers to navigate directly to any question in the section.
  - o These numbers also indicate whether a question has been flagged and/or left blank.
- Flag tool
  - o You can flag a question on the question screen itself or by using the Nav tool.
  - o Flagging a question has no effect besides marking the question for your own purposes.
- Answer Eliminator
  - o Answer choices can be "crossed-off" on-screen.
  - o An answer choice that's been eliminated cannot be chosen and must be "un-crossed-off" first by clicking the answer choice.
- Magnifier
  - o You can use this to magnify specific parts of the screen.
- Line Mask
  - o This tool covers part of the screen. There is an adjustable window you can use to limit what you can see.
  - o This is an excellent tool if you need an aid to help you focus on specific parts of the text or figure.
  - o However, not everyone will find this tool useful, so do not feel obligated to use it!
  - o Note that you cannot highlight the text in the window of the Line Mask.
- Answer Mask
  - o This tool hides the answer choices of a question.
  - o Answers can be revealed one at a time.
- Screen Zoom
  - o This tool changes the zoom of the entire screen (as opposed to the magnifier, which magnifies only one part of the screen).
  - o Your screen zoom setting will remain the same from question to question.
- Highlighter
  - o You can use this tool to highlight parts of passage text, question text, or answer text.
  - o You cannot highlight within figures.
  - o If you highlight in a passage with multiple questions, your highlights will only show up on that question. (In other words, if you highlight, for example, question 1 of a Reading passage, questions 2–10 of that same passage will not show those highlights.)
  - o Turning off the highlighter tool removes your highlights.

- Shortcuts:

Keybind	Function	Keybind	Function
Ctrl + H	Toggle Help	Ctrl + Enter	Answer Question
Ctrl + F	Flag Item	Alt + M	Toggle Magnifier
Ctrl + I	Item Navigation	Alt + H	Toggle Highlighter
Alt + P	Previous Question	Alt + E	Toggle Answer Eliminator
Alt + N	Next Question	Alt + A	Toggle Answer Masking
A-E or 1-5	Select Alternative	Alt + L	Toggle Line Masking

- The Writing test is typed, rather than written by hand.

You will also be given a small "whiteboard" and dry erase pen with which to make notes and do work.

HOW TO APPROACH THE ACT ONLINE TEST

The strategies mentioned in this chapter are thoroughly discussed in our comprehensive guide, *ACT Prep*, so be sure to pick up a copy of that book if you have not already done so. These approaches were created in reference to the pencil-and-paper format, but they still apply to the ACT Online Test with some adjustments. This chapter assumes your familiarity with these strategies and will show you how to make the best use of them given the tools available in the computer-based format.

You will also want to incorporate some computer-based practice into your prep plan. ACT's website has practice sections for each of the four multiple-choice parts of the test and for the essay. We recommend that you do those sections toward the end of your preparation (and close to your test date) to give yourself an opportunity to practice what you've learned on a platform similar to the one you'll be using on the day of the test.

> **Remember!**
> Your goal is to get the best possible score on the ACT. ACT's goal is to assign a number to you that (supposedly) means something to colleges. Focus on your goal!

If you are planning to take the ACT online, you should practice as if you're doing all your work on the computer, even when you're working in a physical book. Use a highlighter, but don't use the highlighter on any figures (as the ACT Online Test won't let you do so). Use your pencil to eliminate answer choices and have a separate sheet of paper or a whiteboard to do any work you need to do, instead of writing on the problem itself.

Also, remember that our approaches work. Don't get misled by ACT's instructions on the day of the test—their way of approaching the test won't give you the best results!

Overall

Your Personal Order of Difficulty (POOD) and Pacing goals will be the same on the ACT Online Test as on the pencil-and-paper version. Because it is easy to change your answers, put in your Letter of the Day (LOTD) when skipping a Later or Never question. Use the Flag tool on the Later questions so you can jump back easily (using either the navigation bar at the bottom of the screen or the Nav tool).

Process of Elimination (POE) is still a vital approach. On both the paper-and-pencil ACT and the ACT Online test, there are more wrong answers than correct ones. Eliminating one you know are wrong helps you to save time, avoid trap answers, and make a better guess if you have to. On the ACT Online Test, you cannot write on the test, but you can use the Highlighter tool. Turn on these tools (and the Line Mask, if desired) at the beginning of the English section and use them throughout.

ENGLISH

The Basic Approaches to both Proofreader and Editor questions are the same on the computerized and the paper versions of the ACT. When you decide to skip a question to come back to it Later (for example, a question asking for the introduction to the topic of the passage before you've read any part of the passage), flag the question so you can easily jump back to it before moving on to the next passage. When you have five minutes remaining, flag your current question and use the Nav tool to make sure you've put in your LOTD for any questions that you haven't done, then return to your spot and work until time runs out.

For a comprehensive review of all sections of the ACT and the strategies mentioned throughout this chapter, check out our book, *ACT Prep.*

When you work Proofreader questions, you can use the Highlighter tool to help you focus on the key parts of the text. Let's see an example:

Sneaking down the corridor, the agent, taking

care not to alert the guards, <mark>spotting</mark> the locked door.

- A. NO CHANGE
- B. spot
- C. are spotting
- D. spots

Use the tools available to help you focus on the key portions of the text. Practice with a highlighter when you're working on paper (instead of underlining with your pencil).

Here's How to Crack It

Verbs are changing in the answer choices, so the question is testing subject/verb agreement. The verb must be consistent with the subject. *The agent* is the subject; highlight it:

Sneaking down the corridor, <mark>the agent</mark>, taking

care not to alert the guards, <mark>spotting</mark> the locked door.

- A. NO CHANGE
- B. spot
- C. are spotting
- D. spots

The agent is singular, so the verb must be singular. Eliminate (B) and (C), as both are plural. *Spotting* cannot be the main verb of a sentence, so eliminate (A). The correct answer is (D).

Similarly, the Highlighter tool is helpful on Editor questions. Use the tool on both the passage and the question to help you focus on the relevant parts of each.

As it's name suggests, the Indian fantail is not native to North America. In fact, its establishment here was quite accidental. In 1926, the San Diego Zoo acquired four pythons from India for its reptile exhibit. The long trip from India required, that, the pythons be provided with food for the journey, and a group of unfortunate fantails was shipped for just that purpose. Two lucky fantails survived, and their beautiful appearance caused the San Diego Zoo to keep and breed them for the public to see. Eventually, some of the animals escaped captivity and developed populations in the wild, all thanks to those two birds!

Given that all the choices are true, which one provides the most relevant and specific information at this point in the essay?

- **A.** NO CHANGE
- **B.** and they have quite an appetite.
- **C.** because no one wanted them to starve.
- **D.** and they are quite picky in what they'll eat.

Here's How to Crack It

The question asks for the *most relevant and specific information*. Highlight those words in the question. The first sentence of the paragraph focuses on the *Indian fantail*, and the sentence after the underlined portion discusses *(t)wo lucky fantails*. The final sentence discusses *the animals* that escaped. Highlight these words in the paragraph.

Your screen should look like this:

As it's name suggests, the Indian fantail is not native to North America. In fact, its establishment here was quite accidental. In 1926, the San Diego Zoo acquired four pythons from India for its reptile exhibit. The long trip from India required, that, the pythons be provided with food for the journey, and a group of unfortunate fantails was shipped for just that purpose. Two lucky fantails survived, and their beautiful appearance caused the San Diego Zoo to keep and breed them for the public to see. Eventually, some of the animals escaped captivity and developed populations in the wild, all thanks to those two birds!

Given that all the choices are true, which one provides the most relevant and specific information at this point in the essay?

- **A.** NO CHANGE
- **B.** and they have quite an appetite.
- **C.** because no one wanted them to starve.
- **D.** and they are quite picky in what they'll eat.

Use POE, focusing on whether the choice is consistent with the highlights in the passage. The sentence as written discusses *a group of unfortunate fantails*; keep (A). Choices (B), (C), and (D) do not talk about the Indian fantail; instead, they focus on the pythons. This is inconsistent with the goal of the sentence and the content of the paragraph; eliminate those answers. The correct answer is (A).

―――――――――○―――――――――

Finally, you can't write in the passage, so you'll need to approach the Vertical Line Test slightly differently. On the paper-and-pencil ACT, you would use this strategy for questions about punctuation, drawing a vertical line where the punctuation breaks up the ideas in the text. On the computerized ACT, you should use the whiteboard to handle these questions.

―――――――――○―――――――――

I'm not searching for a ghost or yeti, my phantom is the Indian fantail. These beautiful creatures are members of the pigeon family, but you could not tell that by looking at them.

- **A.** NO CHANGE
- **B.** yeti: my phantom
- **C.** yeti my phantom
- **D.** yeti, since this

Here's How to Crack It

Punctuation is changing in the answer choices, so the question is testing STOP and GO punctuation. There is Half-Stop punctuation in (B), so use the Vertical Line Test. You cannot draw a line in the text, so draw a "t" on your whiteboard, with "yeti" in the bottom-left and "my" in the bottom-right:

Read each part of the sentence and determine whether it is complete or incomplete. *I'm not searching for a ghost or yeti* is a complete idea; write "C" in the upper-left of the "t." *My phantom is the Indian fantail* is also a complete idea; write "C" (for "complete") in the upper-right of the "t." Your board should look like this:

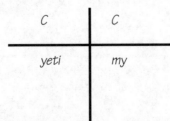

Eliminate any answer that cannot link two complete ideas. Both (A) and (C) use GO punctuation, which cannot link complete ideas; eliminate (A) and (C). Choice (D) adds *since*, which makes the idea to the right of the line incomplete. However, *since* is used to show time or causation, which does not work in the context of the sentence. Eliminate (D). The correct answer is (B).

MATH

First off, you'll still need to bring your calculator to the ACT Online Test—which is a good thing! You're already comfortable with your personal calculator, so there will be one less thing to worry about on the day of the test.

> **Write it down!**
>
> It is tempting to do all your work in your head. Don't fall into this trap! It's easier to make mistakes when you're not writing down your work, and you'll often have to "go back" if you don't have something written down. Use your whiteboard!

When choosing questions to do Later, flag the question so you can easily navigate back to it after doing your Now questions. Do put in your LOTD when doing so; you don't want to accidently leave a question blank! When you get the five-minute warning, finish the question you're working on, flag it (so you can find your spot easily), then put in your LOTD for every unanswered question. Then you can go back to working until time runs out.

Use the Highlighter tool to highlight what the question is actually asking, especially in Word Problems. Of course, you'll want to use your whiteboard when working the steps of a math problem (don't do the work in your head!).

ACT Online Geometry Basic Approach

Because you can't write on the screen, the Basic Approach for Geometry questions needs a few slight tweaks:

1. Draw the figure on your whiteboard (copy if it's provided; draw it yourself otherwise). If the figure would be better drawn differently from the way ACT has drawn it (for instance, a similar triangles question), redraw the figure in a way that will help you answer the question.

2. Label the figure you drew on your whiteboard with the information from both ACT's figure and the question.

3. Write down any formulas you need and fill in the information you know.

Let's see how that works on a question.

In the figure below, triangle *ABC* is similar to triangle *DEF*. What is the length of *EF* ?

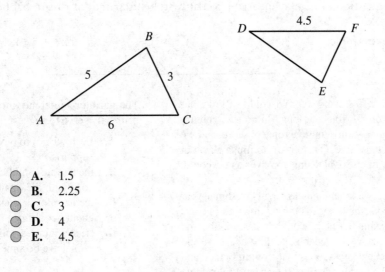

○ **A.** 1.5
○ **B.** 2.25
○ **C.** 3
○ **D.** 4
○ **E.** 4.5

Here's How to Crack It

The question asks for the length of *EF*, so highlight that in the question. Follow the Geometry Basic Approach. Start by drawing the figure on your whiteboard. Because the triangles are similar, redraw triangle *DEF* to be oriented the same way as *ABC*. Label your figure with the given information.

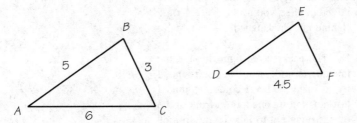

Write down the equation you need and fill in the necessary information. *AC* corresponds to *DF*, and *BC* corresponds to *EF*. Set up a proportion: $\frac{AC}{DF} = \frac{BC}{EF}$. Fill in the information from your figure: $\frac{6}{4.5} = \frac{3}{x}$, where *x* is equal to *EF*. Cross-multiply to get $6x = 3(4.5)$, or $6x = 13.5$. Divide both sides by 6 to get $x = 2.25$. The correct answer is (B).

READING

First off, there are a few differences between the pencil-and-paper ACT and the ACT Online Test. In the ACT Online Test, there are no line references; rather, the relevant part of the text is highlighted. The passage will also "jump" to the highlighted text if it's off the screen when you go to that question. This may disorient you at first: be prepared for this to happen.

Let's see an example.

...protested every step. We could still run, but, Hook worried, for how long? In a cross-country race, only a team's top five runners score, and we weren't those five. Our job was to finish ahead of as many of our rival teams' top fives as we could.

Leah was a senior that year, my freshman year. All season, she'd been counting down to this last race, praying her body wouldn't say *No*. She and I joked that we needed to go to the Knee Store and pick out new knees, ones that wouldn't crack and pop and burn all the time. It was hard to watch a teammate in that much pain, but Leah was a trooper, never slacking from workouts, never stopping to walk, never losing sight of the next person in front of her to catch.

The crack of the starter's pistol sent us surging out of that little crop of trees and onto the race course. I hollered, "See you at the Knee Store!" Behind me, she laughed.

The pack stayed tight through the first quarter-mile, and I was surrounded by so many bodies I couldn't think. I just ran, putting one foot in front of the other, trying not to fall. Trying to look beyond the jostling mass surrounding me, I could barely...

The narrator's references to the Knee Store primarily serve to suggest that:

- **A.** Leah wishes to buy better knee supports.
- **B.** the narrator and Leah use humor to cope with their pain.
- **C.** the narrator desires to learn more about her injury.
- **D.** Leah's injuries, unlike the narrator's, have become unbearable.

> Reading on a computer screen can be disorienting. Practice by reading articles or other passages on the computer when possible.

Here's How to Crack It

The question asks what the *references to the Knee Store...suggest*. The references to the *Knee Store* are highlighted in the text. Note that the text has shifted down to the highlighted portions. The window indicates that Leah and the narrator *joked that we needed to go to the Knee Store*. Leah *laughed* after the narrator referred to the Knee Store. Therefore, the answer should be consistent with joking and laughing. Choice (A) takes the reference too literally; eliminate (A). "Humor" is consistent with the text's references to *joked* and *laughed*; keep (B). There's no indication of the narrator's goal to *learn more about her injury*, nor does the text support the idea that Leah's injuries *have become unbearable*, eliminate (C) and (D). The correct answer is (B).

When you have five minutes remaining, flag your current question and use the Nav tool to make sure you've put in your LOTD for any questions that you haven't done. Then return to your spot and work until time runs out. If you've just started or finished a passage, click through the questions to look for Easy to Find questions in the remaining time, and don't forget to put in your LOTD for any question you don't answer!

The biggest difference between the ACT Online Test and the paper-and-pencil ACT is that you can only see one question on the screen at a time. Rather than looking over the questions at a glance, you must click from question to question. This feature means that the Reading Basic Approach (covered below) needs to be modified in order to be as time efficient as possible.

ACT Online Reading Basic Approach

1. **Preview**
   Read only the blurb—do not go through and map the questions. Instead, write the question numbers on your whiteboard to prepare to Work the Passage.

2. **Work the Passage**
   This step is *even more* optional on the ACT Online Test than on the pencil-and-paper ACT. You haven't mapped the questions, and your highlights only show up on one question. If you do decide to Work the Passage, ensure that you're getting through the passage in 2–3 minutes. More likely, you'll find it best to just skip this step and move on to the questions after reading the blurb and setting up your whiteboard.

   > You don't get points for reading—only for answering questions correctly. Determine whether Working the Passage helps you answer questions correctly and quickly.

3. **Select and Understand a Question**
   When Selecting a Question, if a question is Easy to Find (a portion of the text is highlighted or you Worked the Passage and know where in the passage the content you need is), do it Now. Understand the question, then move on to Step 4.
   If the question is not Easy to Find (in other words, you don't immediately know where in the passage to go), write down the question's lead words on your whiteboard next to the question number. Include EXCEPT/LEAST/NOT if the question includes those words. If there are no lead words, flag the question.

   After you do all the questions with highlights, then Work the Passage, scanning actively for your lead words. Once you find a lead word, do the corresponding question. After answering the questions with lead words, finish with the flagged questions.

4. **Read What You Need**
   Find the 5–10 lines you need to answer the question. Remember that only the quotation will be highlighted—the answer is not necessarily highlighted. You must read the lines before and after the highlighted portion to ensure that you find the correct answer to the question. If you find the Line Mask tool helpful, use it to frame your window.

5. **Mark the Answer in the Passage**

   As you read, look for evidence for the answer to the question in your window and highlight it using the highlighter tool. (You can highlight text that ACT has already highlighted—the color will change to "your" highlighting color.) As always, base your answer on the words in the passage as much as possible.

6. **Use POE**

   Use the Answer Eliminator tool to narrow the answer choices down to one answer. If the question is an EXCEPT/LEAST/NOT question, instead write ABCD on your whiteboard and mark each answer T or F for True or False (or Y or N for Yes or No) and choose the odd one out.

Dual Reading Approach

The questions for Dual Reading passages are grouped with the questions about Passage A, then those about Passage B, then those about both passages. Each question should be labeled with an indicator for the passage the question refers to. Work each passage separately, answering all the Passage A questions you plan to answer before moving onto the Passage B questions.

You should also write down the Golden Thread of each passage on your whiteboard—either after Working the Passage or after finishing the questions on that passage. That will aid you in answering the questions about both passages.

SCIENCE

The overall approach to the Science test is the same on the ACT Online Test as it is on the traditional pencil-and-paper version. There are a few small adjustments to make, but the overall strategy remains the same.

The Flag tool is very important when identifying Later passages and questions. On a Later passage, flag the first question, then put your LOTD for every question on the passage. Make a note on your whiteboard of the first question in the passage so you can easily jump back to the passage.

When working a Now passage, you may still encounter a Later question. For these stand-alone Later questions, flag the question but don't put in your LOTD. When you get to the end of a passage, check the bar at the bottom of the screen to make sure you have answered every question up to that point.

Science Basic Approach

There are a few small changes to the Science approach when taking the ACT Online Test.

1. **Work the Figures**

   You can't highlight the figures. Experiment with taking quick notes about the variables, units, and trends on your whiteboard and determine whether it helps you find the needed information quickly.

2. **Work the Questions**
   Highlight the words and phrases from the figures in the question to help guide you to the relevant information.

3. **Work the Answers**
   Use the Answer Eliminator tool to work POE on answer choices with multiple parts.

Let's look at an example.

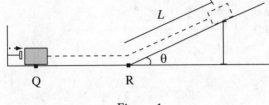

A block is placed on a frictionless horizontal surface at point Q. The block is pushed with a plunger and given initial velocity v along the horizontal surface. At point R, the block slides up a ramp with coefficient of friction f to a maximum distance L along the ramp. The distance between points Q and R is 1.0 m.

Figure 1

Figure 2, below, shows how L varies with v for different f on a ramp with $\theta = 20°$. Figure 3 (on the following page) shows how L varies with v for different θ on a ramp with $f = 0.1$.

Key	
Marker	f
□	0.15
○	0.30
△	0.60
×	0.90

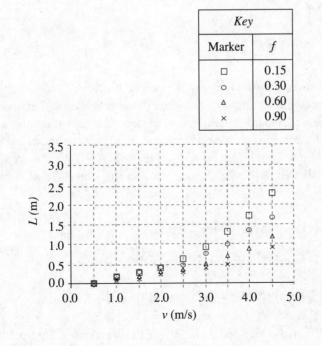

Figure 2

> **Scrolling Passages**
> Most passages in Science will require scrolling down to see all the figures. Look for a scroll bar for every passage!

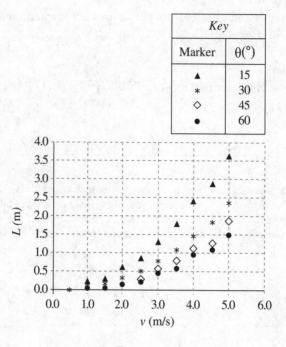

Figure 3

If $f = 0.90$ for the sliding block and $v = 5.5$ m/s, L will most likely be closest to which of the following?

- **A.** 0.3 m
- **B.** 0.7 m
- **C.** 1.5 m
- **D.** 3.0 m

Here's How to Crack It

Start by Working the Figures. Figure 1 shows the points Q and R and variables L and θ, but there are no numbers or trends. Figure 2 shows a direct relationship between L (m) and v (m/s); mark this on your whiteboard. Furthermore, the legend gives values of f; as f increases, L decreases. Mark these relationships on your whiteboard. Figure 3 also shows a direct relationship between L (m) and v (m/s); the legend, however, gives θ (°). As θ increases, L decreases. Put these on your whiteboard as well. Note that Figures 2 and 3 show both L and v; Figure 2 has f, whereas Figure 3 has θ.

Your whiteboard should look like the following:

Figure 2: L (m) ↑ v (m/s) ↑ and f ↑ L ↓

Figure 3: L (m) ↑ v (m/s) ↑ and θ ↑ L ↓

The question refers to the variables f, v, and L; highlight those variables. Figure 2 has all three variables. The highest value of v given in the figure is 4.5, so start there and use the trend to make a prediction about a v of 5.5. At $v = 4.5$ and $f = 0.90$, L is approximately 0.9. The trend is increasing, so a v of 5.5 must result in an L value of greater than 0.9; eliminate (A) and (B).

An *L* value of 3.0 would be higher than any value already in Figure 2, and extending the trend for the line created by the *f* = 0.90 marks would not result in *L* increasing to 3.0 by the time *v* reaches 5.5; eliminate (D). Although you can't physically extend the line because it's on a computer screen, it may be a good idea to use your finger to trace where you would draw on the screen. The correct answer is (C).

You'll still approach the passage that's all or mostly text as if it is a Reading passage. Unlike in Reading, you will want to Map the Questions during the Preview step, as there will not be a group of questions about each passage like there is in the Dual Reading passage. Instead, the questions will not be asked in any particular order, so use your whiteboard to map out which scientist(s) or experiment(s) each question refers to. As with the other sections, at the five-minute warning, flag your question, put in your LOTD on any unanswered question, then keep working until time runs out.

WRITING

As you have probably guessed, you'll be typing the Writing test on the ACT Online Test. But before we get to writing the essay, there are a few minor points to note about the format of this test on the computer.

First, you won't be able to highlight when Working the Prompt or Perspectives, so be sure to write notes on your whiteboard. Second, ACT has given the prompt and perspectives on one screen, then repeated them on the screen that contains a text box. Feel free to do your work on the screen within the text box. If you're used to making your essay outlines on a computer, you can use the text box to do so here, as long as you remember to delete any notes before the section comes to an end.

When writing the essay, all the same points apply to both the pencil-and-paper and online tests (have a clear thesis, make and organize your arguments in a way that is easy to follow, etc.). When you have 5 minutes left, quickly type up a conclusion paragraph (if you haven't already), then go back and finish up your body paragraph ideas. It's more important to have a conclusion than it is to have perfect body paragraphs. Finally, spend a minute or two at the end to quickly fix any obvious typos or grammatical issues.

When you practice the Writing test at home, type your essay in a word processing program instead of writing it by hand. Be sure to turn off spell check, as the ACT does not provide it, so you don't want to rely on it.

That's it! Everything you've learned for the pencil-and-paper ACT can be applied to the ACT Online Test with a few small tweaks. You've got this!

Part II
Reading

Chapter 3
The ACT
Reading Test

Even students with superior reading skills find this test to be tough. To crack the Reading test, you have to learn a strategic approach of *how* to work the passages in an order that makes sense for you. In this chapter, you'll learn how to order the passages and apply a basic approach.

FUN FACTS ABOUT THE READING TEST

The Reading test consists of 4 passages with 10 questions each, for a total of 40 questions that you must answer in 35 minutes. There are many factors about the structure of this test that make it difficult. For one thing, the particular passages will obviously vary from test to test, so you can't predict whether you'll like the topics or find the passages interesting. Moreover, the questions are in neither order of difficulty nor chronological order. And while line references in the questions can make finding answers easier, it's not unusual to have passages with only two or three line-reference questions.

There are, however, several consistent factors on each test. The passages are all roughly the same length. One of the four passages will consist of two shorter passages that are somehow related, but the total word count will still be about the same. The passages always come in the same order: Literary Narrative (including Prose Fiction), Social Science, Humanities, and Natural Science. But just because that's ACT's order doesn't mean it has to be yours.

Possibilities to Note

It's possible that ACT will simply call the last three passages "Informational" rather than specifying that they are Social Science, Humanities, and Natural Science. Regardless of the headings, you can expect to see passages from these categories.

One passage in the Reading test may be accompanied by one or more tables, graphs, or other figures that contain information related to the passage.

PERSONAL ORDER OF DIFFICULTY (POOD)

To get your best score on the Reading test, you have to pick your own order of the passages, and on each passage, your own order of the questions. When time is your enemy, as it is on the ACT, find and work what's easier for you up front. Leave what's difficult for you for last, or skip it altogether.

Proven Techniques

The Passages

You can't risk doing the passages in the order ACT provides *just* because they're in that order. What if the Natural Science passage turned out to be the easiest and you ran out of time before you could get to it?

Every time you take the ACT, for practice and for real, pick the order of the passages that makes sense for you. There are four issues to consider when picking your order. After you've done a few practice Reading tests, you may find there's an order you usually stick to. But pay attention to the particulars of each test and be willing to adapt your order.

1. Your POOD

Use your own POOD to identify the genres and topics you like best. For example, do you rarely read fiction outside of school? Then the Literary Narrative is unlikely to be a smart choice for you to do first. The topics, however, may change your mind. Read the blurbs to see if that day's Social Science, for example, is a topic you know more about than, say, the Humanities.

2. Paragraphs

The passages are all roughly the same length, but how they're arranged in paragraphs will differ. It's much easier to find answers on a passage with a reasonable number of smaller paragraphs than on a passage with just a few huge paragraphs.

3. Questions

The answers to Reading questions with line references are easier to find in the text, so the more questions with line references the better. Glance at the questions. Do you see many with numbers? That's a great sign.

4. Answers

Difficult questions tend to have longer answers. So look for questions with short answers. Just like with line references, the more the better.

Be Flexible and Ruthless

Picking your order isn't a long, deliberative process. Use the practice tests in Chapters 9, 11, 13, and 15 to determine a typical order, but always be prepared to adapt. Take 30 seconds at the start of every Reading section to look at the topics, paragraphs, questions, and answers to confirm or adapt your order.

Need More Practice?
Our *ACT Practice Questions* book provides 6 tests' worth of Reading passages. That's 24 passages and 240 questions.

The Questions

Same song, different verse. You can't do the questions in the order ACT provides. They're not in order of difficulty, and they're not in chronological order. Instead, think of *Now, Later, Never*. First, do Now questions that are either easy to answer OR for which the answer is easy to *find*. After you complete the Now questions, do the Later questions that are both difficult to answer AND for which the answers are difficult to find. Depending on your pacing goal, there may also be some Never questions—remember to use your Letter of the Day on these questions. If you are taking the computer-based ACT, you can flag a question to come back to later.

1. Easy to Answer

ACT describes the questions in two categories: those that ask you to *refer* to what is directly stated and those that require you to *reason* an implied meaning. In other words, reference questions ask what the author *says*, while the reasoning questions ask what the author *means*. It's easier to answer "what does the author say?" than to answer "what is the author *really* saying?"

2. Easy to Find the Answer

A question that's easy to answer won't actually be easy if you can't find the answer in the passage. On the other hand, a reasoning question with a line reference tells you exactly where you can find the answer. Even if it's a tougher question to answer, do it Now if you know where to find the answer.

In a perfect world, we'd give you an exact order to follow every time. The ACT is not a perfect world. Instead, you have to consider the particulars of each test and know how to make an order that works on that test. In general, it's a solid strategy to start with the line-reference questions, and then move on to the other specific questions. Leave general questions for last.

PACING

With just 35 minutes to do 4 passages and 40 questions, you don't have even 9 minutes for every passage. But should you do all 4 passages? Think about the pacing chart we discussed in Chapter 1. You may hit your scoring goals if you take more time to do fewer passages. On the other hand, you may decide that you can't get all of the questions on one passage right no matter how much time you spend. In that case, you may be better off doing all the Now questions on all four passages and skipping all the harder questions.

35 ÷ 4 ≠ 36

Whichever pacing strategy works for you, don't treat all the passages you work equally. That is, even if you work all 4, you shouldn't spend 8.75 minutes on each. Spend more time on your best passages and spend less on your worst. For example, you might spend 12 minutes on your first passage, 10 minutes on your second, 8 minutes on your third, and 5 minutes on your last. This is just an example: practice, practice, and practice to figure out a pacing strategy that will help you reach your target score.

PROCESS OF ELIMINATION (POE)

Many students destroy their pacing with one particular bad habit on the Reading test: they keep rereading and rereading part of the passage, trying to understand the answer to a tough question. But they're ignoring the one advantage of a multiple-choice test: the correct answer is right on the page. Use POE to eliminate three wrong answers to find the correct answer. It's not always easy to answer these questions, but you will likely be able to spot at least one wrong answer. In fact, using POE is a crucial step of our 6-step Basic Approach.

Now that you know how to pick your order of the passages, it's time to learn the Basic Approach.

> The computer-based test requires some modifications to this approach. If you're taking the test on the computer, check out Chapter 2.

THE BASIC APPROACH

The Reading test is an open-book test. You wouldn't read a whole book and answer all the questions from memory, so you shouldn't do that on the ACT. Instead, you need a smart, effective strategy.

Step 1: Preview

This step involves two parts.

First, check the blurb to see if there is additional information other than the title, author, and copyright. There usually isn't, but occasionally there is. You have to check each time to see if this one time is the exception. Here's an example of a blurb from a humanities passage.

HUMANITIES: This passage is adapted from the article "The New Wave of Graphic Arts" by Brian Becker, which originally appeared in *Art Pages* (© 2009 Art Pages).

Second, map the questions. Put a star next to each line or paragraph reference, and underline the lead words. By lead words, we mean words you'll actually find in the passage. Don't underline generic words like "main idea" or "how the author would characterize."

Here are ten mapped questions.

21. One of the main points the author formulates is that:

22. Based on the information in the passage, during which of the following periods were authors LEAST likely to produce works that <u>combined words and images to tell their stories?</u>

23. The passage's author indicates that compared to many of the works that came before it, <u>William Blake's *Vala, or the Four Zoas*:</u>

☆ 24. The main purpose of the fourth paragraph (lines 53–73) is to make clear that <u>contemporary graphic novels</u> are:

☆ 25. As it is used in line 24, the word *marked* could reasonably be said to mean all of the following except:

☆ 26. As it is used in line 39, the word *idle* most nearly means:

27. The passage suggests that before the <u>1700s</u>, compared to the images in graphic novels and comic books, <u>images in illustrated books:</u>

28. According to the passage, an important factor in the <u>difficulty of defining the graphic novel</u> with any precision is that:

29. It can most reasonably be inferred from the passage that one aspect of graphic novels that has made <u>literary critics</u> interested in the genre since the <u>1970s</u> is the ability of graphic novels to:

30. Which of the following is NOT answered by the passage?

Spend no more than 30 seconds mapping the questions. Do not read the questions thoroughly for comprehension at this stage. Just spot the line and paragraph references to star and the lead words to underline.

Do look at the lead words you've underlined, however. They tell you something about the main idea before you've read one word of the passage: this passage is about graphic novels.

Step 2: **Work the Passage**

You have two options for how to work the passage: Up Front or As You Go. We'll work the passage Up Front for now. We'll discuss working As You Go in Chapter 6.

If you opt to work the passage Up Front, spend no more than 3 minutes on the passage. Look for and underline your lead words. If you struggle with time, read only the first sentence of each paragraph. You'll read what you need to answer specific questions.

Here are the first sentences of each paragraph to our passage, with the lead words from some questions found and underlined.

> The graphic novel is a true anomaly in contemporary literature; there is <u>no set definition</u> for what the genre is, so there are many disagreements as to its origins and characteristics.
>
> Many scholars suggest that the first European author to <u>combine words and images</u> in this way was the British poet and artist <u>William Blake.</u>
>
> The Swiss caricaturist Rudolf Töpffer made images even more central in *Histoire de M. Vieux Bois,* published in 1833 and translated into English in 1837 as *The Adventures of Obadiah Oldbuck.*
>
> Graphic novels, however, seem to have bridged the divide: ever since the first graphic novel was published in the <u>1970s,</u> the genre has been hailed as a powerful literary response to film and television.
>
> Because the form of the graphic novel is so new, critics and publishers are still not sure how to document or describe the phenomenon.

Between the stars and the lead words you found in the first sentences of the paragraphs, you have a lot of questions whose answers are easy to find, and you're ready to move on to the next step.

Step 3: Select and Understand a Question

Work the questions in an order that makes sense: do Now the questions that are easy to answer or whose answers are easy to find. Look at the stars on questions 24, 25, and 26. You know where to read to find those answers, and when you worked the passage, you found the locations for questions 22, 23, 28, and 29.

Do Later, or Never, questions that are both difficult to answer and whose answers are difficult to find. Questions 21 and 30 are both good Later/Never questions, because they have no line references or lead words.

Once you have selected a question, make sure you understand what it is asking. The "questions" on ACT Reading are often written as half-finished statements, so translate the statement into a question.

Here's an example.

---

28. According to the passage, an important factor in the <u>difficulty of defining the graphic novel</u> with any precision is that:

Translate: What's an important factor that makes it difficult to precisely define the graphic novel?

Step 4: Read What You Need

Read a window of 5–10 lines from the passage to find the answer.

The beginning of the first paragraph mentioned something about the lack of definition, so read approximately lines 1–10 to find the answer.

> The graphic novel is a true anomaly in contemporary litera-
> ture; there is no set definition for what the genre is, so there are
> many disagreements as to its origins and characteristics. Graphic
> novels may be so difficult to categorize because they incorporate
> 5 so many earlier elements from popular culture, the arts, literature,
> and the cinema. At once a site for fast-paced editing, detailed
> portraiture, and powerful internal reflections, the graphic novel
> may be the art form of the early twenty-first century. Many people
> are familiar with the cinematic adaptations of graphic novels, and
> 10 even this small slice of the genre shows the range of the graphic
> novel form. Daniel Clowes's *Ghost World*, begun in 1993 as a
> graphic novel and made into a film in 2001, is a tragicomic look
> at the life of a suburban teenager. Frank Miller's *300*, published
> in 1998 and released as a film in 2007, is an action epic based
> 15 on a historical event. Marjane Satrapi's *Persepolis*, published in
> French in 2000 and released in theaters in the U.S. in 2008, is a
> coming-of-age story told alongside the history of modern Iran.

Never answer specific questions from memory. Always read a window of 5 to 10 lines to find the answer to each question, using the line references and lead words as a guide.

Step 5: Mark the Answer in the Passage

Underline the phrases or sentences in the passage that answer the question.

Lines 4–6 say that graphic novels are *difficult to categorize because they incorporate so many earlier elements from popular culture, the arts, literature, and the cinema*; this answers question 28, so underline these lines.

Step 6: Use POE

Use Process of Elimination to get rid of answers that do not match what you underlined. For reference questions, the answer will closely match the text.

    F. the genre has not changed since the eighteenth century.
    G. most of the books become movies so quickly that defining them is irrelevant.
    H. critics have been so scornful of the genre that they have avoided discussing it.
    J. the genre incorporates elements from other distinct genres.

Eliminate (F) because there's no mention of the *eighteenth century*. There's also no mention of *critics*, so eliminate (H). Although the paragraph does discuss graphic novels that have become *movies*, there's nothing to support the idea that speedy adaptation to film renders defining them *irrelevant*, so eliminate (G). You're left with (J), which is a good match for what you underlined in the text. The correct answer is (J).

Repeat

Steps 3–6 repeat: make your way through the rest of the questions, making smart choices about the order of your questions, doing every Now question that is easy to answer or whose answer is easy to find. Select and Understand a Question and Read What You Need to answer it. As you read, Mark the Answer in the Passage, and Use POE to find the answers.

Try another question.

---

24. The main purpose of the fourth paragraph (lines 53–73) is to make clear that contemporary graphic novels are:

Translate: What is the main purpose of the fourth paragraph?

This paragraph is a little longer than the typical 5-to-10-line window, but since the question asks about the main purpose of the paragraph, read the whole thing before answering.

> Graphic novels, however, seem to have bridged the divide. Ever since the first graphic novel was published in the 1970s,
> 55 the genre has been hailed as a powerful literary response to film and television. Composed with the same delicacy as a masterful painting or a work of high literary fiction, graphic novels have incorporated both the low- and high-cultural heritage of many twentieth-century art forms. Art critics find in them the techni-
> 60 cal skill of great painters, and literary critics are attracted to the innovative portrayals of the inner lives of characters. Perhaps the best-known graphic novel not turned into a feature film is Art Spiegelman's *Maus* (published 1973–1991), the story of the experiences of a Polish Jew in a concentration camp and the
> 65 way these experiences reverberate through later generations of his family. More recently published is what many would argue is the classic of the genre of the graphic novel, Chris Ware's *Jimmy Corrigan, The Smartest Kid on Earth*, released in 2000. The main narrative concerns the title character's first meeting
> 70 with his father, thirty years after the father abandoned him and his mother. Rich in historical detail, *Jimmy Corrigan* gives a long history of the city of Chicago and intimate psychological portraits of its characters.

The purpose of the paragraph may not be directly stated so that you can underline it, but you should still base your answer on the text.

F. popular with the general public but scorned by critics of literature and the arts.

G. available mainly in book form and not likely to be made into films.

H. accepted by both the general public and literature critics.

J. mainly based on historical events and the experiences of teenagers.

Here's How to Crack It

It's likely that you don't think any of these answer choices "sounds" like the right choice, so use POE. Lines 59–61 discuss what art and literary critics like about graphic novels, so eliminate (F). One example of a graphic novel not turned into a film is discussed in lines 61–66, but there's no mention of how *likely* graphic novels are to be turned into films in general, so eliminate (G). There's nothing specific in the paragraph that contradicts (H), so keep it. There's no mention anywhere in the paragraph of teenagers, so eliminate (J). You're left with (H), the correct answer.

Save for Last

The toughest reasoning questions should be done last (if at all—your pacing strategy may mark them as Never). After you've worked all the specific questions in the passage, you understand the main theme better. Questions 21 and 30 for this passage are both smart choices to do last.

Take a look at question 21, and see how what you learned from answering questions 24 and 28 can help you answer a tougher, general question. You haven't read the whole passage at this point, but see whether you can eliminate any answer choices based on what you have read.

21. One of the main points the author formulates is that:

   A. because of the difficulty of defining what a graphic novel is, the genre will ultimately not succeed.

   B. graphic novels combine elements from many genres in innovative ways that are appealing to a wide range of audiences.

   C. William Blake invented the genre of graphic novel.

   D. although graphic novels are often made into films, the books are usually superior to the films.

Here's How to Crack It

After reading the windows for questions 24 and 28, you can tell that the author has a favorable opinion of graphic novels, so eliminate (A). Both of the paragraphs you looked at did discuss film adaptations of graphic novels, but there was never any discussion of whether the films or the books are *superior*, so eliminate (D). At this point, you may think you can't choose between (B) and (C). But take a look back at the first sentence of each paragraph: the second paragraph discusses William Blake and seems to support (C), but that's just a single paragraph. In other words, it's a detail, not a main idea. On the other hand, (B) agrees with the answers to both the questions you already answered as well as the first sentences of the first, fourth, and fifth paragraphs. That makes it a pretty good bet for the correct answer to the main idea question.

Summary

o   Pick your order of the passages.

o   Use your POOD to identify the genres and topics you like best.

o   Pay attention to your track record in practice.

o   Examine the particulars of each test and be prepared to confirm or change your order each time.

o   Look for passages with a reasonable number of small paragraphs.

o   Look for passages with many line-reference questions.

o   Look for passages with many short answers.

o   Use the 6-step Basic Approach.
    1.   Preview
    2.   Work the Passage
    3.   Select and Understand a Question
    4.   Read What You Need
    5.   Mark the Answer in the Passage
    6.   Use POE

Chapter 4
Working with the Answer Choices

Once you've completed steps 1–5 of the Basic Approach, you will usually have a good idea about what the correct answer will be. However, in order to choose the correct answer, you still have to eliminate three wrong answers. In this chapter, you'll learn how to efficiently eliminate wrong answers and how to work backward from the answers when it is difficult to Mark the Answer in the Passage.

USE POE: A TWO-PASS APPROACH

Step 6 of the Reading Basic Approach is to use Process of Elimination. On questions that are Easy to Answer, you may easily eliminate three answers that don't match the text you underlined in Step 5. In that case, you only need to make one pass through the answers. Actually cross out each answer choice that you eliminate. If you are taking the computer-based ACT, you can eliminate answers with the "Answer Eliminator" option in the Tools menu.

On questions that are harder to answer, however, you may initially see more than one answer that seems to match the text you underlined, or you might find some answers confusing. In that case, make two passes through the answers. On your first pass, eliminate the "junk" answers that clearly don't match the underlined text. Leave in answers that seem to match the text of the passage, marking them with a check if they seem to match well. Mark them with a ~ if they don't seem to match perfectly, but you're not ready to completely eliminate them. Mark answers that you find confusing with a question mark. This should include answers with vocabulary that you're not sure of.

Then, take a second pass through the remaining answers—you can dig deeper once you've narrowed down the possibilities.

Common Trap Answers

ACT creates wrong answers for one reason: to distract test-takers from the correct answer. When they create a wrong answer, they want to make it tempting. How do they do this?

There are three common types of "trap" answers that you will see on the ACT Reading test. When you make your second pass through the answer choices, be on the lookout for these common traps.

Out the Window

These answers are either not mentioned at all in the passage, or they are mentioned in a part of the passage that is outside the window for the question and that is not about the question's topic.

Words Out of Context

These answers recycle *words* from the passage, but they don't quite match the *meaning* of what the passage states.

Right Answer, Wrong Question

These answers include a statement that is true according to the passage, but they don't answer the question that was asked.

Here is an example from a passage that you'll see more of later. The correct answer is circled so that you can focus on the trap answers.

When Matthew reached Bright River there was no sign of any train. The long platform was almost deserted; the only living creature in sight being a girl who was sitting on a pile of shingles at the extreme end. Matthew, barely noting that it was a girl, sidled past her as quickly as possible without looking at her. Had he looked he could hardly have failed to notice the tense rigidity and expectation of her attitude and expression. She was sitting there waiting for something or somebody and, since sitting and waiting was the only thing to do just then, she sat and waited with all her might and main.

1. The primary purpose of the first paragraph is to:

   A. describe Matthew's first encounter with the girl and emphasize how little attention he paid her.

   B. suggest that the station master is not familiar with the train schedule.

Is the *station master* mentioned in the first paragraph? No, this is an Out the Window answer.

   C. explain why Matthew fails to notice the only living creature in the town of Bright River.

Does this answer include words from the text? Yes—*failed to notice, only living creature,* and *Bright River* all appear in the paragraph. Does the answer match the meaning of the text? No— the text says that the girl was the only living creature *in sight* on the *platform*, not the only living creature in the town. This is a Words Out of Context answer.

   D. inform the reader that Matthew and the girl were the only people on the train platform.

Does this answer include a true statement according to the text? Yes—the only person in sight when Matthew arrives is the girl. Does it answer the question that was asked? No—this is one detail from the paragraph, but the paragraph's *main purpose* is not to inform the reader of this fact. This is a Right Answer, Wrong Question answer.

For more practice working with answer choices, try the following questions. Before working the questions, complete Steps 1 and 2.

Step 1: Preview

Check the blurb and map the questions. Remember to underline lead words and star line references in the questions.

PROSE FICTION: This passage is adapted from the novel *Anne of Green Gables* by L.M. Montgomery. The novel was written in 1908. Matthew and Marilla Cuthbert are brother and sister.

1. The primary purpose of the first paragraph is to:

2. The narrator mentions the "ordinary observer" in line 33 in order to

3. According to the narrator, Matthew decides:

4. The stationmaster's description of the girl suggests that she decided to wait outside because:

5. The passage portrays Matthew as:

6. As it is used in line 22, the word *charge* most nearly means:

7. The passage suggests all of the following about the orphan asylum EXCEPT:

8. According to the passage, the stationmaster locks the ticket office:

9. Based on the passage, which character is likely the most talkative?

10. The passage could best be described as:

Step 2: Work the Passage

Read the passage, looking for and circling the lead words from the questions.

When Matthew reached Bright River there was no sign of any train. The long platform was almost deserted; the only living creature in sight being a girl who was sitting on a pile of shingles at the extreme end. Matthew, barely noting that it was a girl, sidled past her as quickly as possible without
5 looking at her. Had he looked he could hardly have failed to notice the tense rigidity and expectation of her attitude and expression. She was sitting there waiting for something or somebody and, since sitting and waiting was the only thing to do just then, she sat and waited with all her might and main.

Matthew encountered the stationmaster locking up the ticket office
10 preparatory to going home for supper, and asked him if the five-thirty train would soon be along.

"The five-thirty train has been in and gone half an hour ago," answered that brisk official. "But there was a passenger dropped off for you—a little girl. She's sitting out there on the shingles. I asked her to go into the ladies'
15 waiting room, but she informed me gravely that she preferred to stay outside. 'There was more scope for imagination,' she said. She's a case, I should say."

"I'm not expecting a girl," said Matthew blankly. "It's a boy I've come for. He should be here. Mrs. Alexander Spencer was to bring him over from Nova Scotia for me."

20 The stationmaster whistled.

"Guess there's some mistake," he said. "Mrs. Spencer came off the train with that girl and gave her into my charge. Said you and your sister were adopting her from an orphan asylum and that you would be along for her presently. That's all I know about it—and I haven't got any more orphans
25 concealed hereabouts."

He walked jauntily away, being hungry, and the unfortunate Matthew was left to do that which was harder for him than bearding a lion in its den—walk up to a girl—a strange girl—an orphan girl—and demand of her why she wasn't a boy. Matthew groaned in spirit as he turned about and
30 shuffled gently down the platform towards her.

She had been watching him ever since he had passed her and she had her eyes on him now. Matthew was not looking at her and would not have seen what she was really like if he had been, but an ordinary observer would have seen this: A child of about eleven, garbed in a very short, very tight,
35 very ugly dress of yellowish-gray wincey. She wore a faded brown sailor hat and beneath the hat, extending down her back, were two braids of very

thick, decidedly red hair. Her face was small, white and thin, also much freckled; her mouth was large and so were her eyes, which looked green in some lights and moods and gray in others.

40   So far, the ordinary observer; an extraordinary observer might have seen that the chin was very pointed and pronounced; that the big eyes were full of spirit and vivacity; that the mouth was sweet-lipped and expressive; that the forehead was broad and full; in short, our discerning extraordinary observer might have concluded that no commonplace soul inhabited the

45   body of this stray woman-child of whom shy Matthew Cuthbert was so ludicrously afraid.

Matthew, however, was spared the ordeal of speaking first, for as soon as she concluded that he was coming to her she stood up, grasping with one thin brown hand the handle of a shabby, old-fashioned carpet-bag; the

50   other she held out to him.

"I suppose you are Mr. Matthew Cuthbert of Green Gables?" she said in a peculiarly clear, sweet voice. "I'm very glad to see you. I was beginning to be afraid you weren't coming for me and I was imagining all the things that might have happened to prevent you. I had made up my mind that if you

55   didn't come for me to-night I'd go down the track to that big wild cherry-tree at the bend, and climb up into it to stay all night. I wouldn't be a bit afraid, and it would be lovely to sleep in a wild cherry-tree all white with bloom in the moonshine, don't you think? You could imagine you were dwelling in marble halls, couldn't you? And I was quite sure you would come for me

60   in the morning, if you didn't to-night."

Matthew had taken the scrawny little hand awkwardly in his; then and there he decided what to do. He could not tell this child with the glowing eyes that there had been a mistake; he would take her home and let Marilla do that. She couldn't be left at Bright River anyhow, no matter what mistake

65   had been made, so all questions and explanations might as well be deferred until he was safely back at Green Gables.

Steps 3, 4, and 5: Select and Understand a Question, Read What You Need, Mark the Answer in the Passage

STEPS
3, 4, and 5

4.   The stationmaster's description of the girl suggests that she decided to wait outside because:

This question asks what the *stationmaster's description* suggests about the girl's reason for waiting *outside*. Since there is no line reference, use the lead words *stationmaster*, *girl*, and *outside* to find the window for the question. The stationmaster is first mentioned in the second paragraph, and he describes the girl in the third paragraph.

"The five-thirty train has been in and gone half an hour ago," answered that brisk official. "But there was a passenger dropped off for you—a little girl. She's sitting out there on the shingles. I asked her to go into the ladies'

15   waiting room, but she informed me gravely that she preferred to stay outside. 'There was more scope for imagination,' she said. She's a case, I should say."

Underline the lines that give information about why the girl waited outside. In lines 14–16, the stationmaster says, *"I asked her to go into the ladies' waiting room, but she informed me gravely that she preferred to stay outside. 'There was more scope for imagination,' she said."* According to the stationmaster, the girl wanted to wait outside because there was more opportunity to use her imagination outside than inside. In other words, the girl found it more interesting to wait outside.

STEP 6 » Step 6: Use POE

Eliminate answers that don't match the text you underlined in Step 5.

> 4. The stationmaster's description of the girl suggests that she decided to wait outside because:
>
>   F. she became worried when she imagined waiting inside the station.
>   G. the outdoor setting provided more interest than did the ladies' waiting room.
>   H. her experience at the orphan asylum had made her defiant towards authority.
>   J. she was uncomfortable with the stationmaster's brusque manner.

Choice (F) is a Words Out of Context trap: the text mentions *imagination*, and says that the girl replied *gravely*, or seriously, but there is no evidence that she was imagining things that worried her. Eliminate (F).

Keep (G) because it matches the text from the passage.

Choice (H) is Out the Window—there is no evidence that the girl is *defiant towards authority*, nor any discussion of her *experience at the orphan asylum*. Eliminate (H).

Eliminate (J) because the stationmaster is described as *brisk*, which means "quick," but not as *brusque*, which means "rude." There is also no indication that the girl is uncomfortable with the stationmaster. Eliminate (J).

The correct answer is (G).

Repeat Steps 3–6 for the following questions. Use two passes of Process of Elimination if you need to, and be on the lookout for trap answers once you've eliminated answers that don't match the text you underlined.

———————————————○———————————————

> 6. As it is used in line 22, the word *charge* most nearly means:
>
>   F. accusation.
>   G. expense.
>   H. supervision.
>   J. leadership.

Here's How to Crack It

This is a vocabulary-in-context question. It asks not just the meaning of *charge*, but the meaning of *charge* as it is used in the context of the passage. Carefully read the window, cross out the word *charge* and fill in another word that fits the meaning of the text. The window states, *"Guess there's some mistake," he said. "Mrs. Spencer came off the train with that girl and gave her into my charge. Said you and your sister were adopting her from an orphan asylum and that you would be along for her presently."* Mrs. Spencer asked the stationmaster to look after the orphan girl until Matthew arrived. Therefore, the word charge must mean something like "care." Eliminate answers that do not match this meaning. Choice (F), *accusation*, does not match "care." Notice that *accusation* is another definition of the word "charge," but it is not supported by the text. This is a Right Answer, Wrong Question trap—this type of trap answer is very common on vocabulary-in-context questions, so be on the lookout for them as you Use POE. Eliminate (F). Choice (G), *expense*, does not match "care." This is another Right Answer, Wrong Question trap answer, so eliminate (G). Keep (H) because it matches the text from the passage. Eliminate (J) because *leadership* does not match "care." The correct answer is (H).

8. According to the passage, the stationmaster locks the ticket office:

    F. to prevent theft during the night.
    G. at approximately 6:00 pm.
    H. during all of his mealtimes.
    J. whenever there is no train in the station.

Here's How to Crack It

This question doesn't have a line reference, so use the lead words *stationmaster* and *ticket office* to find the window. Lines 9–12 state that the stationmaster was *locking up the ticket office* prior to *going home for supper* and that the *five-thirty train* had come and gone *half an hour ago*. Underline these phrases in the passage, then eliminate answers that are not consistent with the text. Choice (F) is an Out the Window answer—there is no mention of preventing *theft*. Eliminate (F). Choice (G) matches the text you underlined—since the five-thirty train came half an hour ago, the time is about six o'clock. Keep (G). Choice (H) is Words Out of Context answer—the text says that the stationmaster is about to have supper, but there is not enough evidence to support the idea that the stationmaster locks the office during *all* mealtimes. Eliminate (H). Eliminate (J) because the passage only mentions one time when the stationmaster locks the office—there is not enough evidence to support the statement that he locks it *whenever there is no train in the station*. The correct answer is (G).

Use Comparison

When you are trying to choose between two answers on your second pass, use a comparison strategy. Compare the answers to each other, to the passage, and to the question. How do the two answers differ from one another? Focus on the difference between them and ask, does the answer truly match what was said in the passage? Does it answer the question that was asked?

Try the comparison strategy with the following questions from the passage you worked above. Two of the answers have been eliminated on the first pass, so only two remain.

---○---

2. The narrator mentions an "ordinary observer" in line 33 in order to:

    F. provide the reader with a sense of the orphan girl's physical appearance.
    G.
    H. foreshadow the unusually spirited and expressive character of the orphan girl.
    J.

Here's How to Crack It

Compare (F) and (H) to see how they differ. Choice (F) focuses on the girl's physical appearance, while (H) focuses on the girl's character. Now, compare these answers back to the question and to the passage. The question asks why the narrator mentions the *ordinary observer*. The window for the question describes what an ordinary observer might see, including the girl's *dress*, *hat*, *hair*, and *face*. This is a physical description, and therefore supports (F). The next paragraph describes the girl's character with phrases such as *full of spirit and vivacity*, *expressive*, and *no commonplace soul*; however, the passage suggests that those observations would be made by an *extraordinary observer*, not an *ordinary observer*. Therefore, (H) does not answer the question about why the ordinary observer is mentioned. Choice (H) is a Right Answer, Wrong Question trap, so eliminate it. The correct answer is (F).

---○---

---○---

3. According to the narrator, Matthew decides:

    A. that he will bring the orphan girl back to Green Gables rather than attempt to sort out the mistake that has been made.
    B.
    C.
    D. that he will leave it up to Marilla to question Mrs. Spencer about why she brought a girl rather than a boy from the orphanage.

Here's How to Crack It

Compare (A) with (D) to see how they differ. Both answers are about the mistake of bringing a girl rather than a boy from the orphan asylum. Choice (A) simply says that Matthew will bring the girl home rather than *attempt to sort out the mistake*, while (D) mentions *Marilla* questioning *Mrs. Spencer* about the mistake. The last paragraph indicates that Matthew could not bring himself to tell the girl that there had been a mistake, and that *he would take her home and let Marilla do that*. In other words, Matthew will let Marilla tell the girl about the mistake. This supports (A). The passage does not mention Marilla questioning *Mrs. Spencer*, so eliminate (D). The correct answer is (A).

---○---

10. The passage could best be described as:

F.

G. a descriptive account of the first meeting of two characters.

H.

J. an evocative introduction of the setting in which a story will unfold.

Here's How to Crack It

Compare (G) and (J) to see how they differ. Choice (G) describes the passage as an *account of the first meeting between two characters*. Choice (J) describes the passage as an *introduction of the setting* of the story. Now, compare these answers back to the passage. This is a general question, so use the correct answers to the previous questions together with what you have read in the passage to help you answer it. Question 1 asked about the purpose of the first paragraph, and the correct answer was to *describe Matthew's first encounter with the girl*. The passage describes both Matthew and the orphan girl in detail, which supports (G). The passage does not include much description of the *setting*, and it does not suggest that the rest of the story will take place at the train station, so eliminate (J). The correct answer is (G).

Work Backward from the Answers

If you find it difficult to Mark the Answer in the Passage, try working backward from the answer choices. Read each answer and then compare it to the window for the question. Is the topic of the answer choice mentioned in the window? If not, it is an Out the Window answer and can be eliminated. If the topic is discussed in the window, does the answer choice truly match what the passage says? If not, it is a Words Out of Context answer and can be eliminated. If the answer matches what the passage says, does it answer the question asked? If not, it is a Right Answer, Wrong Question answer and can be eliminated.

Try working backward on the following questions.

5. The passage portrays Matthew as:

A. committed to his plan of adopting a boy.

B. being in the habit of running late.

C. a keen observer of human nature.

D. uncomfortable about speaking with the girl.

Here's How to Crack It

This is a broad question, and the passage portrays more than one of Matthew's qualities, which makes it difficult to underline the answer. This is a good opportunity for working backward from the answers. Choice (A) says that Matthew is *committed to his plan of adopting a boy*. The text says that Matthew *groaned in spirit* at the thought of asking the orphan girl *why she wasn't a boy*, and later that he *could not tell this child with the glowing eyes that there had been a mistake.* Instead, he decides to take her home and sort it out later. Therefore, the passage does not portray Matthew as *committed to his plan of adopting a boy.* Eliminate (A). Choice (B) says that Matthew is *in the habit of running late.* The text suggests that Matthew arrives late to meet the five-thirty train, but this is only one example and doesn't support the statement that he is *in the habit* of being late. Eliminate (B). Choice (C) says that Matthew is a *keen observer of human nature*, but the passage states that he barely noted the girl when he first walked by her, and later that *Matthew was not looking at her and would not have seen what she was really like if he had been.* The passage does not portray Matthew as a *keen observer of human nature*, so eliminate (C). Choice (D) says that Matthew is *uncomfortable about speaking with the girl.* This answer is supported by the passage, which says that walking up to speak to the girl was *harder for him than bearding a lion in its den,* that he was *ludicrously afraid* of the girl, and that he was *spared the ordeal of speaking first.* The correct answer is (D).

7. The passage suggests all of the following about the orphan asylum EXCEPT:

   A. It is located in Nova Scotia.
   B. It is located some distance from Green Gables.
   C. The orphans who live there are exclusively girls.
   D. The children who live there are not provided with expensive clothes.

Here's How to Crack It

The question asks which statement about the *orphan asylum* is NOT suggested by the passage. An EXCEPT/LEAST/NOT question is a good opportunity for working backward from the answers, since it requires you to find three answers that **are** in the passage and may be located in separate windows. To locate (A), look for the lead words *Nova Scotia.* Matthew states that Mrs. Spencer was to bring a boy orphan *over from Nova Scotia,* which suggests that the orphan asylum is in Nova Scotia. Eliminate (A). Eliminate (B) because the orphan girl arrives on a train, and Matthew travels from Green Gables to the train station in Bright River. This suggests that the orphan asylum is *located some distance from Green Gables.* Keep (C) because the passage suggests that Matthew and Marilla are expecting to adopt a boy, which suggests that the orphanage is a home for both boys and girls. Eliminate (D) because the description of the orphan girl's dress suggests that it doesn't fit her well, and her hat is described as *faded.* This suggests that the orphan asylum is not able to provide *expensive clothes* to the orphans. The correct answer is (C).

9. Based on the passage, which character is likely the most talkative?

   A. Matthew Cuthbert
   B. Mrs. Spencer
   C. The orphan girl
   D. The stationmaster

Here's How to Crack It

This is a general question, so it may be hard to find. This makes it a good candidate for working backward from the answers. The passage says that the idea of talking to the girl is hard for *Matthew*, and he does not say much throughout the passage, so eliminate (A). The passage only mentions one short statement spoken by *Mrs. Spencer*, so eliminate (B). Lines 51–60 are one uninterrupted speech by the *orphan girl*, starting with a question that Matthew never has a chance to answer. This suggests that she may be a *talkative* character. Keep (C). The *stationmaster* answers Matthew's questions, but does not go on at length. When compared with the orphan girl, he is not especially talkative, so eliminate (D). The correct answer is (C).

Bonus Question!

Which of the following phrases is used in the passage to indicate the girl's creative way of seeing the world?

   A. "with all her might and main" (line 8)
   B. "She's a case, I should say" (line 16)
   C. "marble halls" (line 59)
   D. "I was quite sure" (line 59)

Here's How to Crack It

In this question, the answers include line references, which means that you must work backward from the answers. Read a short window around the lines in each answer. The phrase in (A) describes how the girl *waited*; these lines don't describe her *way of seeing the world* or suggest that she is *creative*, making this is a Right Answer, Wrong Question trap. Eliminate (A). The phrase in (B) is spoken by the stationmaster about the girl. These lines don't describe the girl's creative way of seeing the world, so eliminate (B). The girl uses the phrase in (C) to describe how she imagines it would be to sleep in a cherry tree: *You could imagine you were dwelling in marble halls.* This is a creative way of seeing the world, so keep (C). The phrase in (D) shows the girl's certainty that Matthew would come for her. He is actually coming to pick her up, so this doesn't indicate a creative way of seeing the world. Eliminate (D). The correct answer is (C).

(Yes, there are only 10 questions for each passage on the ACT! This one was just a bonus.)

Summary

- o When you Use POE, take two passes through the answers.

  - • On the first pass, eliminate answers that don't match the text you underlined.

  - • One the second pass, use comparison and look for common trap answers.

- o Be on the lookout for common trap answers:

  - • Out the Window

  - • Words Out of Context

  - • Right Answer, Wrong Question

- o Work backward from the answers for:

  - • questions that are hard to find in the passage.

  - • questions for which it's hard to Mark the Answer in the Passage.

  - • EXCEPT/LEAST/NOT questions.

  - • questions with line references in the answers.

Chapter 5
Dual Passages

One of the four passages in each ACT Reading test will consist of two shorter passages. In this chapter, you'll learn to efficiently work these dual passages, including the questions that ask about both passages.

DUAL PASSAGES

One of the four passages in each ACT Reading test will consist of two shorter passages that are somehow related. Your approach to the dual passages should be exactly the same as your approach to the other passages, except that you'll apply it to one shorter passage at a time. Choose one passage to do first (the one that has more questions attached to it is usually a good choice), and then go through the six-step Basic Approach with that passage.

On dual passages, it's useful to make a few notes at the bottom of each passage (or on your white board) about the central idea of each passage for quick reference to keep from mixing them up. You can do this either after working the passage or after answering the questions about a single passage.

There are two options for working the other passage and the questions that ask about both passages.

1, 2, Both

Follow the six-step Basic Approach with the other passage. Leave the questions that ask about both passages for Later (or Never). Before you answer the questions that ask about both passages, jot down the relationship between the passages: what's the connection between them? What do the authors agree or disagree about? You can usually rely heavily on POE on the questions that ask about both passages: any answer choice that mischaracterizes one of the passages can be automatically eliminated.

1, Both, 2

After you work the questions about the first passage and jot down the central idea, go to the questions that ask about both passages. Use POE to eliminate answers that mischaracterize the first passage. Then follow the six-step Basic Approach with the other passage. Jot down the central idea of the second passage and the relationship between the passages. Finally, finish the questions about both passages, eliminating answers that mischaracterize the second passage or the relationship between the passages.

Work Hard, Play Hard
Remember to balance your test preparation with occasional study breaks—walks in a park, trips to the movies, healthy snacks. Don't burn yourself out before test day!

If you find the dual passages especially difficult, you may be inclined to leave them for Later or Never in your POOD. On the other hand, you may be inclined to do the dual passages Now because each passage is half the length of a single passage, making the answers easier to find. You may also be inclined to treat the dual passages just like any other passage and base your POOD decisions on the topic, paragraphs, questions, and answers. Each approach is fine—POOD is, after all, personal—but be sure to practice the dual passages (in the following drill and in Chapters 8, 9, 11, 13, and 15) so you can feel confident in knowing how to attack them if you need to on the test.

Try out the approach with the following set of dual passages.

DUAL PASSAGES DRILL

SOCIAL SCIENCE: Passage A is adapted from the article "First Flight: How Wright Brothers Changed the World" by Willie Drye, NG Image Collection. Passage B is adapted from the article "Wright Brothers Flight Legacy Hits New Turbulence" by Jarret Liotta, NG Image Collection.

Passage A by Willie Drye

Thursday, December 17, 1903, dawned windy and cold on North Carolina's Outer Banks. At Kill Devil Hills, the thermometer hovered around the freezing mark, and a 25-mile-per-hour wind blowing out of the north made it feel
5 even colder. Orville and Wilbur Wright had a few doubts about whether this was a good day to try to get their flying machine off the ground. But they didn't want to go back home to Ohio without knowing once and for all whether this design was going to work. So they decided that this day
10 was as good as any to give it one more shot.

Crewmen John Daniels, Will Dough, and Adam Etheridge came over from the Lifesaving Station. W.C. Binkley of Manteo and Johnny Moore, a teenager from Nags Head, also showed up to lend a hand. The Wrights and their five
15 accomplices pulled the flying machine from the hangar to a specially designed wooden track the brothers had built to launch the flyer. They cranked up the four-cylinder gasoline engine that had been especially designed and built for the flying machine. Orville, at 32 the younger of the pair, was at
20 the controls. A few minutes past 10:30 a.m. Orville climbed onto the lower wing of the flyer, lay stomach-down across it and grasped the controls. At 10:35 a.m. Orville released a wire that held the flying machine to the track, and the contraption chugged slowly forward into the stiff wind. Wilbur
25 trotted alongside, holding the wing to keep the flyer level. Then the flying machine lifted off the track, and Wilbur let go.

Orville's first flight was wobbly and brief. The flyer darted up and down as he tried to figure out how to keep it under control. He didn't want to push his luck. After about
30 12 seconds in the air, he brought the flyer to a landing about 120 feet from where he'd started. It didn't seem like much of an accomplishment, but the brothers were elated. "It was… the first time in the history of the world in which a machine carrying a man had raised itself by its own power into the air
35 in full flight, had sailed forward without reduction of speed, and had finally landed at a point as high as that from which it had started," Wilbur said later.

Passage B by Jarret Liotta

An iconic piece of American history took a nosedive when the 100th anniversary issue of an annual aviation
40 bible known as *Jane's All the World's Aircraft* displaced the Wright brothers as the first fathers of flight. The new name in town is Gustave Whitehead, a German-born inventor many have long believed took to the air more than two years before Orville and Wilbur even left the ground at Kitty Hawk on
45 December 17, 1903.

But while new research from an Australian aviation expert convinced *Jane's* editors it was time to update the books, the Smithsonian National Air and Space Museum in Washington, D.C.—home to the original Wright Flyer—
50 remains skeptical about Whitehead's work, which it views as mostly myth. The Aeronautics Division's senior curator—author and Wright expert Dr. Tom Crouch—believes *Jane's* was "hoodwinked."

John Brown, an Australian flight historian, was respon-
55 sible for swaying *Jane's*. Ironically, it was while working directly with Crouch that Brown came across a large amount of previously overlooked data on Whitehead. "There were a huge number of discoveries," Brown said, including newspaper accounts stating that Whitehead may have been flying
60 as early as 1897—six years before the Wright brothers. He also believes that photographic enhancements confirm that a long-missing picture of Whitehead actually flying his plane in Fairfield, Connecticut, on August 14, 1901—a lithograph of which was published at that time in the *Bridgeport Her-*
65 *ald*—can be seen on the wall of an aviation exhibit in a 1906 photo taken by William Hammer.

"The issue is: Did Gustave Whitehead fly or didn't he fly? Did he have the means? Did he have the motive?"

Brown calls it "indisputable," based on the man's
70 professional background in aeronautics, the documented evidence of the number of airplane motors Whitehead created and sold, affidavits signed by eyewitnesses who saw him fly, newspaper accounts, and more.

Crouch, who has spent much of his career researching
75 and writing about the Wrights, said the Whitehead controversy reemerges "every 20 years, like clockwork," yet never with—in his opinion—definitive evidence to rewrite history. Crouch also discounts the testimony of witnesses who claimed to see Whitehead flying, as well as signed affidavits
80 stating that the Wrights visited Whitehead's shop several months before their first flight and essentially plagiarized many of his methods and tools.

As far as this controversy is concerned, the next chapter is still up in the air.

11. Based on the information about the *five accomplices* (lines 14–15), it can most reasonably be inferred that:

   A. the additional crewmen have since been recognized as essential to the first flight.

   B. the Wright brothers had assistance in designing the machine they flew at Kitty Hawk.

   C. the Wright brothers were trespassing on the land where they set up the track.

   D. Orville and Wilbur Wright were unable to move the flying machine by themselves.

12. Which of the following statements best captures how Passage A characterizes the flight at Kill Devil Hills on December 17, 1903?

   F. It was unremarkable at the time though it is impressive by today's standards.

   G. It was especially impressive because it was the Wright brothers' first attempt at flight.

   H. It was a cause for celebration, particularly because it took place in the Wright brothers' home state of North Carolina.

   J. It was historic, though brief and somewhat unsteady.

13. The statement in lines 2–5 is typical of Passage A in the way it:

   A. includes numerical data in its description of the Wright brothers' first flight.

   B. emphasizes the importance of the location the Wrights chose for the test flight.

   C. downplays the importance of the day's events in contrast with Orville and Wilbur's confidence.

   D. describes the thoughts and actions of the people involved with the historic first flight.

What is the central idea of Passage A?

_____

_____

_____

14. Which of the following terms in Passage B is used more figuratively than literally?

   F. Nosedive (line 38)

   G. Ground (line 44)

   H. Historian (line 54)

   J. Discoveries (line 58)

15. Which of the following statements about Orville and Wilbur Wright is best supported by Passage B?

   A. They have generally, though not universally, been supposed to be the first people to fly.

   B. Their methods and tools may have been plagiarized by Gustave Whitehead.

   C. Their efforts were supported by local men who assisted them with their test flights.

   D. Their original aircraft was built at the Smithsonian National Air and Space Museum in Washington, D.C.

16. Which of the following events referred to in Passage B occurred first chronologically?

   F. John Brown discovered newspaper accounts about Whitehead.

   G. The 100th-anniversary edition of *Jane's* was published.

   H. The Whitehead controversy emerged for the first time.

   J. John Brown and Tom Crouch worked together directly.

17. The purpose of the phrase "like clockwork" in line 76 is most likely to:

   A. introduce the topic of a similar debate.

   B. imply that the controversy reoccurs on a regular basis.

   C. suggest that the new evidence was reliable.

   D. approximate the time Crouch devoted to research.

What is the central idea of Passage B?

_____

_____

_____

What is the relationship between Passage A and Passage B?

_____

_____

_____

_____

Questions 18–20 ask about both passages.

---

18. John Brown would most likely respond to the account of Orville and Wilbur Wright's first flight presented in Passage A by:

    F. providing additional details about weather conditions on that day.
    G. arguing that the flight described took place at a later date.
    H. disputing Wilbur's quote about the historic nature of the event.
    J. affirming the account and dismissing contradictory theories.

19. An element of Passage B that is not present in Passage A is a reference to what aspect of the early development of aviation?

    A. Aviators
    B. Press coverage
    C. Witnesses of early flights
    D. Flight conditions

20. A similarity between the two passages is that they both:

    F. explicitly state the authors' stances on the topics discussed.
    G. discuss events in which the authors were not directly involved.
    H. mention the types of source material that furnish details about past events.
    J. praise innovators from early aviation history.

Check the answers and explanations to this drill starting on the next page.

DUAL PASSAGES DRILL ANSWERS

11. **D**

12. **J**

13. **A**

What is the central idea of Passage A?

The Wright brothers' first flight was risky and uncertain but historic.

14. **F**

15. **A**

16. **H**

17. **B**

What is the central idea of Passage B?

Passage B discusses a controversy about who was first in flight: the Wright brothers or Gustave Whitehead.

What is the relationship between Passage A and Passage B?

Passage A describes the Wright brothers' first flight, which is commonly accepted to be the first time a person flew in an aircraft. Passage B presents a challenge to that belief: some think that Gustave Whitehead was the first person in flight.

18. **H**

19. **B**

20. **G**

DUAL PASSAGES DRILL EXPLANATIONS

11. **D**   This reasoning question asks what can be inferred about the *five accomplices* in lines 14–15. Read a window around the line reference. The previous sentence says that there were five men that *showed up to lend a hand* to the Wright brothers. Together, the brothers and the five men moved the *flying machine* to prepare for flight. Look for an answer choice that matches this idea. Eliminate (A) because the text does not imply that the five men were *essential to the first flight*; it says that they helped to move the flying machine. Eliminate (B) because the text does not say that the five men helped to *design* the machine. This is a Words Out of Context trap answer. Eliminate (C) because the text does not suggest that the Wright brothers were *trespassing*. Keep (D) because it is supported by the text: since all of the men helped to move the machine, it can be inferred that the brothers probably could not move it on their own. The correct answer is (D).

12. **J**   This reasoning question asks for the statement *that best captures how Passage A characterizes the flight at Kill Devil Hills on December 17, 1903*. Although this question seems specific, it asks about evidence throughout the passage; it is a general question and should be done after all the specific questions. Look for the Golden Thread (correct answers to other questions that can help answer this one—more on this strategy in Chapter 6). Passage A says that *Orville and Wilbur Wright had a few doubts about whether this was a good day to try to get their flying machine off the ground*. It then says that *Orville's first flight was wobbly and brief*, but "It was…the first time in the history of the world in which a machine carrying a man" had flown on its own. Look for a choice that matches this description. Eliminate (F) because the text does not indicate that the flight was *unremarkable*. Eliminate (G) because the text does not say that the December 17 flight *was the Wright brothers' first attempt at flight*; in fact, it indicates that they had attempted flight before. Eliminate (H) because the flight was a cause for *celebration*, but not *because it took place in the Wright brothers' home state of North Carolina*. Keep (J) because the text supports the statement that the flight was *historic, though brief and somewhat unsteady*. The correct answer is (J).

13. **A**   This reasoning question asks why a particular statement is *typical of Passage A*. Although this question includes a line reference, it asks about evidence throughout the passage; it is a general question and it should be done after all the specific questions. Read the sentence that is referenced and consider how it matches other details in the passage. The sentence describes the temperature and the wind speed of *25-mile-per-hour*. Passage A uses other numeric data such as specific times, (*10:30 a.m.* and *10:35 a.m.*) duration (*12 seconds*) and distance (*120 feet*) to describe the first flight. Look for an answer choice that is consistent with this idea. Keep (A) because it is true that the sentence *includes numerical data* as supporting material and that the passage does this as well. Eliminate (B) because the sentence does not discuss the *importance of the location* of the *test flight*.

Eliminate (C) because the sentence does not discuss *Orville and Wilbur's confidence*. Eliminate (D) because the sentence does not describe the *thoughts and actions of the people involved with the historic first flight*. The correct answer is (A).

14. **F**   This reasoning question asks for the term that is *used more figuratively than literally*. The choices have line references, so read a window around each line reference. The lines for (F) say, *An iconic piece of American history took a nosedive when...Jane's All the World's Aircraft displaced the Wright brothers as the first fathers of flight*. In this sentence, *nosedive* does not refer to a literal motion; it figuratively describes what happened to an *iconic piece of American history*. Keep (F). The lines for (G) say that *Gustave Whitehead...took to the air more than two years before Orville and Wilbur even left the ground*. The word *ground* is used literally, since the sentence discusses leaving the ground by flying. Eliminate (G) because *ground* is not used figuratively. The lines for (H) mention *John Brown, an Australian flight historian*. The word *historian* is used literally to describe Brown's profession. The word *historian* is not used figuratively, so eliminate (H). The lines for (J) say, *There were a huge number of discoveries*. The word *discoveries* refers to evidence about Whitehead that Brown found, so it is used literally, not figuratively; eliminate (J). The correct answer is (F).

15. **A**   This reasoning question asks which statement *about Orville and Wilbur Wright is best supported by Passage B*. Use the lead words *Orville and Wilbur Wright* together with lead words from the answers to find the window for this question. Choice (A) says that the Wright brothers have *generally, though not universally, been supposed to be the first people to fly*. The first paragraph mentions the belief that *the Wright brothers* were *the first fathers of flight* and calls this an *iconic piece of American history*, which supports the statement that the Wright brothers have *generally* been thought to be *the first people to fly*. The first paragraph also states that many people believe that Gustave Whitehead *took to the air more than two years before Orville and Wilbur*; therefore, it is not *universally* believed that the Wright brothers were first. Keep (A). Choice (B) indicates that the Wright brothers' *methods and tools may have been plagiarized by Gustave Whitehead*. This is a Words Out of Context trap answer. Lines 78–82 indicate that some people have claimed that the Wright brothers plagiarized Whitehead's work, but not that Whitehead plagiarized the Wright brothers' work. Eliminate (B). Though Passage A discusses *local men* helping the brothers, Passage B does not. Eliminate (C). Choice (D) is a Words Out of Context trap answer. Lines 46–51 say that *the Smithsonian National Air and Space Museum* is *home to the original Wright flyer*. In other words, the flyer is kept at the museum; the text does not indicate that the flyer was *built* at the museum. Eliminate (D). The correct answer is (A).

16. **H**   This reasoning question asks which event *referred to in Passage B occurred first chronologically*. Because this is a general question, it should be done after all the specific questions. Work backward and use lead words from the answers to find the events in the passage. Consider (F). Look for the lead words *John Brown* and *newspaper*. Lines 55–59 say that *it was while working directly with Crouch that Brown came across a large amount of previously overlooked data on Whitehead...including newspaper accounts*. Consider (G). Look for the lead words *100th-anniversary*. Lines 39–41 say that the *100th-anniversary issue of...Jane's All the World's Aircraft displaced the Wright brothers as the first fathers of flight*, and lines 54–55 say that *John Brown... was responsible for swaying Jane's*. Therefore, the *100th-anniversary issue* must have been published after John Brown's work. Eliminate (G) because the publication came after the research mentioned in (F). Consider (H). Look for the lead words *Whitehead controversy*. Lines 74–76 say that *Crouch, who has spent much of his career researching and writing about the Wrights, said the Whitehead controversy reemerges "every 20 years, like clockwork,"* which means that the controversy surrounding Whitehead existed prior to Brown's research. Keep (H) and eliminate (F). Consider (J). Look for the lead words *Brown* and *Crouch*. Lines 55–57 say that *it was while working directly with Crouch that Brown came across a large amount of previously overlooked data on Whitehead*. Therefore, Brown and Crouch worked together during research. The research happened after the controversy first emerged, so eliminate (J). The correct answer is (H).

17. **B**   This reasoning question asks for the *purpose of the phrase "like clockwork" in line 76*. Read a window around the line reference. The text says that *the Whitehead controversy reemerges "every 20 years, like clockwork."* Therefore, the phrase *like clockwork* indicates that the controversy reemerges with regularity. Look for an answer choice that matches this idea. Eliminate (A) because the phrase does not *introduce the topic of a similar debate*. Keep (B) because it matches the text from the passage. Eliminate (C) because the phrase does not *suggest that the new evidence was reliable*. This is a Words Out of Context trap answer; the phrase "like clockwork" describes something that occurs on a regular basis, and is therefore reliable, but in the context of the passage, the phrase describes the *controversy*, not the *evidence*. Eliminate (D) because the phrase does not *approximate the time Crouch devoted to research*. The correct answer is (B).

18. **H**   This reasoning question asks how *John Brown would most likely respond to the account of Orville and Wilbur Wright's first flight presented in Passage A*. Because this question asks about both passages, it should be done after the questions that ask about each passage individually. Consider the Golden Thread of both passages. Passage A describes Orville and Wilbur Wright's first flight, and in Passage B, *John Brown* provides evidence to discredit the idea that the Wright brothers were the first

people to fly. Therefore, John Brown would likely claim that the flight described in Passage A was not the first time a person flew in aircraft. Look for an answer choice that matches this claim. There is no indication that Brown was aware of *weather conditions* on the day of the Wright brothers' flight. Eliminate (F). There is no indication that Brown believes the *date* of the brothers' first flight is wrong; he asserts that another person flew before this date. Eliminate (G). In lines 32–35, Wilbur Wright is quoted as saying that the flight was *the first time in the history of the world in which a machine carrying a man had raised itself by its own power into the air in full flight*. Since Brown does not support the idea that the Wrights were first in flight, he would likely dispute this quote. Keep (H). Brown would not affirm the account of the flight or dismiss contradictory theories, since he asserts that the account is wrong. Eliminate (J). The correct answer is (H).

19. **B** This reference question asks for *an aspect of the early development of aviation* that is mentioned in *Passage B* but not in *Passage A*. Because this question asks about both passages, it should be done after the questions that ask about each passage individually. Eliminate any answer choices that misrepresent either passage. Both passages discuss early *aviators*—Orville and Wilbur Wright in Passage A, and both the Wrights and Gustave Whitehead in Passage B—so eliminate (A). Passage B mentions *newspaper accounts* about Whitehead's flights and a photograph of Whitehead flying that was *published at that time in the* Bridgeport Herald. Therefore, Passage B mentions *press coverage*. Passage A does not mention press coverage, so keep (B). Both passages mention *witnesses of early flights*—Passage A mentions the men who assisted with the flight, and Passage B mentions *witnesses who claimed to see Whitehead flying*—so eliminate (C). Only Passage A discusses *flight conditions*, such as temperature and wind speed, so eliminate (D). The correct answer is (B).

20. **G** This reasoning question asks for a *similarity between the two passages*. Because this question asks about both passages, it should be done after the questions that ask about each passage individually. Consider the Golden Thread of both passages. Passage A gives an account of the Wright brothers' first flight. Passage B discusses the aviation activities of Gustave Whitehead. Passage A does not *explicitly state* the author's perspective, so eliminate (F). Both passages *discuss events in which the authors were not directly involved*, so keep (G). Only Passage B discusses *source material* that furnishes *details about past events* (for example, newspaper accounts, photographs, and eyewitness testimony). Eliminate (H). While both passages discuss early aviators who have been praised, each author presents the information in a neutral way. Neither author praises the innovators, so eliminate (J). The correct answer is (G).

Summary

o   Work the passages one a time, following the Basic Approach.

- Start with the passage that has more individual questions.

- Jot down the central idea of the first passage.

o   1, 2, Both

- Repeat Steps 1–6 with the other passage.

- Jot down the central idea of the second passage.

- Jot down the relationship between the two passages.

- Work the questions about both passages.

o   1, Both, 2

- Go to the questions about both passages and Use POE based on the first passage.

- Repeat Steps 1–6 with the other passage.

- Jot down the central idea of the second passage.

- Jot down the relationship between the two passages.

- Finish the questions about both passages.

Chapter 6
Additional Reading Strategies

In this chapter, you'll practice alternative strategies you can use to Work the Passage, including reading just the first sentence of each paragraph and working the passage "As You Go." You'll also practice using the "Golden Thread" to help Mark the Answer in the Passage and Use Process of Elimination.

WORK JUST THE FIRST SENTENCES

If you find you have trouble finishing Step 2: Work the Passage in three minutes, you may want to consider reading just the first sentence of each paragraph. We'll try this with the next passage. First, complete Step 1: Preview—check the blurb and map the questions.

SOCIAL SCIENCE: This passage is adapted from the article "This courageous historian fought to make Black History Month possible," by Erin Blakemore, NG Image Collection.

11. Which of the following statements best describes how the passage characterizes Woodson's response to Congress's designation of February as National Black History Month?

12. In the passage, the author emphasizes Woodson's educational achievements by discussing them in the context of:

13. The primary function of the sixth paragraph (lines 31–44) is to:

14. In the context of the passage, the reference to President Gerald Ford primarily serves to:

15. As used in line 36, the word *observing* most nearly means:

16. The passage most strongly suggests that the week founded by Woodson to celebrate black literature and history was first expanded to a month-long celebration in which year?

17. Which of the following questions is most directly answered by the passage?

18. It can most reasonably be inferred from the passage that in the 1920s, some local business owners:

19. The passage author includes the quote in lines 47–52 primarily to:

20. The main purpose of the passage is to:

Try reading just the first sentence of each paragraph. Circle lead words if you see them.

In the early 20th century, historian Carter G. Woodson chafed at the world's silence on black achievement. ————————————————

————————————————————————————————

5 ————————————————————————————————

————————————

The son of formerly enslaved parents who could not read, Woodson had struggled to obtain an education. ————————————

————————————————————————————————

10 ————————————————————————————————

————————————————————————————————

————————————

Over time, Woodson became convinced that the world needed a better understanding of black people's contributions to society to counter racist 15 misperceptions about their abilities and aspirations. ————————————

————————————————————————————————

————————————

In 1915, as the nation celebrated the 50th anniversary of emancipation, Woodson founded the Association for the Study of Negro Life and History, which is now known as the Association for the Study of African American Life and History (ASALH). ─────────────────────────────

───
───
───

25 ──
──

"Woodson overwhelmed his audiences with a wealth of information in his speeches, starting with African history and working his way through all of African-American history," writes biographer Jacqueline Goggin. ───

30 ───

Woodson continually looked for other ways to spread the word about black history and accomplishments, like Africans' contribution to animal domestication and farming techniques and the revolutionary activities of Crispus Attucks, who is thought to be the American Revolutionary War's first casualty. ──

───
───
───

40 ──
───
───
───
──

For Woodson, disseminating information about black history served the dual purposes of building up a sense of black pride and countering racist arguments about the supposed inferiority of black achievements. ──────

50 ──
───
──

Over the years, Woodson's celebration gained steam. ────────────

55 ──
───
───
───

60 Woodson died in 1950, but the week he had founded continued to gain popularity. ───

───
───

65 ──

Other presidents issued messages acknowledging the month each year until February 1986, when Congress passed a law designating that month as National Black (Afro-American) History Month. ─────────────────

70 ──
───
──

Which questions will be easy to find, either because they have line references, or because you found their lead words in the first sentences of the paragraphs?

_____

_____

What does the first sentence of paragraph 10 (lines 67–69) suggest about the topic discussed at the end of the previous paragraph?

_____

_____

In which paragraph will you likely find the answer to question 14?

_____

_____

What difference do you see between the length of the celebration mentioned in the first sentence of paragraph 9 (lines 60–61) and the length of the celebration mentioned in the first sentence of paragraph 10 (lines 67–69)?

_____

_____

What does this difference suggest about where you will find the answer to question 16?

_____

_____

When should you work question 17?

_____

_____

What lead words will help you find the answer to question 18?

_____

_____

What does the first sentence of paragraph 7 (lines 45–47) suggest about the answer to question 19?

_____

_____

When should you work question 20?

_____

_____

Check the answers to this drill at the end of the chapter.

WORK THE PASSAGE "AS YOU GO"

So far, we've covered the approach for working the passage Up Front. You can also work the passage As You Go through the questions.

If you choose to work the passage As You Go, start with Step 1: Preview. Then, move on to Step 3: Select and Understand a Question. Start with a line reference question, choosing the line reference that is nearest the beginning of the passage.

Try Step 1: Preview and Step 3: Select and Understand a Question with the following blurb and set of questions.

Step 1: Preview

NATURAL SCIENCE: This passage is adapted from the article "Cities serve as testbeds for evolutionary change" by Carolyn Beans (published in 2019 by PNAS).

31. The central purpose of the passage is to:

32. It is reasonable to infer that the author would characterize the studies described in the passage as:

33. As it is used in line 26, the phrase *on his home turf* most nearly means:

34. Based on the description in the fifth paragraph (lines 43–55) which factor influencing evolution is most likely at play in the loss of *herbivore defense* in white clover?

35. As it is used in line 7, the word *classic* most nearly means:

36. Based on the passage, Marina Alberti's team found that in comparison with animals and plants in rural areas, those living in urban areas:

37. The third paragraph (lines 22–34) most strongly suggests that Johnson's attitude toward urban environments has shifted from one of:

38. According to the passage, the coloration of the peppered moth shifted due to changes in:

39. Which of the following views most nearly reflects the *mindset* (line 15) that the author claims is changing?

40. According to the passage, white clovers that don't produce a particular defense against pests may:

Step 3: Select and Understand a Question

Which question is best to start with, and why?

In this set, question 35 is the best choice because it includes a line reference, which makes it easy to find, and it comes from the beginning of the passage. If you are going to work the passage As You Go, it makes sense to work the questions in the order they appear in the passage.

35. As it is used in line 7, the word *classic* most nearly means:

What is the question asking?

The question asks what the word *classic* means in context.

Step 4: Read What You Need

Here is the first paragraph of the passage. Read a window around the word *classic*.

    Every student of evolution knows the story of the peppered moth. The species comes in two colors: one a peppered white, the other black. During Britain's industrial revolution, hungry birds spotted the lighter morph in soot-coated forests surrounding cities. Meanwhile, the rarer and better
5 camouflaged darker morph avoided becoming lunch and carried the darker gene variant to a higher frequency in the population. When pollution cleared, the lighter morph again became more common. Yet despite this classic case of natural selection under urban conditions, so iconic that the peppered moth adorns the logo of the Society for the Study of Evolution, biologists have
10 mainly chosen to study evolution in places with less human disturbance. "Most people didn't think that cities were really interesting biologically, that they were kind of anti-life," says evolutionary ecologist Marc Johnson, who directs the Centre for Urban Environments at the University of Toronto Mississauga.

Step 5: **Mark the Answer in the Passage**

The window for this question states, *Every student of evolution knows the story of the peppered moth.* The text describes how the appearance of the peppered moth changed during a time of heavy pollution. Then it states, *Yet despite this classic case of natural selection under urban conditions, so iconic that the peppered moth adorns the logo of the Society for the Study of Evolution, biologists have mainly chosen to study evolution in places with less human disturbance.* Therefore, the word *classic* must mean something like "widely recognized" or "iconic."

Step 6: **Use POE**

Eliminate answers that do not match the text from the passage.

> **35.** As it is used in line 7, the word *classic* most nearly means:
>
> **A.** elegant.
> **B.** ancient.
> **C.** flawless.
> **D.** well-known.

Elegant, ancient, and *flawless* do not match "widely-recognized," so eliminate (A), (B), and (C). *Well-known* matches "widely-recognized," so keep (D). The correct answer is (D).

Repeat Steps 3 through 6

After you have worked the first question, find the next line reference question, working in order of where they appear in the passage. Which one is next?

Question 39 includes a line reference from the second paragraph. You'll read the window for question 39 in a moment, but don't skip right to the second paragraph. Instead, check the first paragraph for lead words from the other questions. This is Working the Passage As You Go through the questions.

Remind yourself of the lead words you underlined during Step 1—specifically, the lead words from the questions that don't include line references. Here are a few: *Marina Alberti* (question 36), *peppered moth* (question 38), *white clovers* (question 40).

Recognize anything? How about *peppered moth*? You've already located *peppered moth* in the first paragraph, so work question 38 next.

38. According to the passage, the coloration of the peppered moth shifted due to changes in:

The question asks what caused the change in color of the peppered moth. The first paragraph states,

> ...During Britain's industrial revolution, hungry birds spotted the lighter morph in soot-coated forests surrounding cities. Meanwhile, the rarer and better
> 5 camouflaged darker morph avoided becoming lunch and carried the darker gene variant to a higher frequency in the population. When pollution cleared, the lighter morph again became more common.

Changes in the level of pollution were behind the pepper moths' coloration changes. Eliminate answers that don't match the text from the passage.

38. According to the passage, the coloration of the peppered moth shifted due to changes in:

   F. food sources.
   G. pollution.
   H. biological studies.
   J. tree coloration.

Of these answers, only (G)—*pollution*—matches the passage. The correct answer is (G).

Now you're ready for question 39.

39. Which of the following views most nearly reflects the *mindset* (line 15) that the author claims is changing?

The question asks which mindset is changing. The window for this question states,

> ..."Most people didn't think that cities were really interesting biologically, that they were kind of anti-life," says evolutionary ecologist Marc Johnson, who directs the Centre for Urban Environments at the University of Toronto Mississauga.
> 15 That mindset is changing as Johnson and others use cities as powerful testbeds for evolutionary mechanisms.

The changing *mindset* is the view that cities are not interesting places to study biological evolution. Eliminate answers that don't match this idea.

39. Which of the following views most nearly reflects the *mindset* (line 15) that the author claims is changing?

    A. Biologists generally maintain that it is not possible to directly compare the evolutionary mechanisms that shape different species.

    B. Ecologists believe that studies should be carefully conducted to lessen human disturbance of natural habitats.

    C. Some researchers hypothesize that species exist exclusively within or outside of city borders.

    D. Many biologists believe that cities do not provide an interesting setting for studies of evolution.

Choices (A), (B), and (C) each use some words from the passage, such as *evolutionary*, *Ecologists*, and *city*, but these are all Words Out of Context trap answers. Eliminate (A), (B), and (C). Choice (D) matches the text from the passage, so keep it. The correct answer is (D).

———————◯———————

The next line reference question is question 33. First, scan the rest of the second paragraph for lead words. In this case, there aren't any, so go on to question 33.

———————◯———————

33. As it is used in line 26, the phrase *on his home turf* most nearly means:

The question asks what the phrase *on his home turf* means in context. The window for this question states,

          Some urban evolutionary biologists initially entered the field in search of species to study closer to home. For Johnson, it was something of an adaptation to new circumstances. "I've spent most of my life trying to get out
25 of cities. Once I became a professor and had a young family, it was harder to go away." So he looked for evolution on his home turf.

The phrase *on his home turf* indicates that Johnson decided to study evolution closer to home. Eliminate answers that do not match this idea.

33. As it is used in line 26, the phrase *on his home turf* most nearly means:

    A. where he is comfortable.

    B. at his own university.

    C. near where he lives.

    D. in rural settings.

Choice (A), *where he is comfortable*, may be true, but it is not supported by direct evidence from the passage. Eliminate (A). Choice (B) is also plausible, but the text does not say whether or not Johnson is completing the studies at his *university*—it only indicates that he is doing the studies in the city near where he lives. Eliminate (B). Keep (C) as it matches the text from the passage. Eliminate (D), which is contradicted by the passage. The correct answer is (C).

———————◯———————

Question 37 also references the third paragraph, so work it next.

---

37. The third paragraph (lines 22–34) most strongly suggests that Johnson's attitude toward urban environments has shifted from one of:

The question asks how Johnson's attitude toward urban environments has shifted. The third paragraph states:

> …For Johnson, it was something of an adaptation to new circumstances. "I've spent most of my life trying to get out
> 25 of cities. Once I became a professor and had a young family, it was harder to go away." So he looked for evolution on his home turf. Aspects of city living such as intensified noise, light, and heat could change which traits natural selection favors. Infrastructure such as buildings and roads could block gene flow—the movement of genes from one population into another
> 30 that occurs when individuals migrate or release genetic material such as seeds or pollen. And because urban populations of plants and animals are often smaller and tucked into isolated patches of green space, they may be more susceptible to genetic drift—random fluctuations in the frequency of gene variants within a population.

Johnson initially tried not to spend time in cities, but then he began to study the effect of *aspects of city living* on *evolution*. Eliminate answers that don't match this text from the passage.

37. The third paragraph (lines 22–34) most strongly suggests that Johnson's attitude toward urban environments has shifted from one of:

    A. avoidance to one of interest in conditions that could shape evolutionary development.

    B. enjoyment to one of ambivalence because his young family prefers opens space.

    C. comfort in familiarity to one of dismay due to growing environmental threats.

    D. uncertainty to one of distaste for conditions of increased noise and light.

Choice (A) matches the text, so keep (A). Choice (B) is contradicted by the passage—at first, he did not enjoy cities, but after he had a family, he spent more time in the city. Eliminate (B). Eliminate (C) because the paragraph doesn't discuss *environmental threats*, nor was Johnson comfortable in cities at first. Eliminate (D) because *distaste* is negative, and there's no evidence that Johnson now has a negative attitude toward the city. In addition, this answer takes Words Out of Context: *noise* and *light* are mentioned as conditions that *could change which traits natural selection favors*; there is no information about how Johnson feels about these conditions. Eliminate (D). The correct answer is (A).

The next paragraph reference comes from question 34, which asks about the fifth paragraph. Before you go there, scan the third and fourth paragraphs for the remaining lead words: *Marina Alberti* and *white clovers*. White clovers are mentioned in the fourth paragraph, so work question 40 next.

40. According to the passage, white clovers that don't produce a particular defense against pests may:

The question asks what *white clovers that don't produce a particular defense against pests* may do. The fourth paragraph states:

> ...Johnson focuses on one particular white clover trait:
> 40 the ability to make hydrogen cyanide. Individual white clovers wielding
> this chemical defense are better at warding off insects and other herbivores.
> Those that can't produce the defense better tolerate freezing temperatures.

The white clovers that don't produce the chemical defense may *better tolerate freezing temperatures*. Eliminate answers that don't match this text from the passage.

40. According to the passage, white clovers that don't produce a particular defense against pests may:

F. be less susceptible to freezing temperatures.
G. not be favored in natural selection.
H. produce alternative defense mechanisms.
J. reproduce around the globe.

Choice (F) matches the text, so keep it. Choices (G), (H), and (J) are not supported by the passage, so eliminate those answers. The correct answer is (F).

Now you're ready for question 34.

34. Based on the description in the fifth paragraph (lines 43–55) which factor influencing evolution is most likely at play in the loss of *herbivore defense* in white clover?

The question references the fifth paragraph, but the answer choices include line references from the third paragraph. You'll need to read both, but start with the fifth paragraph:

> In a recent study, Johnson and his team explored how urbanization influ-
> ences the frequency of hydrogen cyanide producers in 20 cities in southern
> 45 Ontario. In each city, they tested for hydrogen cyanide production in clovers
> along a transect from the city center to rural surroundings. The researchers
> discovered that urban white clovers were more likely to lack the herbivore
> defense, with hydrogen cyanide producers increasing in frequency by about
> 0.6% with every kilometer of distance from an urban center. Despite the fact
> 50 that cities are often warmer than surrounding regions, Johnson's previous
> work had suggested that some city centers in northern climes actually have
> colder minimum winter temperatures than nearby natural areas, in part
> because there's less insulating snow cover. It seemed likely, then, that these
> cooler city temperatures act as a selective pressure pushing white clover to
> 55 lose the herbivore defense in favor of cold tolerance.

So far, you know that *urban white clovers were more likely to lack the herbivore defense*, and that it *seemed likely* that *cooler city temperatures act as a selective pressure pushing white clover to lose the herbivore defense in favor of cold tolerance*. In order to answer the question, you need to read the references in the answer choices to identify the factor that matches the description that the *cooler city temperatures act as a selective pressure*.

34. Based on the description in the fifth paragraph (lines 43–55) which factor influencing evolution is most likely at play in the loss of *herbivore defense* in white clover?

    F. Natural selection (line 28)
    G. Gene flow (line 29)
    H. Genetic drift (line 33)
    J. Fluctuation in gene variant frequency (lines 33–34)

The window that includes lines 28-34 states:

> …Aspects of city living such as intensified noise, light, and heat could change which traits natural selection favors. Infrastructure such as buildings and roads could block gene flow—the movement of genes from one population into another
> 30 that occurs when individuals migrate or release genetic material such as seeds or pollen. And because urban populations of plants and animals are often smaller and tucked into isolated patches of green space, they may be more susceptible to genetic drift—random fluctuations in the frequency of gene variants within a population.

Lines 26–28 state that conditions in the city including temperature *could change which traits natural selection favors*. This matches the description that *cooler city temperatures act as a selective pressure pushing white clover to lose the herbivore defense in favor of cold tolerance*. Keep (F). Lines 28–31 describe *gene flow*, and mention *buildings and roads* blocking the movement of genes. This doesn't match the description of what happened with the white clovers, so eliminate (G). Lines 31–34 describe *genetic drift* as *random fluctuations in the frequency of gene variants*. Neither of these matches the description of what happened with the white clovers, so eliminate (H) and (J). The correct answer is (F).

———————○———————

There is one more specific question left—question 36.

———————○———————

36. Based on the passage, Marina Alberti's team found that in comparison with animals and plants in rural areas, those living in urban areas:

The question asks for a comparison between animals and plants in urban areas and those in rural areas. Read the sixth paragraph, looking for the lead words *Marina Alberti*. The text states:

> Despite clear and repeatable examples of urban evolution, researchers still can't say how commonly city species evolve to embrace urban landscapes. In a recent meta-analysis of experimental and observational studies reporting more than 1,600 phenotypic changes across species, urban

60 ecologist Marina Alberti of the University of Washington and her team
conclude that animal and plant traits shift more rapidly in urban areas. But
most studies in the analysis didn't measure natural selection or identify an
underlying genetic basis to the change. Evolutionary biologists need more
tests of adaptation caused by clear selective pressures to determine which
65 factors influence whether it happens and how consistently.

According to the window, the traits of animals and plants in urban areas change more quickly than those of rural animals and plants. Eliminate answers that do not match this idea.

36. Based on the passage, Marina Alberti's team found that in comparison with animals and plants in rural areas, those living in urban areas:

   F. are more likely to survive quick changes in weather.
   G. undergo more rapid changes in their characteristics.
   H. are more likely to display traits with a clear genetic basis.
   J. experience more gradual shifts in their traits.

Choice (F) mentions *quick changes in weather*, but the passage discusses changes in the animals' and plants' *traits*. Eliminate (F). Keep (G) as it matches the text from the passage. Eliminate (H) because it takes Words Out of Context: the text says that most of the studies didn't *identify an underlying genetic basis to the change*. It does not compare the genetic basis of traits in urban and rural species. Eliminate (J) because it states the opposite of what is indicated by the text. The correct answer is (G).

The two remaining questions are general questions. Now that you have worked the passage while answering the specific questions, you're ready to tackle them.

31. The central purpose of the passage is to:

The question asks for the *central purpose of the passage*. Think back on what you've read, and what you've learned about the passage from the specific questions. The author begins by explaining that until recently, evolutionary biologists have not done much research in urban areas. Then she states that this *mindset is changing*, and she gives examples of recent research into how city environments affect the evolution of plants and animals. The central purpose of the passage is to discuss this new area of research. Eliminate answers that do not match this purpose.

31. The central purpose of the passage is to:

   A. highlight increasing disparities in survival rates between urban and rural members of the same species.
   B. discuss the growing area of urban research within the field of evolutionary biology.
   C. persuade readers to protect plant and animal species threatened by buildings and roads in cities.
   D. convince researchers from other fields to study evolution within cities.

Eliminate (A) because the passage does not discuss *survival rates*. Keep (B) because it matches the passage. Eliminate (C) because the passage is informative; the author does not try to *persuade readers* to take action. There is also no discussion of protecting species, and *roads and buildings* are just one detail rather than a central focus of the passage. At the end of the passage, the author does state that evolutionary biologists need to do more research about evolution in cities, but she does not try to *convince researchers from other fields* to do this research. Eliminate (D). The correct answer is (B).

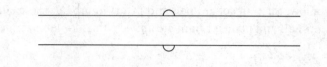

32. It is reasonable to infer that the author would characterize the studies described in the passage as:

The question asks how *the author would characterize the studies described in the passage*. The author presents the studies as examples of researchers' growing interest in urban evolution, and she concludes by stating, *Evolutionary biologists need more tests of adaptation caused by clear selective pressures to determine which factors influence whether it happens and how consistently*. Eliminate answers that do not match this text from the passage.

32. It is reasonable to infer that the author would characterize the studies described in the passage as:

    F. comprehensive; taken together, the studies provide a thorough picture of the mechanisms of urban evolution.

    G. inapplicable; the studies focus on subjects that are only tangentially related to urban evolution.

    H. promising; the studies provide a foundation for additional research in urban evolution.

    J. disappointing; the studies do not provide conclusive evidence of instances of urban evolution.

Eliminate (F) because the author does not consider the studies to be *comprehensive*; she concludes that *more tests* are needed. Eliminate (G) because the author presents the studies as examples of research on urban evolution, saying, *Johnson and others use cities as powerful testbeds for evolutionary mechanisms*. Keep (H) because it matches text from the passage—the author finds the research *promising*, presenting findings from the studies and saying that there are *clear and repeatable examples of urban evolution*, and she also advocates for additional research. Eliminate (J) because it is contradicted by the author's statement that there are *clear and repeatable examples of urban evolution*. The correct answer is (H).

FIND THE GOLDEN THREAD

In an ACT Reading passage, the correct answers agree with each other and with the main idea of the passage. This means that you can use the answers to specific questions to help you answer general questions. Sometimes, you can even use the answer to one specific question to help you answer another specific question.

Take a look at the following set of questions (there is no passage). The correct answer to question 11 is circled. How many of the other answers can you identify because they agree with question 11?

FIND THE GOLDEN THREAD DRILL

SOCIAL SCIENCE: This passage is adapted from the study "The Power of the Urban Canvas: Paint, Politics, and Mural Arts Policy" by Maura E. Greaney (© 2003 by Maura E. Greaney).

11. One of the main points that the author of the study seeks to make in the passage is that public art murals:

 A. do little more than cover up old and abandoned infrastructure.

 B. are more meaningful in large cities than in smaller communities.

 C. improve their communities by encouraging artistic expression and dialogue about local issues.

 D. are only embraced by members of intellectual communities.

12. According to the passage, which of the following is NOT an effect of urban mural programs?

 F. The promotion of cultural appreciation

 G. The elimination of all graffiti on abandoned building

 H. The repurposing of public spaces

 J. The protection of artistic expression

13. The author would most likely agree that:

 A. funding for public murals should come from private donors.

 B. a mural created for the city of Boston might not have the same cultural impact if it were painted in Los Angeles.

 C. national political issues are the most meaningful subjects for public murals.

 D. professional art training is a necessary prerequisite for those participating in public mural creation.

14. When the author argues that *communal bonds* (line 17) are a necessary part of the urban mural programs, she most likely means that public murals:

 F. should be funded by the people in the communities in which the art will be created.

 G. do not matter to individuals outside the neighborhoods in which they were created.

 H. only matter to "at-risk" youths and disadvantaged groups.

 J. require collaboration and discussion among community members.

15. Based on the passage, a public mural would be LEAST effective at inspiring conversations about:

 A. political challenges.

 B. art styles.

 C. economic inequity.

 D. social justice.

16. As it is used in line 63, the word *tension* most nearly means:

 F. conflict.

 G. stress.

 H. tautness.

 J. balance.

17. The author maintains that city policy makers must:

 A. allow people of a community to participate in the creation of murals.

 B. carefully research topics for mural subjects.

 C. actively push others to create murals that increase the city's economic value.

 D. limit their involvement in public art projects.

18. According to the lines 46–47, the author would most likely agree that which of the following constitutes an effective subject for a public mural?

 F. A street scene of a neighboring town

 G. A picket line at a local factory

 H. An abstract design

 J. A family reunion

19. In the sixth paragraph, the phrase "Culture is an indispensable weapon in the freedom struggle" (lines 82–83) supports the idea that:

 A. violence plays a role in the subjects of many public murals.

 B. maintaining a productive public art program is a challenging endeavor.

 C. public art gives underrepresented people a way to express their ideas.

 D. meaningful cultural expression is only possible in homogenous neighborhoods.

20. In the passage, the author argues that public art has the ability to:

 F. empower the community to celebrate local culture.

 G. teach residents the meaning of fine art.

 H. engage artists who would otherwise be unemployed.

 J. increase property values by incorporating fashionable design.

DRILL ANSWERS

Work Just the First Sentences Drill Answers

Which questions will be easy to find?

> Question 11 – The lead words *Congress*, *designating*, and *Black History Month* appear in the last paragraph.

> Question 12 – The lead word *education* appears in the second paragraph.

> Question 13 – The question includes a line reference.

> Question 15 – The question includes a line reference.

> Question 19 – The question includes a line reference.

What does the first sentence of paragraph 10 (lines 67–69) suggest about the topic discussed at the end of the previous paragraph?

> The words "Other presidents" suggests that the end of the previous paragraph discussed something about what one president did.

In which paragraph will you likely find the answer to question 14?

> You will most likely find it in paragraph 9 (lines 60–66).

What difference do you see between the length of the celebration mentioned in the first sentence of paragraph 9 (line 63) and the length of the celebration mentioned in the first sentence of paragraph 10 (lines 67–69)?

> The first sentence of paragraph 9 mentions the *week* he founded, but the first sentence of paragraph 10 mentions acknowledging the *month* each year.

What does this difference suggest about where you will find the answer to question 16?

> It will most likely be answered in paragraph 9, after the mention of the *week* but before the mention of the *month*.

When should you work question 17?

> You should work it after you work all of the easy-to-find questions. Working the easy-to-find questions will familiarize you with the structure and content of the passage, which will make it easier to find the right locations in the passage for question 17.

What lead words will help you find the answer to question 18?

You should look for *1920s* and *business owners*.

What does the first sentence of paragraph 7 (lines 45–47) suggest about the answer to question 19?

The topic sentence of a paragraph is a good place to look for a clue about the purpose of details included in the paragraph. The first sentence of paragraph 7 says, *For Woodson, disseminating information about black history served the dual purposes of building up a sense of black pride and countering racist arguments about the supposed inferiority of black achievements.* The purpose of the quotation in paragraph 7 is probably to support this point.

When should you work question 20?

Question 20 is a general question that asks about the passage as a whole, so you should work it after you work the specific questions. You will read most of the passage and identify many correct answers while working the specific questions, which will give you a sense of the main idea of the passage.

Find the Golden Thread Drill Answers

11. **C**
12. **G**
13. **B**
14. **J**
15. **B**
16. **F**
17. **A**
18. **G**
19. **C**
20. **F**

Summary

- ○ If you have trouble finishing Step 2: Work the Passage in three minutes, consider reading just the first sentence of each paragraph.

- ○ You can Work the Passage As You Go through the questions instead of Up Front.

  - • Work the specific questions in line reference order.

  - • Look for lead words in between the line references.

  - • Work general questions last.

- ○ Find the Golden Thread.

  - • The correct answers agree with one another and with the main idea.

  - • Use the Golden Thread to help with general questions and questions that are hard to answer.

Chapter 7
Advanced Reading Strategies

Build your skills for working challenging Reading passages and questions.

ADVANCED STRATEGIES

If you encounter a question that is hard to answer, or a passage that is tough to understand, remember Personal Order of Difficulty: leave the tough passage or question for Later or Never, and make sure you've worked the more straightforward passages or questions first. When you're ready to work one of the tougher questions or passages, try the strategies outlined in this chapter.

We'll learn the strategies as we work the questions for a challenging passage. First, Preview by checking the blurb and mapping the questions, then Work the Passage.

> **HUMANITIES:** This passage is adapted from the book *Merce Cunningham*, edited by James Klosty (© 1975 by James Klosty).

21. The author describes Cunningham as all of the following EXCEPT:

22. Based on the passage, it can most reasonably be inferred that Cunningham's critics objected to:

23. When the author uses the phrase, "Cunningham chose to begin at the root," (lines 38–39), he most nearly means that:

24. As used in line 34, the word *kinetic* most likely refers to:

25. The passage author most strongly implies that Martha Graham's response to a choreographic work by Cunningham would most likely be one of:

26. Which of the following quotations most directly relates to the author's view of what made Cunningham unique as a choreographer?

27. The passage author responds to Cunningham's critics by:

28. The author uses the statement "If ballet-goers couldn't *name* the steps they nonetheless could *hum* them" (lines 48–49) most nearly to:

29. The main purpose of the fourth paragraph (lines 25–32) is to:

30. The passage as a whole is best described as:

Merce Cunningham. Dancer. Choreographer. Teacher. Born in Centralia, Washington, an obscure number of years before the stock market crashed. Draws careful studies of plants for pleasure. Charming in public. Fierce in self-discipline. At ease in motion. At home in secrecy. By example and
5 accomplishment has done more to generate and influence the contemporary arts than any other choreographer.
Cunningham's revolution, begun in the early 1950s, was undertaken not to startle or to scandalize, but to discover a way of working comfortable for his personality and compatible with his personal vision. His ideas were not
10 unique. They were shared by friends: composers (John Cage, Earle Brown, Morton Feldman, Christian Wolff); and painters (Robert Rauschenberg,

Jasper Johns, etc.). But the ideas were not shared by his compatriots in the world of dance. In fact, Cunningham's ideas were *antithetical* to commonly held concepts of serious dancing, to many ideals of classical ballet, and
15 particularly to the aesthetic of Martha Graham, in whose company Cunningham's career had begun.

Cunningham was urged to leave Graham by John Cage, soon to become America's most controversial composer, as well as a respected poet, philosopher, graphic artist, and mycologist. The two men gave several concerts
20 together in the 1940s, and when Cunningham began to assemble his own company of dancers, Cage did whatever had to be done to keep the company going. At one time or another he has been its program designer, agent, pianist, composer, chauffer, food gatherer, impresario, apologist, fund raiser, chef de cuisine, comedian, and spiritual mentor.

25 Cunningham's association with Cage was as much an idea as it was a fact. Their working together brought forth a new aesthetic holding that dance is dance and music is music—an aesthetic so simple that few were able to accept it with equanimity. Both men shared the belief that neither dance nor music need function as a dependent of the other, that the two
30 have nothing arbitrarily in common but custom, that their combination is less necessity than reflex, and that they can be advantageously freed of one another's syntax.

Cunningham proceeded to develop a choreography and a technique based on the kinetic integrity of the body unconstrained by the rhythmic,
35 melodic, or formal proposals of an external music. It was a concept of dance quite beyond plotless Balanchine or Ashton's *Symphonic Variations*, those highly refined examples of an art that has always been subsumed in implied or explicit musical structures. Cunningham chose to begin at the root. He turned dance back upon itself, focusing on its primary component:
40 each movement as an atomic gesture in time. He felt that dancing need not concern itself with narrative nor with philosophical, psychological or mythical pretensions. Presumably, if one danced, and danced well, that ought to be enough—both for the dancer and for his audience. Martha Graham and Jose Limon were clearly of another mind. True, for modern dance's Doris
45 Humphrey and certain ballet choreographers nonnarrative dancing was quite respectable, but the whitest of "white" ballets was still about music in some sense, still about the great ongoing affair between dancer and orchestra or dancer and piano. If ballet-goers couldn't *name* the steps they nonetheless could *hum* them. But the music at Cunningham performances was new
50 and unusually experimental. It was difficult to listen to, no less to hum. And Cunningham's dancers, as an ultimate insult, attempted to do neither! Ballet without meanings was one thing, since music helped to underline the dancing for one's eyes through one's ears. But an enterprise in which music was as irrelevant as narrative? Thus are anarchists and *enfants terribles* born!
55 Dionysiacs too—to use the epithet for Cunningham one critic preferred.

But the cries of "anarchy" were far-fetched, as outlandish as the reference to Dionysus. Far from Bacchic abandon, the rule for Cunningham's dancers is absolute definition. Traditional ballet is a far more Dionysian enterprise, for the dancer can ride the musical pulse, using it as a kind of
60 surrogate heartbeat on which bodily functions play without consciousness. Absence of metrical accompaniment only intensifies the mental effort needed to establish the strict order that supports each dancer's part. Cunningham dancing is a rigorously Apollonian activity: it is the dancer, not the music, who recreates the spatial and temporal structure that is each dance.
65 To perform a work of several sections, each several minutes in duration, with one's muscle memory the only "clock," and to come within seconds of a required time at each performance, is a task no Dionysian would contemplate, nor attempt, nor accomplish.

Translate

Translating will help you answer tough reasoning questions and questions involving difficult vocabulary. It can also help you to understand the main point, determine the purpose, and identify tone. Translating comes in handy particularly on dense, difficult passages, but it's a skill we use for all reading comprehension.

Use translating to work the following questions.

---

25. The passage author most strongly implies that Martha Graham's response to a choreographic work by Cunningham would most likely be one of:

The question asks how Martha Graham would likely respond to Cunningham's choreographic work. Use the lead words *Martha Graham* to find the window for the question, and then Read What You Need. *Martha Graham* appears in the second paragraph.

> Cunningham's revolution, begun in the early 1950s, was undertaken not to startle or to scandalize, but to discover a way of working comfortable for his personality and compatible with his personal vision. His ideas were not
> 10 unique. They were shared by friends: composers (John Cage, Earle Brown, Morton Feldman, Christian Wolff); and painters (Robert Rauschenberg, Jasper Johns, etc.). But the ideas were not shared by his compatriots in the world of dance. In fact, Cunningham's ideas were *antithetical* to commonly held concepts of serious dancing, to many ideals of classical ballet, and
> 15 particularly to the aesthetic of Martha Graham, in whose company Cunningham's career had begun.

The window for this question includes a fairly difficult vocabulary word, *antithetical*. In order to Mark the Answer in the Passage, you will need to translate. Use the surrounding context for clues, starting with the pieces of information that you understand best.

The previous sentence states that Cunningham's *ideas were not shared by his compatriots in the world of dance.* This indicates that other artists in the dance world did not agree with Cunningham's ideas.

Next, look at the sentence including the word *antithetical*: *Cunningham's ideas were antithetical to commonly held concepts of serious dancing.* Together with the previous sentence, this suggests that *antithetical to* means something like "in opposition to."

The text states, *Cunningham's ideas were antithetical to commonly held concepts of serious dancing, to many ideals of classical ballet, and particularly to the aesthetic of Martha Graham.* Based on the translation you've done, you know that *antithetical to* means *opposed to.* Therefore, Martha Graham would most likely be opposed to Cunningham's style of choreography.

Use Process of Elimination to eliminate answers that do not match the translation based on the text from the passage.

25. The passage author most strongly implies that Martha Graham's response
    to a choreographic work by Cunningham would most likely be one of:

    A. supportive guidance of his development.
    B. opposition to his artistic principles.
    C. criticism of his lack of originality.
    D. appreciation for his revolutionary approach.

Choice (A) is a Words Out of Context trap answer—the text says that Cunningham began his career as a member of Graham's company, but the text also says that Cunningham's ideas were *antithetical… particularly to the aesthetic of Martha Graham*. Therefore, the text does not support the idea that Graham would respond to Cunningham's work with support. Eliminate (A). Choice (B) matches the text from the passage, so keep it. The word *criticism* in (C) matches the passage, but the text says that Cunningham's ideas were opposed to the *aesthetic of Martha Graham*; therefore, she would critique his work because it was aesthetically (artistically) different from hers, not because of *his lack of originality*. This answer takes Words Out of Context. Earlier in the paragraph, the text says that Cunningham's *ideas were not unique* because they were shared by artists in other disciplines: *composers* and *painters*. However, the text suggests that Cunningham's approach was unique within the dance world at that time. Eliminate (C). Choice (D) also takes Words Out of Context: the text does mention *Cunningham's revolution*, but the text from the passage indicates that Martha Graham would respond to his *revolutionary approach* with opposition, not *appreciation*. Eliminate (D). The correct answer is (B).

———○———

Use translation based on context clues to answer the following questions:

———○———

28. The author uses the statement "If ballet-goers couldn't *name* the steps they
    nonetheless could *hum* them" (lines 48–49) most nearly to:

The question asks why the author includes the quote in the question. Use the given line reference to find the window, then Read What You Need.

                                  True, for modern dance's Doris
45 Humphrey and certain ballet choreographers nonnarrative dancing was
   quite respectable, but the whitest of "white" ballets was still about music in
   some sense, still about the great ongoing affair between dancer and orchestra
   or dancer and piano. If ballet-goers couldn't *name* the steps they nonetheless could *hum* them. But the music at Cunningham performances was new
50 and unusually experimental. It was difficult to listen to, no less to hum. And
   Cunningham's dancers, as an ultimate insult, attempted to do neither! Ballet
   without meanings was one thing, since music helped to underline the dancing for one's eyes through one's ears. But an enterprise in which music was
   as irrelevant as narrative?

The quote in the question is about *ballet-goers*. This is a lead word: use it to help you sort through the text and focus on the most useful information. The quote also mentions that the ballet-goers could *hum* the steps. The idea of humming a dance step may seem odd, but this is also a clue: the information you are looking for may be about music. The text states that ballet *was still about music in some sense, still about the great ongoing affair between dancer and orchestra or dancer and piano.* Later the text says, *Ballet without meanings was one thing, since music helped to underline the dancing for one's eyes through one's ears.* This information suggests that music was important in ballet, and that music helped people watching ballet to understand or appreciate the dancing.

Use Process of Elimination to eliminate answers that do not match this translation.

28. The author uses the statement "If ballet-goers couldn't *name* the steps they nonetheless could *hum* them" (lines 48–49) most nearly to:

   F. establish that dancing Cunningham's choreography was a rigorously Apollonian activity.
   G. demonstrate the essential role that Cage's music played in shaping the structure of Cunningham's choreography.
   H. convey that arts patrons were familiar with the musical compositions to which ballet was choreographed.
   J. emphasize that traditional dance choreography was closely related to the music that accompanied it.

Choice (F) is an Out the Window answer—the discussion about *Apollonian activity* occurs in the final paragraph and does not explain why the author uses the statement mentioned in question 28. Eliminate (F). Choice (G) is contradicted by the passage, which implies that *music* was *irrelevant* to Cunningham's choreography. This is a Words Out of Context answer that mistakenly applies what the passage says about the essential relationship between *ballet* and its music to Cunningham's choreography. Eliminate (G). Choice (H) is a Right Answer, Wrong Question trap—the statement that ballet-goers *could hum* the steps indicates that they probably were familiar with the music that accompanied the ballet; however, that fact does not answer the question that was asked. The question asks *why* the author uses the statement, and the author uses the statement to convey that music helped people watching ballet to understand or appreciate the dancing. Eliminate (H). Choice (J) matches the text from the passage, so keep it. The correct answer is (J).

23. When the author uses the phrase, "Cunningham chose to begin at the root," (lines 38–39), he most nearly means that Cunningham:

The question asks what the author means by the statement, *Cunningham chose to begin at the root.* Use the given line reference to find the window, then Read What You Need.

Cunningham proceeded to develop a choreography and a technique based on the kinetic integrity of the body unconstrained by the rhythmic,
35 melodic, or formal proposals of an external music. It was a concept of dance quite beyond plotless Balanchine or Ashton's *Symphonic Variations,* those highly refined examples of an art that has always been subsumed in implied or explicit musical structures. Cunningham chose to begin at the root. He turned dance back upon itself, focusing on its primary component:
40 each movement as an atomic gesture in time. He felt that dancing need not concern itself with narrative nor with philosophical, psychological or mythical pretensions.

When a question asks what is meant by a particular word or phrase, the answer is often found in the surrounding text. To Mark the Answer in the Passage, translate the phrase based on the context. After the quoted phrase, the next sentence states that Cunningham focused on dance's *primary component: each movement as an atomic gesture in time*. To state this simply, Cunningham focused on each individual movement in his dances.

Use Process of Elimination to eliminate answers that do not match this translation.

23. When the author uses the phrase, "Cunningham chose to begin at the root," (lines 38–39), he most likely means that Cunningham:

A. turned back time by drawing his choreographic inspiration from movements that were present in the earliest forms of dance.

B. sought to unify dance rhythm and style with the rhythm and melody of external music.

C. focused on movement itself rather than on conveying stories or ideas through movement.

D. developed his dance based on the foundation created by his predecessors, such as Balanchine and Ashton.

Choice (A) is a Words Out of Context answer: the text says that Cunningham *turned dance back upon itself*, not that he *turned back time*. Furthermore, there is no mention of early forms of dance. Eliminate (A). Choice (B) is contradicted by the passage: the text says that Cunningham's choreography was *unconstrained by* (which means "not limited by") *external music*. It does not say that he tried to *unify* dance with external music. Notice how important one word can be in translating correctly. As you work through the answer choices, make sure each word matches the meaning in the text. Eliminate (B). Keep (C) because it matches the idea that Cunningham focused on *each movement*. The text also says that Cunningham *felt that dancing need not concern itself with narrative nor with philosophical, psychological or mythical pretensions*, which matches *rather than…conveying stories or ideas*. Choice (D) is contradicted by the passage: the text says that Cunningham's *concept of dance* was *quite beyond plotless Balanchine or Ashton's Symphonic Variations*, which the author says are examples of dance that was *subsumed in* (absorbed in) *external musical structures*. Since Cunningham's dance was *unconstrained by* external music, the author is contrasting Cunningham with Balanchine and Ashton. Eliminate (D). The correct answer is (C).

---

24. As used in line 34, the word *kinetic* most likely refers to:

The question asks what the word *kinetic* refers to. Use the given line reference to find the window for the question, then Read What You Need. This question uses the same window as question 23.

> Cunningham proceeded to develop a choreography and a technique based on the kinetic integrity of the body unconstrained by the rhythmic,
> 35 melodic, or formal proposals of an external music. It was a concept of dance quite beyond plotless Balanchine or Ashton's *Symphonic Variations*, those highly refined examples of an art that has always been subsumed in implied or explicit musical structures. Cunningham chose to begin at the root. He turned dance back upon itself, focusing on its primary component:
> 40 each movement as an atomic gesture in time. He felt that dancing need not concern itself with narrative nor with philosophical, psychological or mythical pretensions.

To Mark the Answer in the Passage, translate based on the context in the window. The text says that Cunningham's technique was based on the *kinetic integrity of the body*, so the word *kinetic* is likely related to the body. This sentence also indicates that the word *kinetic* is related to something that Cunningham based his choreography on. Later, the text says that Cunningham focused on *each movement*, so the word *kinetic* may be related to movement.

Use Process of Elimination to eliminate answers that do not match this idea.

> **24.** As used in line 34, the word *kinetic* most likely refers to:
>
> **F.** story.
> **G.** movement.
> **H.** rhythm.
> **J.** melody.

The text says that Cunningham felt that dancing did not need to *concern itself with narrative*, and the word *narrative* means "story." Since Cunningham felt that story was not important, he probably did not base his choreography on story. Therefore, the word *kinetic* probably does not refer to *story*. Eliminate (F). Keep (G) because it matches the passage. The text says that Cunningham's choreography was *unconstrained by the rhythmic* and *melodic proposals* of music. As noted in question 23, *unconstrained by* means *not limited by*, so Cunningham's choreography was not based on *rhythm* or *melody*. Eliminate (H) and (J). The correct answer is (G).

Topic Sentences and Transition Words

Making predictions as you read will help you read passages more efficiently, because it helps you know what to look for before you read. Predictions based on surrounding text can also help you find the correct windows for questions and identify correct answers. Topic sentences (first sentences) of each paragraph often provide a good map of the passage's structure. Transition words such as "but," "however," "furthermore," and "for example" are also important clues to the structure of an author's message.

For more on transition words, see the Princeton Review's companion book, *ACT English Prep*.

Where would you expect to find the windows for the following two questions?

> **22.** Based on the passage, it can most reasonably be inferred that Cunningham's critics objected to:

> **27.** The passage author responds to Cunningham's critics by:

These questions don't include line references, and they don't have very good lead words, either. They include the capitalized word *Cunningham's*, but the whole passage is about Cunningham. They ask about *critics*, but that word is not very easy to spot in the text.

Use the topic sentences of the paragraphs to get a sense of where the discussion of *Cunningham's critics* might be. The first sentence of the first paragraph is simply, *Merce Cunningham*.

This paragraph may be a general introduction to Merce Cunningham and his work. The first sentence of the second paragraph reads, *Cunningham's revolution, begun in the early 1950s, was undertaken not to startle or to scandalize, but to discover a way of working comfortable for his personality and compatible with his personal vision.* The second paragraph may be about Cunningham's motivations for doing things his own way. The first sentences of the third and fourth paragraphs both mention *John Cage.* These two paragraphs likely discuss John Cage and the partnership between Cage and Cunningham. The first sentence of the fifth paragraph says, *Cunningham proceeded to develop a choreography and a technique based on the kinetic integrity of the body unconstrained by the rhythmic, melodic, or formal proposals of an external music.* This paragraph will likely include details about Cunningham's approach to choreography. So far, we haven't seen any indication of a discussion of critics. The first sentence of the last paragraph says, *But the cries of "anarchy" were far-fetched, as outlandish as the reference to Dionysus.* The phrase *cries of "anarchy"* sounds critical, so the windows for question 22 and question 27 are likely near this line. However, the windows won't be exactly the same. Where will you find the objections of the critics, and where will you find the author's response to the critics? Read the topic sentence carefully—it begins with the transition word *but,* and it says that *the cries of anarchy were far-fetched.* The author has probably just discussed *the cries of "anarchy"* at the end of the previous paragraph, and the word *but* indicates a change in direction. Therefore, the window for question 22 is likely the end of the previous paragraph, and the window for question 27 most likely includes the last paragraph.

Try working the two questions.

---

22. Based on the passage, it can most reasonably be inferred that Cunningham's critics objected to:

The question asks what *Cunningham's critics objected to.* Now that you have found the window for the question, Read What You Need and Mark the Answer in the Passage.

> …But the music at Cunningham performances was new
> 50 and unusually experimental. It was difficult to listen to, no less to hum. And
> Cunningham's dancers, as an ultimate insult, attempted to do neither! Ballet
> without meanings was one thing, since music helped to underline the danc-
> ing for one's eyes through one's ears. But an enterprise in which music was
> as irrelevant as narrative? Thus are anarchists and *enfants terribles* born!
> 55 Dionysiacs too—to use the epithet for Cunningham one critic preferred.

Now you can see the lead word, *critic,* in the last sentence of the paragraph. Translate the text, looking for words that indicate a critical point of view. The text says that the *music* was *difficult to listen to, no less to hum. And Cunningham's dancers, as an ultimate insult, attempted to do neither!* What does the word *neither* refer back to? It refers back to listening to the music and humming the music. Then, the text indicates that in ballet, *music helped to underline the dancing for one's eyes through one's ears,* which indicates that the music was closely related to the dancing in ballet. The next sentence starts with another opposite direction transition, *but,* and says, *an enterprise in which music was as irrelevant as narrative.* This sentence contrasts Cunningham's choreography with ballet and indicates that the music was irrelevant to Cunningham's choreography. In the next sentence, you may not understand *enfants terribles,* but *anarchists* are people who rebel against the established way of doing things. Therefore, putting all of the translation together, Cunningham's critics objected to the fact that the music was not relevant to the dancing in Cunningham's choreography, which was not like what they were used to in more traditional dance.

Use Process of Elimination to eliminate answers that do not match this translation.

22. Based on the passage, it can most reasonably be inferred that Cunningham's critics objected to:

F. Cunningham's apparent belief that narrative was irrelevant to dance.
G. the contempt that Cunningham showed for choreographers who were otherwise highly regarded.
H. Cunningham's disregard for the traditional relationship between dance and music.
J. the lack of technical training required for dancers in Cunningham's company.

Choice (F) is a Words Out of Context answer: *narrative* was not relevant to Cunningham's dance, but the passage discusses other choreographers who also created non-narrative dance and suggests that critics accepted this, saying, *Ballet without meanings was one thing, since music helped to underline the dancing for one's eyes through one's ears.* Therefore, the lack of *narrative* was not what critics objected to, so eliminate (F). Choice (G) is not supported by the passage; according to the text, Cunningham did things differently from other choreographers, but there is no indication that he showed *contempt* for them. Eliminate (G). Keep (H) because it matches the text from the passage. Eliminate (J) because there is no mention of the dancers' *technical training*. The correct answer is (H).

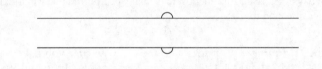

27. The passage author responds to Cunningham's critics by:

The question asks how the *author responds to Cunningham's critics*. We have already identified the final paragraph as the window for question 27, so Read What You Need.

> But the cries of "anarchy" were far-fetched, as outlandish as the reference to Dionysus. Far from Bacchic abandon, the rule for Cunningham's dancers is absolute definition. Traditional ballet is a far more Dionysian enterprise, for the dancer can ride the musical pulse, using it as a kind of
> 60 surrogate heartbeat on which bodily functions play without consciousness. Absence of metrical accompaniment only intensifies the mental effort needed to establish the strict order that supports each dancer's part. Cunningham dancing is a rigorously Apollonian activity: it is the dancer, not the music, who recreates the spatial and temporal structure that is each dance.
> 65 To perform a work of several sections, each several minutes in duration, with one's muscle memory the only "clock," and to come within seconds of a required time at each performance, is a task no Dionysian would contemplate, nor attempt, nor accomplish.

Now use translation to help you determine the correct answer. The transition word *but* at the beginning of the paragraph indicates that that the author disagrees with the critics, and indeed, he describes the critics' objections as *far-fetched* and *outlandish*. It may be difficult to understand the details about *Dionysian* and *Apollonian* activity in this paragraph, but you can eliminate answers that do not indicate disagreement.

> **27.** The passage author responds to Cunningham's critics by:
>
> **A.** countering the suggestion that Cunningham's dance lacks discipline.
> **B.** providing additional details to support the description of Cunningham's choreography as anarchic.
> **C.** objecting to the critics' focus on Apollonian and Dionysian qualities in dance.
> **D.** providing an overview of the change in critical response throughout Cunningham's career.

Eliminate (B) because it indicates that the author supports the critics' description of Cunningham's work as *anarchy*. Eliminate (D) because it indicates that the author is neutral with regard to the critics' objections. There is also no discussion of a *change* in critical response. You have a 50/50 chance of guessing correctly on this question now, so remember POOD: it may be time to guess and move on to another question.

If your pacing target tells you that you need to keep working on this question, focus on the differences between the two remaining answers and continue translating. Choice (A) says that the author counters a suggestion that the critics made, while (C) says that the author objects to what the critics focus on. In the passage, the author says that the critics' *reference to Dionysus* is *outlandish*, and then states that *the rule for Cunningham's dancers is absolute definition*, which he describes as being *far from Bacchic abandon*. He describes ballet as *Dionysian* and mentions that in ballet the dancers can follow the music *without consciousness*. He contrasts this with Cunningham's choreography, which he says is *Apollonian*; he also describes how the lack of *metrical accompaniment* increases *the mental effort needed to establish the strict order that supports each dancer's part*. He also argues that Cunningham's dancers had to *perform a work of several sections, each several minutes in duration, with one's muscle memory the only "clock," and to come within seconds of a required time at each performance*. Putting these pieces of information together, the author uses the terms *Apollonian* and *Dionysian* to contrast Cunningham's choreography with ballet, so he seems to accept these qualities as a valid focus when discussing dance. Therefore, (C) can be eliminated. The author's use of terms such as *mental effort* and *strict order* and his description of the challenging tasks Cunningham's dancers had to perform indicate that he believes the dancers had *discipline*, which supports (A). The correct answer is (A).

Try working a purpose question.

> **29.** The main purpose of the fourth paragraph (lines 25–32) is to:

The question asks *why* the author includes the fourth paragraph. Questions that ask *why* something was said can seem more challenging than questions that simply ask *what* was said. However, just like the reference questions, these reasoning questions are based on evidence in the text. The topic sentence of a paragraph can provide an important clue to the author's purpose in that paragraph.

First, Read What You Need: the window for this question is the fourth paragraph.

> 25 Cunningham's association with Cage was as much an idea as it was a fact. Their working together brought forth a new aesthetic holding that dance is dance and music is music—an aesthetic so simple that few were able to accept it with equanimity. Both men shared the belief that neither dance nor music need function as a dependent of the other, that the two
> 30 have nothing arbitrarily in common but custom, that their combination is less necessity than reflex, and that they can be advantageously freed of one another's syntax.

Remember that you are looking for an answer that explains *why* the author included this paragraph. The topic sentence of the paragraph references *Cunningham's association with Cage*. Therefore, the correct answer will likely be about the partnership between Cunningham and Cage. The rest of the topic sentence says that their association *was as much an idea as it was a fact*. The exact meaning of this piece of information is not quite as clear, so use the details given in the paragraph to help you translate. Start with the pieces of information that are easiest to understand. The paragraph mentions music and dance several times. We know from working other questions that Cunningham was a choreographer and Cage was a composer, so this reference to dance and music makes sense. The text says that both Cunningham and Cage *shared the belief that neither dance nor music need function as a dependent of the other*. In other words, they believed that music did not need to be dependent on dance, and dance did not need to be dependent on music. The rest of that sentence makes the same point in different ways: dance and music have nothing in common but tradition, combining dance and music is not necessary, and dance and music can be freed of one another. The second sentence of the paragraph says that Cunningham and Cage *working together brought forth a new aesthetic*. Putting these pieces together, the paragraph's purpose is to convey that, working together, Cunningham and Cage did something new: they separated music from dance.

Use Process of Elimination to eliminate answers that do not match this idea.

> **29.** The main purpose of the fourth paragraph (lines 25–32) is to:
> **A.** highlight how difficult Cunningham and Cage's approach was for the wider dance community to accept.
> **B.** emphasize the innovative nature of Cunningham's artistic relationship with John Cage.
> **C.** establish that Cunningham had a greater influence on dance innovation than did Cage.
> **D.** persuade the reader that dance is dance and music is music.

Choice (A) is a Right Answer, Wrong Question trap: the text says that *few were able to accept* Cunningham and Cage's new aesthetic *with equanimity*, but highlighting this fact is not the purpose of the paragraph. This answer focuses on what was said instead of on *why* it was said. Eliminate (A). Keep (B) because it addresses the relationship between Cunningham and Cage and says that the partnership was *innovative*, which matches text from the passage. Eliminate (C) because there is no comparison between Cunningham and Cage suggesting that one was more influential than the other. Choice (D) is another Right Answer, Wrong Question trap:

the passage states that in Cage and Cunningham's work, *dance is dance and music is music.* However, the purpose of the passage is not to *persuade the reader* of this. Again, this answer focuses on what was said instead of why it was said. Eliminate (D). The correct answer is (B).

Work Backward from the Answers

We discussed working backward from the answers in Chapter 4, and this skill is especially helpful when working hard-to-find and hard-to-answer questions.

Try the following EXCEPT/LEAST/NOT question.

---

21. The author describes Cunningham as all of the following EXCEPT:

The question asks for a description of Cunningham that does *not* match the passage. Use lead words from the answer choices to find the window for question.

21. The author describes Cunningham as all of the following EXCEPT:
- **A.** a teacher.
- **B.** a composer.
- **C.** a dancer.
- **D.** a choreographer.

The words *dancer, choreographer,* and *teacher* all appear in the first paragraph, and are used to describe *Merce Cunningham.* The word *composer* appears in lines 10 and 18, but it is used to describe other people, including *John Cage.* It does not describe Cunningham.

Notice that on this question, it was not possible to Mark the Answer in the Passage. For an EXCEPT/LEAST/NOT question, simply eliminate answers that are supported by the passage, and choose the answer that is *not* supported by the passage. Eliminate (A), (C), and (D). The correct answer is (B).

Try working backward on a question that includes line references in the answers.

---

26. Which of the following quotations most directly relates to the author's view of what made Cunningham unique as a choreographer?

The question asks for a quotation that reflects the *author's view* of what made Cunningham's choreography *unique.* Use the line references from the answers to find what you need in the passage.

As with question 21, it is not possible to Mark the Answer in the Passage. Instead, use Process of Elimination, eliminating answers that do not answer the correct question. Remember to read a small window around each line reference so that you understand the context.

> 26. Which of the following quotations most directly relates to the author's view of what made Cunningham unique as a choreographer?
>
> F. "At home in secrecy" (line 4)
> G. "whatever had to be done" (line 21)
> H. "the great ongoing affair between dancer and orchestra" (line 47)
> J. "music was as irrelevant as narrative" (lines 53–54)

The lines for (F) describe Cunningham as a person, but they do not describe his choreography, so eliminate (F). The lines for (G) describe what John Cage did. Since these lines are not about Cunningham, eliminate (G). The lines for (H) refer to ballet, not to Cunningham's choreography, so eliminate (H). The lines for (J) describe an aspect of Cunningham's choreography. As we have seen while working other questions, throughout the passage the author discusses the fact that Cunningham separated dance from music, which made his work different from ballet and other modern dance. Therefore, this quotation relates to the author's view of what made Cunningham's choreography unique. The correct answer is (J).

Use Previous Questions and the Golden Thread

In question 26, you used what you had read while working other questions to help you. Working a hard-to-find question Later can help because as you work the questions, you become more familiar with the structure of the passage, which makes it easier to find the questions. Working a hard-to-answer question Later can help because as you work the questions, you become more familiar with the passage's Golden Thread, which can help you predict the correct answer based on the text and Use Process of Elimination. (There is more on the Golden Thread in Chapter 6).

Use your previous work on this passage to answer the last question.

> 30. The passage as a whole is best described as:

This is a general question that asks for a description of the passage as a whole, so look for the Golden Thread. The passage discusses the choreography of Merce Cunningham, emphasizing that his work was unique in the dance world at that time. In particular, the author focuses on the fact that Cunningham's choreography was not dependent on the music that accompanied it— a fact that critics at the time objected to.

Use Process of Elimination to eliminate answers that do not match this idea.

30. The passage as a whole is best described as:

    F. an introduction to the innovative and controversial choreographic work of Merce Cunningham.

    G. a comparison between the choreography of Merce Cunningham and the work of artists in other fields such as painting and composing.

    H. a critique of Merce Cunningham's collaboration with John Cage as a missed opportunity to create meaningful connections between composing and choreography.

    J. a detailed biographical portrait of Merce Cunningham's life including his early career as a dancer.

Choice (F) matches the text—the passage supports the description *innovative* because Cunningham's work was unique in the dance world at that time, and it supports *controversial* because critics objected to the work. Keep (F). Choice (G) is a Right Answer, Wrong Question trap: the second paragraph provides some *comparison* of Cunningham's choreography with the work of certain painters and composers, but this is one detail and does not describe *the passage as a whole*. Eliminate (G). Choice (H) has the wrong tone: the author is complimentary about the innovative collaboration between Cunningham and Cage, whereas (H) is more in keeping with the views of the critics discussed in the passage. Eliminate (H). Eliminate (J) because the passage does not provide many *biographical* details about Cunningham; instead it focuses on Cunningham's choreography. The correct answer is (F).

Summary

○ Follow your Personal Order of Difficulty: leave harder passages and questions for Later or Never.

○ When you are ready to work a harder passage or question, try these strategies:

- Translate based on context.

- Use Bite-Sized Pieces and start with the information you understand best.

- Use topic sentences and transition words as guides.

- Work backward from the answers.

- Use the Golden Thread and your work on previous questions to help with Later questions.

Chapter 8
Reading
Practice Drills

Put all of your Reading skills together to work the
two practice drills in this chapter.

PRACTICE DRILL 1

NATURAL SCIENCE: This passage is adapted from the article, "Hole's on First? New Evidence Shows Black Hole Growth Preceding Galactic Formation" by John Matsos (Reproduced with permission. © 2011 Scientific American, a division of Nature America, Inc. All Rights Reserved).

The co-evolution of black holes, almost unfathomable in their bulk, and the even more massive galaxies that host them remains poorly understood—a kind of chicken-and-egg problem on mammoth scales. Do black holes, such as
5 the lunker in our own Milky Way Galaxy, which contains the mass of four million suns (that's about eight undecillion, or 8×10^{36} kilograms), drive the evolution of galaxies around them; or do galaxies naturally nurture the gravitational gobblers at their centers; or perhaps do they come into being
10 together, as a matched pair?

A serendipitous discovery in a relatively close-by dwarf galaxy may help answer that question. Amy Reines, a graduate student in astronomy at the University of Virginia (U.V.A.), was looking at bursts of star formation in a galaxy
15 known as Henize 2-10, which serves as a kind of observational proxy for galaxies that existed in the early universe. She noticed a suspicious radio wave source coming from a small region of the galaxy, a good distance removed from the active stellar nurseries. A comparison with archival
20 data showed X-ray radiation from the same location within Henize 2-10; the balance of radiation levels in different wavelengths pointed to the presence of a giant black hole accreting material from its surroundings.

That is notable because Henize 2-10 lacks a detectable
25 spheroid, or galactic bulge, in its center, which is usually directly related to the mass of a galaxy's black hole. "That suggests that you just don't need one to make a black hole," Reines says. "People have thought that galaxies and their black holes have grown synchronously," she adds. "This
30 really challenges this notion and suggests that a massive black hole could form ahead of its galaxy." Reines and her colleagues from U.V.A. and the National Radio Astronomy Observatory, headquartered in Charlottesville, Va., reported the finding online January 9 in *Nature*. (*Scientific American*
35 is part of Nature Publishing Group.)

The presence of the black hole is also of interest because the galaxy, about 30 million light-years from Earth, is still forming stars at a rapid clip and is thought to resemble galaxies that were prevalent many billions of years ago. "We think
40 we may be witnessing an early stage of galaxy formation and black hole evolution," Reines says.

Without a telltale galactic bulge it can be difficult to locate a black hole, which may be why Henize 2-10 and similar galaxies have not been known to harbor massive
45 black holes. "We've been avoiding galaxies like this, because where's the center?" says Jenny Greene, an astronomer at the University of Texas at Austin who wrote a commentary to accompany the research in *Nature*. "We've just avoided them like the plague because you just don't know where to
50 look for a black hole."

But if giant black holes in star-forming dwarf galaxies prove to be common—that is, if Henize 2-10 is not an outlier but a representative of a larger population—they may have much to tell about the formation of primordial black holes
55 and galaxies in the early universe. "There are all kinds of interesting relationships" between black holes and their host galaxies, says astronomer James Ulvestad, director of the National Science Foundation's Division of Astronomical Sciences. "But we don't really know very well how that
60 happens or how these things get started." (Ulvestad commented on the research as an astronomer in the field, not as an NSF representative.)

There are reasons to think that diminutive star-formers such as Henize 2-10 were prevalent in the early universe,
65 before mergers incorporated those dwarfs into larger galaxies. "The early galaxies in the universe were all kind of like this," Ulvestad says. But the kinds of objects that astronomers can actually see in the early universe, by peering far across the cosmos, all give off far more radiation than the
70 black hole found in Henize 2-10, so the question of how many black holes of that ilk existed early on remains open.

The key to the new discovery, Greene says, "is really opening a new realm for us to search." There exist many more dwarf galaxies that may also have black holes, which
75 would hold even more clues to the history and evolution of black holes and their galaxies. "If you can find a few more of them nearby then that tells you that it's common," Ulvestad says. "Then you can say by extrapolation, 'okay, we're looking at some common phenomenon that was happening
80 early in the universe.'"

31. The primary purpose of the passage is to:
   A. discuss the possible relationships between dwarf galaxies and black holes and reasons for studying them.
   B. persuade readers that the research of astronomers is conclusive with regard to the relationship between dwarf galaxies and black holes.
   C. present new data that astronomers have gathered through visual examination of Henize 2-10.
   D. inspire readers to learn more about certain galaxies and black holes.

32. The passage mentions Reines observing all of the following about Henize 2-10 EXCEPT:

    F. evidence of the reason the galaxy lacks a spheroid.

    G. a radio wave source coming from a region outside of the active stellar nurseries.

    H. bursts of star formation similar to those in galaxies in the early universe.

    J. radiation levels pointing to the existence of a black hole.

33. Information in the second paragraph (lines 11–23) indicates that dwarf galaxy research utilizes all of the following EXCEPT:

    A. radio wave measurements.

    B. observations of the early universe.

    C. archival data.

    D. X-ray radiation detection.

34. According to the passage, when does Reines think the massive black hole in Henize 2-10 may have developed?

    F. Before the dwarf galaxy developed

    G. At the same time that the dwarf galaxy developed

    H. After the dwarf galaxy developed

    J. Before other nearby galaxies developed

35. In the context of the fifth paragraph (lines 42–50), lines 48–50 primarily serve to emphasize the:

    A. flawed research astronomers conduct when avoiding Henize 2-10 and other galaxies.

    B. analysis used by astronomers to determine the size of a galactic bulge.

    C. challenges astronomers have when trying to identify the center of a black hole.

    D. reason black holes may not have been discovered in Henize 2-10 and similar galaxies.

36. Which of the following questions is NOT answered by information given in the passage?

    F. Why are astronomers interested in dwarf galaxies?

    G. How does the size of the Milky Way Galaxy black hole compare to the size of Henize 2-10?

    H. What reason do astronomers give for not studying black holes in dwarf galaxies more extensively?

    J. What is one method astronomers use to detect black holes?

37. The main purpose of the last paragraph is to:

    A. convince readers to search for dwarf galaxies.

    B. show the faults in Ulvestad's reasoning about black hole evolution.

    C. detail the events of the evolution of dwarf galaxies and black holes.

    D. emphasize the implications of finding more examples of a particular phenomenon.

38. As it is used in line 67, the word *this* most likely refers to:

    F. a dwarf galaxy.

    G. a larger galaxy.

    H. a burst of star formation.

    J. an outlier in the population.

39. The author would most likely agree with which of the following statements?

    A. Research on black holes and dwarf galaxies can provide information about the early universe.

    B. The age of the Milky Way Galaxy is less than the age of the Henize 2-10 galaxy.

    C. The sizes of black holes are best determined by measuring the sizes of galactic bulges.

    D. A lack of funding will prevent researchers from understanding the co-evolution of black holes and galaxies.

40. Jenny Greene most nearly indicates that attempts to study dwarf galaxies without galactic bulges have been:

    F. thoroughly planned.

    G. lacking funding.

    H. somewhat limited.

    J. comprehensive.

Check the answers and explanations for this drill starting on page 102.

PRACTICE DRILL 2

PROSE FICTION: Passage A is adapted from the short story "A Different Ending" by Shaily Menon (© 2016 by Shaily Menon). Passage B is adapted from *The Boat* by Nam Le (© 2008 by Nam Le. Used by permission of Alfred A. Knopf, an imprint of the Knopf Doubleday Publishing Group, a division of Penguin Random House LLC. All rights reserved.).

Passage A by Shaily Menon

On the wall next to the bed, and above the table with Da's typewriter and Da's big dictionary, were Da's bookshelves. The bookshelves were filled with many heavy books. I had to stand on a chair to read the titles.

5 One man wrote a book about war and peace. Another man wrote about crime and punishment. He also wrote a book about an idiot. I tried to sound out his name. Da helped me. *Dos-to-yev-sky,* he said slowly, so I could repeat it. He said he liked the Russian authors. There was pathos in those
10 stories. I looked up *pathos* in Da's big dictionary. I loved that dictionary.

Sometimes, after dinner Da and I took turns reading aloud from one of the books on his shelf. I liked listening to Da read. On Sunday mornings he read interesting stories
15 from the newspaper. "Would you like to hear an interesting tidbit?" he asked. "The Nobel Prize for Literature has been announced. It will go to Pablo Neruda, from the country of Chile, for his poetry that brings alive a continent's destiny and dreams." I loved those tidbits.

20 But my favorite reading time of all with Da was after we returned from the peanut seller's shop with paper cones of warm roasted peanuts. On Sunday afternoons, after the vegetable vendor with the basket of cucumbers, tomatoes, and bitter gourd on his head had come and gone, and after
25 the dhobi had delivered freshly laundered clothes that smelled like the sun, and after everyone had woken from their afternoon naps, the vendor of savory snacks would call out from the street. "Bhel puri! Pani puri!" he would shout, and kids would come running to buy bowls of tasty,
30 mouth-watering concoctions.

I was not allowed to eat street food, but dry-roasted peanuts were an exception to that rule. Da and I would walk to the peanut seller's shop and we would order three small cones of peanuts–one for me, one for Da, and one for Ma–
35 and bring them home. Then we would eat the peanuts and drink warm, spicy chai that Ma had brewed for us.

I used to think the warm peanuts were the most delicious part of the cones, until I discovered the writing on the paper. The peanut seller tore sheets out of paperback books
40 to make the cones, and after the peanuts were all gone, I would smooth out the sheet and read both sides. Sometimes I really liked the story and wanted to know what happened next. Da took me to the British Council Library and helped me search out the book the story was from. If we found the
45 book, we would bring it home for me to read. Sometimes the story in the book was not as good as the bit of story on the page. Other times, it was even better.

Passage B by Nam Le

My father arrived on a rainy morning. I was dreaming about a poem, the dull *thluck thluck* of a typewriter's keys
50 punching out the letters. It was a good poem—perhaps the best I'd ever written. When I woke up, he was standing outside my bedroom door, smiling ambiguously. He wore black trousers and a wet, wrinkled parachute jacket that looked like it had just been pulled out of a washing machine.
55 Framed by the bedroom doorway, he appeared even smaller, gaunter, than I remembered. Still groggy with dream, I lifted my face toward the alarm clock.

"What time is it?"

"Hello, Son," he said in Vietnamese. "I knocked for a
60 long time. Then the door just opened."

The fields are glass, I thought. Then tum-ti-ti, a dactyl, end line, then the words *excuse* and *alloy* in the line after. *Come on*, I thought.

"It's raining heavily," he said.

65 I frowned. The clock read 11:44. "I thought you weren't coming until this afternoon." It felt strange, after all this time, to be speaking Vietnamese again.

"They changed my flight in Los Angeles."

"Why didn't you ring?"

70 "I tried," he said equably. "No answer."

I twisted over the side of the bed and cracked open the window. The sound of rain filled the room--rain fell on the streets, on the roofs, on the tin shed across the parking lot like the distant detonations of firecrackers. Everything
75 smelled of wet leaves.

"I turn the ringer off when I sleep," I said. "Sorry."

He continued smiling at me, significantly, as if waiting for an announcement.

"I was dreaming."

80 He used to wake me, when I was young, by standing over me and smacking my cheeks lightly. I hated it—the wetness, the sourness of his hands.

"Come on," he said, picking up a large Adidas duffel and a rolled bundle that looked like a sleeping bag. "A day lived,
85 a sea of knowledge earned." He had a habit of speaking in Vietnamese proverbs. I had long since learned to ignore it.

I threw on a T-shirt and stretched my neck in front of the lone window. Through the rain, the sky was as gray and striated as graphite. *The fields are glass* . . . Like a shape in
90 smoke, the poem blurred, then dissolved into this new, cold, strange reality: a wind-blown, rain-strafed parking lot; a dark room almost entirely taken up by my bed; the small body of my father dripping water onto the hardwood floors.

Questions 1–3 ask about Passage A.

1. Which of the following questions is specifically answered in Passage A?

   A. Why does Da encourage the narrator to read?
   B. Why wasn't the narrator allowed to eat street food?
   C. Why does Da take the narrator to the British Council Library?
   D. Where does the peanut seller get the book pages for the peanut cones?

2. It can most reasonably be inferred from Passage A that the narrator enjoys the roasted peanut cones because they:

   F. taste better than the snacks that Ma prepares at home.
   G. are popular with other children the narrator's age.
   H. are sold by a vendor who is the narrator's friend.
   J. are wrapped with pages from books, which the narrator reads.

3. As they are used in lines 9–10, what do the words *those stories* refer to?

   A. Entries in Da's dictionaries
   B. Russian literature
   C. Newspaper articles
   D. Pablo Neruda's poems

Questions 4–7 ask about Passage B.

4. The narrator of Passage B most likely dreamed of the sound of a typewriter because:

   F. his father was knocking on his door.
   G. the rain falling on the tin shed made a loud, percussive sound.
   H. he uses a typewriter to compose his poetry.
   J. his father is lightly smacking his cheeks to wake him.

5. Passage B most strongly suggests that the narrator's bedroom:

   A. is in his parents' home.
   B. leaks during heavy rain.
   C. is fairly small.
   D. is where the narrator usually composes poetry.

6. Throughout Passage B, the narrator's reaction to his father is to:

   F. convey happiness at reconnecting with his father.
   G. express anger about unresolved family issues.
   H. speak to his father about close family members.
   J. show disappointment that his father interrupted a dream.

7. In Passage B, which of the following pairs of actions most clearly indicates that the narrator's father arrives unexpectedly, while the narrator is asleep?

   A. The narrator's question about the time and the groggy expression of his father
   B. The groggy lifting of the narrator's face toward the alarm clock and his question about the time
   C. The narrator's dreaming about a poem and the smiling expression of the narrator's father
   D. The slight smacking of the narrator's cheeks by his father and the groggy lifting of the narrator's face toward the alarm clock

Questions 8–10 ask about both passages

8. Which of the following elements is most clearly similar in the two passages?

   F. The primary characters' familial relationship
   G. The use of imagery related to the weather
   H. The ages of the narrators
   J. The interspersing of childhood recollections within description of the present

9. Among the characters in both passages, which one is portrayed as feeling most distant from a family member?

   A. The narrator of Passage A
   B. The father in Passage B
   C. The son in Passage B
   D. Ma in Passage A

10. Which of the following statements best describes the portrayals of Da in Passage A and the father in Passage B, respectively? In Passage A, Da is portrayed as:

    F. a person who appreciates literature, whereas the father in Passage B is portrayed as lacking respect for poetry.
    G. a figure who is looked up to by his daughter, whereas the father in Passage B is portrayed as somewhat vulnerable.
    H. meticulous about his possessions, whereas the father in Passage B is portrayed as careless with his appearance.
    J. somewhat cold and distant, whereas the father in Passage B is portrayed as regretful about the time he has spent apart from his son.

Check the answers and explanations for this drill starting on page 106.

PRACTICE DRILL ANSWERS AND EXPLANATIONS

Drill 1 Answers

31. **A**

32. **F**

33. **B**

34. **F**

35. **D**

36. **G**

37. **D**

38. **F**

39. **A**

40. **H**

Drill 1 Explanations

31. **A** This reasoning question asks about the *primary purpose* of the passage. Because this is a general question, it should be done after all the specific questions. Look for the Golden Thread. The passage discusses the discovery of a *black hole* in a *dwarf galaxy*, which may help answer questions about the *co-evolution* of black holes and galaxies. Look for an answer that matches this idea. Choice (A) refers to *dwarf galaxies and black holes and the reasons for studying them*, which matches the text from the passage. Keep (A). Choice (B) states that *the research of astronomers is conclusive with regard to the relationship between dwarf galaxies and black holes*. This is a Words Out of Context trap answer: while the use of the terms *dwarf galaxies and black holes* may make this an attractive answer choice, the passage never states that *the research of astronomers is conclusive*. If anything, this research is portrayed as new and speculative. Eliminate (B). Choice (C) states that the purpose of the passage is to *present new data that astronomers have gathered through visual examination of Henize 2-10*. This is also a Words Out of Context answer: although the *new data* in the passage was obtained through *examination of Henize 2-10*, the text states that Amy Reines *noticed a suspicious radio wave source* coming from Henize 2-10. Therefore, the examination was not *visual*. Eliminate (C). Choice (D) states that the purpose of the passage is to *inspire readers to learn more about certain galaxies and black holes*. While the author does discuss galaxies and black holes, he does not try to *inspire readers to learn more*; instead, he informs readers about a recent discovery and its potential implications. Eliminate (D). The correct answer is (A).

32. **F** This reference question asks what *Reines* did not observe about *Henize 2-10*. When a question asks what is *not* mentioned in the passage, eliminate answers that are mentioned. Look for the lead word *Reines* to find the window for the question. *Reines* is discussed in the second and third paragraphs. Choice (F) states that Reines found *evidence of the reason the galaxy lacks a spheroid*. In the third paragraph, the author states that *Henize 2-10 lacks a detectable spheroid*, but no *reason* is given as to why that is. Keep (F). Eliminate (G) because in the second paragraph, the text states that Reines *noticed a suspicious radio wave source coming from a small region of the galaxy, a good distance removed from the active stellar nurseries*. Eliminate (H) because the second paragraph states that Reines *was looking at bursts of star formation* and suggests that Henize 2-10 is similar to *galaxies that existed in the early universe*. Eliminate (J) because the second paragraph states that *the balance of radiation levels in different wavelengths pointed to the presence of a giant black hole*. The correct answer is (F).

33. **B** This reference question asks what tools *dwarf galaxy research* does not use. When a question asks what is *not* mentioned in the passage, eliminate answers that are mentioned. Read the second paragraph and look for lead words from the answers. Choice (A) is *radio wave measurements*. The text states that *she noticed a suspicious radio wave source* while examining the dwarf galaxy Henize 2-10. Eliminate (A). Choice (B) is *observations of the early universe*. Though the author mentions the early universe in the second paragraph, the text states that Henize 2-10 *serves as a kind of observational proxy for galaxies that existed in the early universe*. Therefore, observations of the early universe are not used as a research tool to study dwarf galaxies. Instead, observations of dwarf galaxies are used as tools to study galaxies from the early universe. Keep (B). Choice (C) is *archival data*. The author states that *archival data showed X-ray radiation from the same location within Henize 2-10*, so *archival data* was used as a research tool for studying a dwarf galaxy. Eliminate (C). The same line shows that *X-ray radiation detection* was used in studying Henize 2-10, so eliminate (D). The correct answer is (B).

34. **F** This reference question asks when *Reines* thinks *the massive black hole in Henize 2-10* developed. Look for the lead word *Reines* to find the window for the question. *Reines* is discussed in the second and third paragraphs. In the third paragraph, Reines states that the evidence *suggests that a massive black hole could form ahead of its galaxy*, showing that she believes that the black hole may have developed before the galaxy. This closely matches (F), which says that the black hole developed *before the dwarf galaxy*, so keep (F). Choice (G) is a Right Answer, Wrong Question trap answer: the passage states that other *people have thought that galaxies and their black holes have grown synchronously*, but this is not what Reines believes. Eliminate (G). Eliminate (H) because Reines indicates that the black hole may have developed before the galaxy, not *after* it. Eliminate (J) because Reines does not compare the ages of *other nearby galaxies* to the age of the black hole. The correct answer is (F).

35. **D** This reasoning question asks what the given quotation emphasizes. Read a window around the given line reference. Lines 42–45 state that *without a telltale galactic bulge it can be difficult to locate a black hole, which may be why Henize 2-10 and similar galaxies have not been known to harbor massive black holes*. The quote referenced in question 35 explains that astronomers have avoided studying galaxies like Henize 2-10 *because you just don't know where to look for a black hole*. Look for an answer that matches this text from the passage. Choice (A) states that the astronomers' research was *flawed*, but

the text never states that the research was poorly done, just that astronomers have avoided it. Eliminate (A). Choice (B) refers to determining *a size of the galactic bulge*, but determining size is not mentioned as a topic of research. Eliminate (B). Choice (C) refers to *the center of a black hole*. While the text does mention *the center*, it refers to the centers of galaxies, not the centers of black holes. Eliminate (C). Choice (D) closely matches the text, so keep (D). The correct answer is (D).

36. **G** This reference question asks which question *is not answered* in the passage. When a question asks what is *not* mentioned in the passage, eliminate answers that are mentioned. The question in (F) is answered in lines 51–54, which state that *if giant black holes in star-forming dwarf galaxies prove to be common … they may have much to tell about the formation of primordial black holes and galaxies in the early universe*. Eliminate (F). The question in (G) is about the relative sizes of the *Milky Way black hole* and *Henize 2-10*. Though the size of the *Milky Way black hole* is referenced in the first paragraph, and Henize 2-10 is referred to as a dwarf galaxy, the sizes of the two are never compared. Keep (G). The question in (H) is answered in lines 49–50, which state that astronomers have avoided studying black holes in dwarf galaxies *because you just don't know where to look for a black hole*. Eliminate (H). The question in (J) is answered in lines 21–22, which explain that the researcher observed *the balance of radiation levels in different wavelengths* as a way to detect *the presence of a giant black hole*. Eliminate (J). The correct answer is (G).

37. **D** This reasoning question asks for the *purpose of the last paragraph*. Read the last paragraph as the window. The paragraph states that if more dwarf galaxies with black holes are discovered near Henize 2-10, then researchers *can say by extrapolation, 'okay, we're looking at some common phenomenon that was happening early in the universe.'* The paragraph emphasizes what could be learned from finding additional examples similar to the black hole in Henize 2-10. Look for an answer that matches this idea. Choice (A) states that the last paragraph is meant to *convince readers to search for dwarf galaxies*. While the author is clearly in favor of further research, he does not appeal to *readers* to personally help in the search. Eliminate (A). Choice (B) states that the last paragraph shows *the faults in Ulvestad's reasoning*, but the author does not indicate that Ulvestad is mistaken. Eliminate (B). Choice (C) states that the purpose of the last paragraph is to *detail the events of the evolution of dwarf galaxies and black holes*. Though the last paragraph is certainly about *dwarf galaxies and black holes*, no specific events are detailed. Eliminate (C). Choice (D) states that the purpose of the last paragraph is to *emphasize the implications of finding more examples of a particular phenomenon*. This matches the text from the passage, so keep (D). The correct answer is (D).

38. **F** This reference question asks what the word *this* in line 67 refers to. Read a window around the line reference. The text mentions *diminutive star-formers such as Henize 2-10* and then says that the *early galaxies in the universe were all kind of like this*. Therefore, the word *this* refers to *diminutive star-formers such as Henize 2-10*. Look for an answer that matches this text from the passage. Keep (F), as *Henize 2-10* is a *dwarf galaxy*. Choice (G) is a Right Answer, Wrong Question trap answer: the phrase *larger galaxies* is mentioned, but the passage says that small galaxies were common in the early universe, and only later merged into larger galaxies. The word *diminutive* means "small," and *Henize 2-10* is repeatedly referred to as a dwarf galaxy. Eliminate (G). Choice (H) is Out the Window: the phrase *a*

burst of star formation is found much earlier in the passage; it does not appear in the window for the question and therefore it is not what the word *this* refers to. Eliminate (H). Eliminate (J) because the passage states that galaxies like *Henize 2-10* were common in the early universe, whereas the word *outlier* refers to something rare. Eliminate (J). The correct answer is (F).

39. **A** This reasoning question asks which statement the author would agree with. There is not a good lead word in this question, so work it later. Choice (A) states that *research on black holes and dwarf galaxies can provide information about the early universe*. In lines 53–55, the author states that giant black holes *may have much to tell about the formation of primordial black holes and galaxies in the early universe*. Keep (A). Choice (B) states that the Milky Way Galaxy is younger than Henize 2-10, but ages are never given for either galaxy. Eliminate (B). Choice (C) states that the *sizes of black holes are best determined by measuring the sizes of galactic bulges*. This is a Words Out of Context trap answer: while lines 25–26 say that the galactic bulge is *usually directly related to the mass of a galaxy's black hole*, there is not enough evidence to support the statement that measuring a galactic bulge's size is the *best* method to determine a black hole's size. Eliminate (C). Choice (D) refers to a *lack of funding*, which is never mentioned in the passage. Eliminate (D). The correct answer is (A).

40. **H** This reference question asks what *Jenny Greene* indicates about *attempts to study dwarf galaxies without galactic bulges*. Look for the lead words *Jenny Greene* and *galactic bulges* to find the window for the question. In lines 46–50, Jenny Greene states that astronomers have *avoided* looking for black holes in such galaxies in the past. Look for an answer that matches this idea. The text does not mention the planning involved with the research, so eliminate (F). *Funding* is not discussed in the window, so eliminate (G). The fact that researchers have *avoided* looking for black holes in certain types of galaxies indicates that the attempts to study these galaxies have been *somewhat limited*, so keep (H). The word *comprehensive* means "thorough;" (J) is contradicted by Greene's statements, so eliminate (J). The correct answer is (H).

Drill 2 Answers

1. **C**

2. **J**

3. **B**

4. **F**

5. **C**

6. **J**

7. **B**

8. **F**

9. **C**

10. **G**

Drill 2 Explanations

1. **C** This referral question asks which question is *answered in Passage A*. There is no good lead word in this question, so work the question later. Work backward and use lead words from the answers to find the window for this question. Although the narrator describes reading together with Da throughout the passage, she never mentions *why* he encourages her to read, so eliminate (A). In line 31, the narrator says, *I was not allowed to eat street food*, but she does not explain *why* she was not allowed to, so eliminate (B). In the final paragraph, the narrator says that she liked to read the pages that the peanut cones were made from. She says, *Sometimes I really liked the story and wanted to know what happened next. Da took me to the British Council Library and helped me search out the book the story was from*. This explains why *Da* takes *the narrator to the British Council Library*, so keep (C). Although the passage states that the peanut cones were made from book pages, and that the narrator sometimes found copies of the book the stories were from at the library, the text does not explain where the peanut seller gets the book pages, so eliminate (D). The correct answer is (C).

2. **J** This reasoning question asks why *the narrator enjoys the roasted peanut cones*, according to Passage A. Look for the lead words *roasted peanut* and *cones* to find the window for the question. Lines 32–35 say that the narrator and *Da* would *walk to the peanut seller's shop* to order *three small cones of peanuts… and bring them home*. Lines 39–41 indicate that the *peanut seller tore sheets out of paperback books to make the cones*. The narrator would then *read both sides* of the page and would sometimes go to the *British Council Library* with *Da* to find the book that the page came from. Look for an answer choice that matches this idea. The narrator does not indicate that the roasted peanuts *taste better*

than the snacks that Ma prepares at home, so eliminate (F). Choice (G) is a Words Out of Context trap answer because the passage indicates that *kids would come running to buy* other street food, but not the peanuts specifically, and this isn't the reason the author likes buying peanuts. Eliminate (G). The text does not indicate that the peanut seller was the *narrator's friend*, so eliminate (H). Keep (J) because it matches the text from the passage. The correct answer is (J).

3. **B** This reasoning question asks what the words *those stories* refer to, as they are used in lines 9–10. Read a window around the given line reference. Lines 8–10 state, *He said he liked the Russian authors. There was pathos in those stories.* Therefore, the words *those stories* refer to the stories by the Russian authors. Look for an answer that matches this idea. Choice (A) is a Words Out of Context trap answer: the next sentence mentions that the narrator looked up a word in *Da's big dictionary*, but the words *those stories* do not refer to dictionaries, so eliminate (A). Keep (B) because *Russian literature* matches the text from the passage. Choices (C) and (D) are Out the Window trap answers: the next paragraph mentions Da reading out loud from the *newspaper*, as well as *Pablo Neruda's* poetry, but those topics are not included in the window for question 3, nor do they explain what the words *those stories* reference. Eliminate (C) and (D). The correct answer is (B).

4. **F** This reasoning question asks for the most likely reason that the narrator of Passage B *dreamed of the sound of a typewriter*. Look for the lead words *dream* and *typewriter* to find the window for this question. The first paragraph of Passage B states, *My father arrived on a rainy morning. I was dreaming about a poem, the dull* thluck thluck *of a typewriter's keys punching out the letters…When I woke up, he was standing outside my bedroom door.* Then the narrator's father says that he had *knocked for a long time.* This suggests that the narrator may have heard the knocking as the sound of the typewriter in his dream. Look for an answer that matches this idea. Keep (F) because it matches the text from the passage.. Choice (G) mentions the sound of the *rain falling on the tin shed*. This sound is described in the passage, but the sound of the rain only became audible after the narrator opened the window. This happened after the narrator woke up, so it does not explain why the narrator heard a certain sound in his dream. This is an Out the Window trap answer; eliminate (G). Eliminate (H) because the passage does not specify whether or not the narrator actually uses a typewriter when he writes poetry; this is a Words Out of Context trap answer. Choice (J) is an Out the Window trap answer: the passage says that the narrator's father *used to* wake him by lightly smacking his cheeks, but this did not happen on the day described in the passage, so it does not explain why the narrator heard a certain sound in his dream. Eliminate (J). The correct answer is (F).

5. **C** This reasoning question asks what Passage B suggests about *the narrator's bedroom*. There is not a good lead word in this question (the *bedroom* is mentioned in multiple places in the passage), so answer the question later. The final paragraph describes the bedroom as *a dark room almost entirely taken up by my bed*. Look for an answer that matches this text from the passage. Eliminate (A) because the narrator's father knocks when he arrives, indicating that the narrator and the father do not live in the same home. Choice (B) says that the bedroom *leaks* in the rain; although the passage describes heavy rain outside, there is no indication that the water is leaking into the bedroom. This is a Words Out of Context trap answer, so eliminate (B). Choice (C) says that the bedroom is *small*; this is supported by

the statement that the room was *almost entirely taken up by* the bed. Keep (C). Eliminate (D) because, although the narrator is trying to compose a poem in his bedroom during the events in the passage, the text does not give information about where he *usually* composes poetry. The correct answer is (C).

6. **J**   This reasoning question asks about *the narrator's reaction to his father* throughout the passage. Because this is a general question, it should be done after all of the specific questions. Look for the Golden Thread. The passage begins with the father's arrival, and the narrator says, *I was dreaming about a poem…a good poem—perhaps the best I'd ever written.* He never greets his father; instead he asks what time it is, frowns, and asks why his father didn't call to let him know that he would be arriving early. He recalls how his father used to wake him when he was young, saying, *I hated it.* Throughout the passage, the narrator continues trying to compose the poem from his dream even as he talks to his father. In the final paragraph the narrator states, *Like a shape in smoke, the poem blurred, then dissolved into this new, cold, strange reality*, which indicates that he has forgotten or lost his train of thought about the poem. The narrator's reaction to his father is somewhat negative, and he seems concerned about the poem he is trying to compose. Look for an answer that matches this idea. Eliminate (F) because the narrator's reaction is somewhat negative; there is no indication that he is happy to reconnect with his father. Eliminate (G) because, although the narrator's reaction is somewhat negative, the word *anger* is too extreme to match the tone of the passage, and there is no mention of *unresolved family issues*. Eliminate (H) because the narrator and his father do not talk about other *family members*. Keep (J) because *disappointment* is somewhat negative, and the statement that the father *interrupted a dream* matches the text from the passage. The correct answer is (J).

7. **B**   This reasoning question asks for the pair of actions in Passage B that *most clearly indicates that the narrator's father arrives unexpectedly, while the narrator is asleep*. Look for the lead word *arrive* to find the window for the question. Passage B begins with the narrator stating, *My father arrived on a rainy morning.* He then discusses the events surrounding his father's arrival. The narrator indicates that he *was dreaming about a poem*, and that when his father arrived, he *lifted* his *face toward the alarm clock* to check the time, though he was still *groggy with dream.* He then asks about the *time*. Look for an answer choice that matches this idea. The passage indicates that the narrator was *groggy*, not that his *father* was. Eliminate (A). Keep (B) because it matches the text from the passage. Eliminate (C) because *the smiling expression of the narrator's father* does not indicate that the narrator was asleep when his father arrived. Though the *slight smacking of the narrator's cheeks by his father* occurred when the narrator was asleep, this action occurred earlier in the narrator's life, not when his father arrived on this occasion. Eliminate (D). The correct answer is (B).

8. **F**   This reasoning question asks for the element that is *most clearly similar in the two passages*. Because this question asks about both passages, it should be done after the questions that ask about each passage individually. Consider the Golden Thread of both passages. Passage A discusses the narrator's relationship with her father, and Passage B discusses the narrator's relationship with his father. Keep (F) because the *primary characters* of both passages have the same *familial relationship*: father and child. Though Passage B uses *imagery related to weather*, Passage A does not. Eliminate (G). It can be inferred from Passage A that the narrator is recalling memories of her childhood, so the stories

take place when she is a child. In Passage B, the narrator lives alone when his father comes to visit, and he has been apart from his Vietnamese-speaking family for some time. From this, it can be inferred that the narrator is a teenager or an adult. However, neither passage reveals the present age of the narrator or the narrator's exact age in the passage, so eliminate (H). While Passage B features *childhood recollections* interspersed *within description of the present*, Passage A is entirely a *childhood recollection*, with no mention of the *present*. Eliminate (J). The correct answer is (F).

9. **C**   This reasoning question asks for the character in either passage that *is portrayed as feeling most distant from a family member*. Because this question asks about both passages, it should be done after the questions that ask about each passage individually. Consider the Golden Thread of both passages. Choice (A) asks about the *narrator* of Passage A, so scan Passage A looking for general indications of family relations. In Passage A, the narrator only mentions two family members: Da and Ma. She recalls happy memories about Da: how Da would read to her from the *Sunday morning* newspaper and take her to the *British Council Library* and help her *search out* a story she was looking for. In lines 35–36, she indicates that she, Da, and Ma would gather for *dry-roasted peanuts* and *chai*. None of these ideas indicates that the narrator is *distant from a family member*, so eliminate (A). Choice (B) asks about the *father* in Passage B. In lines 51–52, the narrator says that his father *was standing outside my bedroom door, smiling ambiguously*. The father then explains that he *knocked for a long time. Then the door just opened.* The father is portrayed as eager to connect with his son, not as feeling *distant* from him, and the passage does not mention the father's relation to any other family member. Eliminate (B). Choice (C) asks about the *son* in Passage B, who is the narrator. In lines 58–67, the narrator greets his father not by saying hello but by asking what time it is. He then says, "*I thought you weren't coming until this afternoon*" and indicates that it *felt strange...to be speaking Vietnamese again*. These statements indicate that the narrator is not necessarily excited to see his father, suggesting that he feels *distant* from his father. Keep (C). Choice (D) asks about *Ma* in Passage A. Use the lead word *Ma* to find the window. Lines 35–36 indicate that *Ma* would brew *chai* for the family to accompany the *dry-roasted peanuts* that *Da* would buy. This statement does not indicate that Ma felt *distant from a family member*. Eliminate (D). The correct answer is (C).

10. **G**   This reasoning question asks about the *portrayals of Da in Passage A and the father in Passage B, respectively*. Because this question asks about both passages, it should be done after the questions that ask about each passage individually. Consider the Golden Thread of both passages. In Passage A, Da is portrayed as a devoted father who is admired by his daughter. In Passage B, the narrator's father arrives with clothes soaked from the rain and is described as *even smaller, gaunter than I remembered*. Look for an answer choice that matches this text from the passage. Passage A indicates that Da *appreciates literature*, but Passage B does not reveal the father's lack of *respect for poetry*, as the son does not tell his father about the poem from his dream. Eliminate (F). Keep (G) because it matches the text from the passage. Passage A indicates that Da shared his books openly with the narrator, not that he was *meticulous* with them. Furthermore, though the father in Passage B arrives soaked from the rain, the passage does not indicate that he is *careless with his appearance*. Eliminate (H). Eliminate (J) because Da is not portrayed as *cold and distant* in Passage A, and the father in Passage B does not indicate regret *about the time he has spent apart from his son*. The correct answer is (G).

Part III
Reading
Practice Tests

Chapter 9
Reading
Practice Test 1

READING TEST

35 Minutes—40 Questions

DIRECTIONS: There are four passages in this test. Each passage is followed by several questions. After reading each passage, choose the best answer to each question and blacken the corresponding oval on your answer document. You may refer to the passages as often as necessary.

Passage I

LITERARY NARRATIVE: The following passage is adapted from the short story "Between Two Homes" by Herbert Malloy (© 1993 by Herbert Malloy).

The fact that air travel allows me to fall asleep on the west coast and wake up on the east coast is bittersweet magic. On a red-eye flight, the continent passes stealthily underneath like an ugly secret we prefer not to acknowledge. Passengers drift
5 in and out of an unsteady slumber, reluctantly awakening to the realization that they are still stuck on an airplane. Sometimes I open my eyes wide enough to gaze out the window at the twinkling lights of the towns and cities below.

I try to decipher which city glimmers below from the size
10 of its grid of light, as well as my perception of how long I have been flying. Could that be Denver? Have I already napped a third of the flight? I look around the cabin to see how many other people are having trouble sleeping and become instantly jealous of the families and couples who have the luxury of
15 leaning on each other.

The aura of cool sunlight begins to infiltrate the cabin as we near Dulles, Virginia. We see flocks of birds sharing the sky with us. By the time we arrive, we will have flown through three time zones, compressing a normal night by removing three of
20 its sacred hours. We are not only cheating space by crossing a continent in the course of a long nap, but also cheating time by turning back our watches and rushing prematurely toward the sunrise.

My hometown is still a car ride away, but the vicinity of
25 the airport is close enough to be a tonic to my nostalgic yearnings. As soon as I see the dense stands of oak and hickory blanketing the hills, I know I am back home. There's no trace of palm trees, no unrelenting flat stretches of compacted and perpendicular city streets. Left behind in our plane's exhaust,
30 Southern California is still fast asleep.

*   *   *   *   *   *

My dad has driven to the airport to pick me up, but I very nearly miss him—I'd forgotten he now drives a different car. I'm sure I've heard him speak of his new blue Toyota, but I always expect him to be driving the brown Lexus he owned
35 when I moved away. Happily, the smell inside the car remains the same: stretched leather, cologne, and the faint hint of a cigarette that was meant to go undetected. I covertly scan the

side of his face while he drives, hoping to see the same face I remember. Instead I see new wrinkles, new spots on his face,
40 new folds of skin on his neck.

We pass by familiar landmarks as we near our house, as well as some not-so-familiar ones. The performance stage in the town center that was merely a proposal when I left is now up-and-running, according to the marquee listing its upcom-
45 ing shows. The Olde Towne Tavern is apparently now called Summit Station. The old dance studio above the apartment buildings on West Deer Park seems to have finally closed — I always wondered how it stayed in business. The cluster of shops that famously burned to the ground near the high school
50 has open doors and cars gliding in and out of the parking lot.

We've arrived at the house, and as soon as I walk through the door, I am flooded with further reminders of my absence — trinkets on the wall I don't recognize, rearranged furniture in the kitchen and living room, sugary cereals and snacks strangely
55 absent from the top of the fridge. What was once my home has become someone else's house — my parents' house.

I suddenly see the mundane routines of my parents cast in a tragic light: my mother's agitation at the grackles that scare the goldfinches away from the bird-feeders, my father's habit
60 of pretending to read the newspaper on the porch (just an op-portunity to keep an eye on the neighborhood), the uninspired television they watch at night, often in separate rooms, and, most depressingly, the way they often fall asleep in front of the television, mouths gaping.

*   *   *   *   *   *

65 The in-flight movie on the way back to California portrays the story of a physicist who awakens after spending ten years in a coma. His initial joy gradually subsides and ultimately leads to confusion and sadness as he attempts to reintegrate into a world that has moved on without him. Even science, that rock
70 of immutable truths, has changed in his absence. He finds the entire body of research he had been working on prior to his coma now obsolete—years of advances in his field had furnished the answers he was pursuing.

As a physicist, he knew that time is a relative phenomenon,
75 a concept that only has meaning in relation to an individual's succession of experiences and ordering of memories. Clearly, though, his world, like mine, had continued to age, changing despite his lack of participation in it. Years are passing whether you're there to observe them or not.

1. It can reasonably be inferred from the passage that the narrator thinks air travel is:

   A. the most enjoyable way to travel.
   B. an ordinary part of the world.
   C. more uncomfortable than convenient.
   D. somewhat unnatural in what it makes possible.

2. The first three paragraphs (lines 1–23) establish all of the following about the narrator EXCEPT that he is:

   F. onboard an airplane.
   G. traveling east.
   H. departing from Denver.
   J. noticing sights below.

3. The point of view from which the passage is told is best described as that of:

   A. a young adult returning from a vacation to Southern California.
   B. an adult relating his reactions to visiting to his hometown.
   C. a young adult awakening from a long coma.
   D. an adult who prefers Southern California to his new home.

4. According to the narrator, which of the following things is relatively new to his parents' house?

   F. Certain trinkets on the wall
   G. The fridge
   H. His father's brown Lexus
   J. The bird-feeders

5. The passage contains recurring references to all of the following EXCEPT:

   A. difficulty sleeping.
   B. birds.
   C. lights of a city.
   D. dancing.

6. The narrator indicates that the most upsetting habit of his parents is:

   F. buying new cars.
   G. how and where they fall asleep.
   H. what they watch on television.
   J. how many trinkets they buy.

7. According to the passage, the coma victim has a sense of time as a relative phenomenon because:

   A. ten years had gone by quickly.
   B. he was a physicist.
   C. it was a side effect of his medical treatments.
   D. it was the focus of his research before his coma.

8. Based on the narrator's account, all of the following are part of the present, rather than the past, in his hometown EXCEPT:

   F. the closed dance studio.
   G. the upcoming show marquee.
   H. Summit Station.
   J. the burnt remains of a shopping center.

9. Details in the passage most strongly suggest that one characteristic of the narrator's hometown is:

   A. flat stretches.
   B. palm trees.
   C. oak trees.
   D. perpendicular streets.

10. When the narrator refers to science as "that rock of immutable truths" (lines 69–70), he is most likely directly referring to:

   F. the unchanging nature believed to be characteristic of scientific knowledge.
   G. the physicist's inability to understand the recent advances in science.
   H. the body of research conducted in the physicist's field during his coma.
   J. the ten years' worth of scientific advances that the narrator had missed.

Passage II

SOCIAL SCIENCE: Passage A is adapted from "Indigenous Goes Global" by Sally Mayfield (© 2002 by Sally Mayfield). Passage B is adapted from "Rethinking Fair Trade" by Harriet Steeley (© 2018 by World Press).

Passage A by Sally Mayfield

MayaWorks is a nonprofit organization that attempts to promote fair trade practices with Mayan artisans who would otherwise have little commercial outlet for their talents. In a broader sense, the organization aims to help traditionally
5　marginalized Guatemalan women attain the literacy, advanced skills, business acumen, and confidence they need to contribute to the economic well-being of their families.

When representatives from MayaWorks first reached out to women in Agua Caliente in 1994, the men of the village were
10　deeply suspicious. The women were extremely shy, avoiding almost all eye contact with the strangers. Ultimately, though, the women of the village agreed to the idea of forming a weaving cooperative and came up with an initial product order they felt they could fill. Each of eight women was to weave a dozen
15　brightly colored wall hangings that spelled the word "peace" in a number of languages. Weeks later, with great pride, the women delivered their order, using local material for the hanging rods and the finest yarn they could find, dyed and then washed to prevent staining.

20　"When we returned to pick up the finished products and pay them, there was a remarkable change in the way we were received by the villagers," Hogan reflects with deep satisfaction. "The women were beaming with self-confidence." The variety of wares created by MayaWorks artisans has greatly expanded
25　over time. Corn husks are used to make decorative angels. Yarn is woven into brightly-colored placemats, napkins, pouches, Beanies, and footbags. Some groups even make religious items, such as stoles for Christian priests and yarmulkes, or kippahs, for Jewish observers.

30　The capacity of these artisans for learning, adapting, and innovating has delighted the founders of MayaWorks. As relationships develop between MayaWorks and individual groups of artisans, new equipment and training is introduced to broaden their design capacity. 36-inch treadle-foot looms now allow
35　weavers to create fabrics that can be sold by the yard side-by-side with mass-manufactured textiles.

Another component of MayaWorks is coordinating and encouraging the financing of microcredit loans, small loans offered to those who have no collateral or credit history (and
40　thus could never qualify for a traditional banking loan). By providing these Mayan villagers with much-needed capital, MayaWorks helps them to upgrade their weaving equipment, install water pumps (which reduces health problems associated with meager and contaminated water sources), and buy
45　crops such as blackberries and potatoes. These measures both increase the sustainability of the community and encourage entrepreneurship. So far, MayaWorks reports, 100% of their microcredit loans have been paid back in full and on time.

Passage B by Harriet Steeley

Fair trade is a movement that aims to create equity in inter-
50　national trading, better conditions for producers in developing countries, and more sustainable environmental practices. Fair trade organizations offer certification to producers who meet certain standards, which include fair trading practices, fair payment, and capacity-building for the producers—for example,
55　developing programs to increase management skills.

One benefit attributed to fair trade is ensuring that smaller producers have access to international markets: small farmers or craft producers join together in a cooperative that sells their products, allowing them to compete with larger businesses.
60　The fair trade system also offers these cooperatives a minimum price to protect producers from variability in market prices and from buyers who might take advantage of smaller producers by paying them too little.

Many people acknowledge fair trade's good intentions
65　and recognize some of its benefits. However, there's a growing concern that fair trade systems in place today may not be as effective at reducing poverty as was once hoped.

One example comes from fair trade coffee. A minimum price floor for fair trade coffee is set, and it's designed to rise
70　when the market price for non-specialty coffee rises, so the fair trade price is always at least $0.20 more than the non-specialty market price. However, the market price for higher-quality beans can exceed the fair trade price, and in recent years, the market price for those specialty beans has been significantly
75　higher. When that happens, it's more beneficial for producers to sell their higher-quality beans at market prices, and there's no incentive to sell high-quality coffee beans to fair trade buyers.

Another problem critics cite is that the price premium for fair trade coffee goes to the cooperative, and not to the coffee
80　farmers themselves. The farmers are members of the cooperatives, so they get to vote on how the money is spent, but the profits don't come directly to them. In some cases, the money may go towards community development that improves the members' quality of life. However, in some cases it goes to the
85　cooperative's operating expenses. Although these expenditures may help the cooperative with its sales, evidence shows that the full benefit of the premium prices is not reaching the farmers themselves. In addition, workers who help produce the coffee, but don't own the farms, are not eligible for membership in the
90　cooperatives. Finally, there are costs involved with meeting the standards to become fair-trade certified, and ultimately, these costs may not be offset by fair trade prices.

11. In the context of Passage A, the statement "the men of the village were deeply suspicious" (lines 9–10) serves to emphasize that the Mayan men were:

    A. not accustomed to the idea of employing their village's women.

    B. unconvinced that MayaWorks representatives were who they said they were.

    C. rarely visited by people who could speak Spanish.

    D. skeptical that the women of the village had artistic talents.

16. The author of Passage B criticizes fair trade systems for which issue that is directly impacted by market prices?

    F. Buyers from outside local villages

    G. Guaranteed price floors

    H. Expanded market access

    J. Coffee quality

17. As it is used in line 92, the word *offset* most nearly means:

    A. displaced.

    B. profited.

    C. shifted.

    D. compensated for.

12. It can most reasonably be inferred from Passage A that regarding MayaWorks, the author feels:

    F. appreciative of the organization's methods and intentions.

    G. convinced that mountain villagers in other countries will join MayaWorks.

    H. doubtful about the quality of the artisans' wares.

    J. confused by the organization's conflicting priorities.

18. Which of the following best captures a difference in the purposes of the two passages?

    F. Passage A provides a critique of a fair trade arrangement, while Passage B provides a comparison between coffee and other fair trade enterprises.

    G. Passage A contrasts MayaWorks's initial and eventual reception in Agua Caliente, while Passage B provides an alternative to fair trade systems.

    H. Passage A provides a snapshot of one fair trade organization, while Passage B provides a critique of fair trade systems.

    J. Passage A provides an overview of MayaWorks's development as an organization, while Passage B argues for doing away with fair trade.

13. As it is used in line 29, *observers* most nearly means:

    A. experimenters.

    B. onlookers.

    C. believers.

    D. photographers.

14. Which of the following is most likely to be found among the products made by MayaWorks artists?

    F. Screen-printed T-shirts

    G. Sequined purses

    H. Hand-woven scarf

    J. Disposable silverware

19. Compared to Passage B, Passage A provides more information regarding how fair trade organizations:

    A. choose the products they will buy.

    B. invest in producers' communities.

    C. respond to critical reactions to their approaches.

    D. set minimum prices.

15. The main function of the last paragraph of Passage A (lines 37–48) is to:

    A. discuss the specific terms and requirements of several types of loans.

    B. describe some important ways that outside investment has helped Mayan communities grow.

    C. itemize some of the ways Mayan artisans have reinvested their earnings.

    D. demonstrate that Mayan villagers are as trustworthy in business as they are skilled in art.

20. The authors of Passage A and Passage B both speak positively of fair trade organizations for practices that:

    F. encourage artisans' innovation.

    G. guarantee producers a fair price for goods.

    H. provide producers with access to buyers.

    J. help individuals contribute to their cooperatives' economic well-being.

Passage III

HUMANITIES: This passage is adapted from the article "Life in the Pits" by Bob Gullberg (© 2003 by Hennen Press).

Mozart and Handel refer to Wolfgang Amadeus Mozart (1756–91), Classical-era composer, and George Frideric Handel (1685–1759), Baroque-era composer.

Looking back over a twenty-year career of playing, composing, and now conducting orchestra music, I often feel a sense of wonder—not at what I have accomplished, but how someone with my agrarian, rather workaday upbringing should
5 have chosen such a path at all. It would have been easy for me to stay on the family farm, eventually to become part-owner, as my brother did quite successfully. However, rewarding as this existence was, it was somehow unfulfilling; my youthful imagination, much to my parents' dismay, often cast about for
10 other, greater pursuits to occupy it. Still, growing up as I did in a household where the radio dispensed milk prices instead of Mozart and hog futures instead of Handel, the thought of embarking on a career in classical music went beyond even my wildest imagination.

15   Perhaps what started me down this unforeseen path was my fascination with other languages. At church services I would hear snippets of Latin and Greek; I was learning Spanish at school; I was instantly drawn to the German, Italian, and Yiddish words and phrases I heard in movies and on TV.
20 Surrounded as I was by the fairly common language of farm and field, these "glamorous" expressions seemed to fill a void in me, and I collected them with the energy of a lepidopterist netting butterflies. As my interest in other languages grew, so did my awareness that music is itself a language, just as capable
25 of expressing and inspiring emotion or thought as the spoken word—sometimes even more so. Take The Tempest, the piece I'm currently rehearsing with my orchestra. It begins in a major key, with just the stringed instruments playing lightly, evoking a sense of peace and contentment—a calm, sunny summer's
30 day. In the second movement, the key diminishes; the mood darkens—clouds and apprehension are building. As the piece progresses, wind instruments, as if blown by the storm, begin to howl, horns blare and shout, overwhelming the senses, thrilling and frightening at once. As the "storm" reaches its height,
35 timpani-roll thunder echoes, and cymbal-clash lightning bolts crash relentlessly, until, when it becomes almost unbearable, the music eases, hope and reason are restored, and soothing notes help the listener forget the chaos and fear he or she felt only moments ago. I've read many accounts of severe weather,
40 even seen them in movies and on TV, but few of them, if any, have been able to replicate not only the sensory experience of a thunderstorm, but also the emotional one the way this piece of music can.

I believe it was music's emotive influence—particularly
45 powerful in my impressionable youth—that ultimately led me to pursue a career in music. Once I began to experience music on an emotional level, I remember having the feeling that others just didn't "get it" like I did, as if somehow music were meant just for musicians. It was only later that I became
50 aware of music's true value—it is a universal language, able to speak to all people, regardless of the linguistic differences that may exist between them. Eventually, of course, music began to eclipse the numerous other "passions" I had throughout my adolescence. Years before I began to pursue music in earnest,
55 I had developed quite an interest in all things motorized. I've always had a mechanical bent (which has served me well in later life, allowing me to turn my hand to almost any musical instrument), and being around farm equipment from an early age certainly gave me an outlet to exercise my abilities. How-
60 ever, my real focus was on cars—I virtually never set down *Automobile Monthly*, a magazine for auto enthusiasts, and I eagerly devoured articles describing which models had the highest horsepower or quickest times in the quarter-mile, and effortlessly committing that information to memory. Eventu-
65 ally, though, like my previous infatuations with archery, and before that dinosaurs, my fixation on cars was to take a "back seat" to a new, greater, and this time lasting, passion for music.

So what made the difference? What made my passion for music continue to burn where other passions had fizzled out?
70 Maturity, perhaps—I know I'd like to think that's the case—or maybe it was just a process of compare-and-contrast; trying different things until I found the one that "fit." If I'm honest with myself, however, I'm forced to admit the answer isn't a "what" or "when," but a "who." For me, like many who find
75 themselves adrift on a sea of uncertainty, it took a mentor to help me find my way to dry land. In my case, that mentor was the conductor of my high-school orchestra, Ms. Fenchurch. A woman of boundless energy and enthusiasm, and with an all-consuming love for music, it was she who first taught me the
80 joy of composition and creation, and helped me to realize that making music is more than just playing notes in a particular order, no matter how well it's done—it's about expression, and perhaps more important, communication. Just like a language.

21. The author mentions *Automobile Monthly* and his mechanical bent primarily to suggest that his:

    A. infatuation with cars was at one time as intense as his passion for music.
    B. interest in and love of all things motorized has remained unchanged throughout his life.
    C. experience with motorized things accounts for his mechanical style of playing music.
    D. obsession with automotive knowledge distracted him from focusing on music.

22. In the first paragraph, the author most nearly characterizes his upbringing as:

   F. easy and usually spent working with his brother.

   G. frustrating yet able to translate easily into music.

   H. somewhat satisfying yet ultimately unable to captivate.

   J. unfulfilling and invariably resulting in his parents' approval.

23. Based on the passage, which of the following was most likely the first to engage the author's passionate interest?

   A. Automobiles

   B. Archery

   C. Dinosaurs

   D. Music

24. Viewed in the context of the passage, the statement in lines 39–43 is most likely intended to suggest that:

   F. music more vividly conveys some experiences than do visual or written accounts.

   G. movies can provide a misleading experience of what a thunderstorm is like.

   H. news reports should more accurately reflect emotional experiences.

   J. thunderstorms are among the hardest experiences to accurately replicate.

25. The passage suggests that the lepidopterist netting butterflies represents:

   A. the author as a child, relishing learning foreign expressions.

   B. the author presently, enjoying his most recent passion.

   C. Ms. Fenchurch, with her boundless energy.

   D. the opening movement of The Tempest.

26. In the context of the passage, lines 34–39 are best described as presenting images of:

   F. jealously, mercy, and resentment.

   G. hate, fear, and disbelief.

   H. conflict, optimism, and love.

   J. chaos, resolution, and relaxation.

27. The author discusses "playing notes in a particular order" (lines 81–82) as part of Ms. Fenchurch's teaching that:

   A. the order of notes matters less than the speed at which they are played.

   B. all music consists of the same parts but rearranged in creative ways.

   C. while one aims to be skilled at performing notes, one should also aim to convey their meaning.

   D. although communication is important, there is more joy to be found in composition itself.

28. Which of the following does NOT reasonably describe a transition presented by the author in lines 27–34?

   F. Lightness to darkness

   G. Calm to thrilling

   H. Apprehension to fright

   J. Overwhelmed to peaceful

29. The main purpose of the last paragraph is to:

   A. describe the lasting influence of Ms. Fenchurch's encouragement.

   B. present an anecdote that conveys Ms. Fenchurch's unique conducting style.

   C. provide detailed background information about Ms. Fenchurch.

   D. illustrate the effect music has on teachers such as Ms. Fenchurch.

30. The passage is best described as being told from the point of view of a musician who is:

   F. telling a linear story that connects momentous events from the beginning of his career to some from the end.

   G. describing how modern works of music such as *The Tempest* have advanced the vision of classical composers such as Mozart and Handel.

   H. suggesting that people who have an interest in universal languages would be well served in studying music.

   J. marveling at his eventual choice of career and considering the people and interests that contributed to it.

Passage IV

NATURAL SCIENCE: This passage is adapted from the article "Debunking the Seahorse" by Clark Millingham (© 2002 by Halcyon Press).

Scientists and laymen alike have long been fascinated by fish known colloquially as seahorses, due to the species' remarkable appearance, unusual mating habits, and incredibly rare reversal of male and female parental roles. The scientific
5 name for the genus is Hippocampus, which combines the Greek word for "horse," *hippos*, with the Greek word for "sea monster," *kampos*. Its distinctive equine head and tapered body shape are a great disadvantage when it comes to the seahorse's swimming ability. It manages to maneuver about by fluttering
10 its dorsal fin up to 35 times a second, but it lacks the caudal, or "tail" fin, which provides the powerful forward thrust for most fish. Instead of swimming to find food, the seahorse coils its signature prehensile tail around stationary objects while using its long snout like a straw to suck in vast numbers of
15 tiny larvae, plankton, and algae. Because the seahorse lacks teeth and a stomach, food passes quickly through its digestive tract, resulting in the need for nearly incessant consumption of food (a typical seahorse can ingest more than 3,000 brine shrimp per day).

20 The peculiar physical features of the seahorse are intriguing, but its mating and reproductive habits are most often the subject of scientists' fascination and debate. Seahorses' courtship rituals often involve a male and a female coordinating their movements, swimming side by side with tails intertwined or coiling around
25 the same strand of sea grass and spinning around it together. They even "dress up" for these rituals, turning a whole array of vivid colors—a sharp contrast to the dull browns and grays with which they typically camouflage themselves among the sea grasses. Courtship typically lasts about two weeks, during
30 which the female and her potential mate will meet once a day, while other males continue to compete for the female's attention, snapping their heads at each other and tail-wrestling.

By the end of the courtship, the female has become engorged with a clutch of around 1,000 eggs, equivalent in mass to one-
35 third her body weight. It is the male, however, who possesses the incubating organ for the eggs, a brood pouch located on his ventral (front) side. The male forces sea water through the pouch to open it up, signifying his readiness to receive the eggs. Uncoiling their tail-grips, the two attach to each other and begin
40 a spiraling ascent towards the surface. The female inserts her ovipositor, a specialized biological apparatus for conducting the eggs into the male's pouch, and the eggs are transferred over the course of eight or nine hours. After that, the male stays put while the female ventures off, only to check in briefly once a
45 day for the next few weeks.

Inside the male's brood pouch, the eggs are fertilized and receive prolactin, the same hormone mammals use for milk production. The pouch delivers oxygen to the eggs via a network of capillaries and regulates a low-salinity environment. As the
50 gestation continues, the eggs hatch and the pouch becomes increasingly saline to help acclimate the young seahorses to the salt water that is waiting outside. The male typically gives birth at night, expelling anywhere from 100 to 1,500 live fry from its pouch. By morning, he once again has an empty pouch
55 to offer his partner if she is ready to mate again.

Because male parenting is such a rarity in the animal kingdom, and male gestation almost unheard-of, scientists often speculate on why male seahorses assume birthing duties. Since giving birth is so energy-intensive and physically
60 limiting, it greatly increases one's risk of death and therefore needs an explanation in terms of evolutionary cost. Bateman's principle holds that whichever sex expends less energy in the reproductive process should be the sex that spends more energy competing for a mate. Only with seahorses do we see the males
65 both compete for mates and give birth. A study conducted by Pierre Robinson at the University of Tallahassee argued that, contrary to appearances, the total energy investment of the mother in growing the clutch of eggs inside of her still outweighed the energy investment of the male in the incubation and birthing
70 process. Male oxygen intake rates go up by 33% during their parental involvement, while the female spends twice as much energy when generating eggs.

In addition to male pregnancy, seahorses also have the distinction of being one of a very small number of monoga-
75 mous species. Scientists believe this is due to the tremendous investment of time and energy that goes into each clutch of eggs a female produces. If her eggs are ready to be incubated and the female does not have a trustworthy male partner ready to receive them, they will be expelled into the ocean and months
80 will have been lost. Additionally, by transferring incubation and birthing duties to the male, a stable monogamous couple can develop an efficient birthing cycle in which he incubates one clutch of eggs while the female begins generating the next.

31. The passage notes that the courtship rituals of seahorses include:

  A. males snapping their heads at females.
  B. camouflaging their body coloring.
  C. allowing sea water to open the brood pouch.
  D. daily meetings for two weeks.

32. The passage states that the seahorse's swimming ability is hindered by its:

  F. tapered body shape.
  G. weak caudal fin.
  H. fluttering dorsal fin.
  J. lack of teeth.

33. Which of the following pieces of information does the most to resolve scientists' confusion as to why male seahorses both compete for mates and give birth?

  A. The fact that the female seahorse possesses an ovipositor
  B. Pierre Robinson's research on the total energy investment of each sex
  C. The habit of seahorses to mate with only one partner
  D. The length of time male seahorses devote to courtship rituals

34. One of the main ideas established by the passage is that:

  F. seahorses are actually quite capable swimmers, despite their unusual appearance.
  G. scientists cannot come up with any coherent explanation for why male seahorses have the evolutionary burden of gestation.
  H. the brood pouch of the male is located on its ventral side.
  J. it is not customary in the animal kingdom for animals to keep the same mating partner for life.

35. As it is used in line 13, the word *signature* most nearly means:

  A. distinctive-looking.
  B. very useful.
  C. autograph.
  D. legally obligated.

36. The main purpose of the fourth paragraph (lines 46–55) is to describe the:

  F. process linking fertilization to hatching.
  G. intricacies of the seahorse's capillary network.
  H. quantity of fry to which males give birth.
  J. amount of salinity seahorse eggs can tolerate.

37. The passage most strongly emphasizes that the monogamy of seahorse mates is most advantageous for the transition from:

  A. low-salinity to high-salinity.
  B. one birthing cycle to the next.
  C. fertilization to incubation.
  D. courtship to mating.

38. As it is used in line 80, the word *lost* most nearly means:

  F. mislaid.
  G. disoriented.
  H. squandered.
  J. defeated.

39. According to the passage, which of the following aspects of a male seahorse's pregnancy provides the best evidence that the seahorse species conforms to the idea behind Bateman's Principle?

  A. Brood pouch
  B. Ovipositor
  C. Prolactin
  D. Oxygen intake

40. The passage indicates that the brood pouch becomes increasingly saline because young seahorses:

  F. would otherwise run the risk of prematurely hatching.
  G. begin gestation in a low salinity environment but ultimately get released into the surrounding water.
  H. have salt extracted from them by the capillary network that delivers oxygen to the brood pouch.
  J. receive the hormone prolactin but do not have the exposure to salt that other mammals do.

END OF TEST
STOP! DO NOT TURN THE PAGE UNTIL TOLD TO DO SO.
DO NOT RETURN TO A PREVIOUS TEST.

Chapter 10
Reading
Practice Test 1
Answers and
Explanations

READING PRACTICE TEST 1 ANSWERS

1.	D		21.	A
2.	H		22.	H
3.	B		23.	C
4.	F		24.	F
5.	D		25.	A
6.	G		26.	J
7.	B		27.	C
8.	J		28.	J
9.	C		29.	A
10.	F		30.	J
11.	A		31.	D
12.	F		32.	F
13.	C		33.	B
14.	H		34.	J
15.	B		35.	A
16.	G		36.	F
17.	D		37.	B
18.	H		38.	H
19.	B		39.	D
20.	H		40.	G

SCORE YOUR PRACTICE TEST

Step A

Count the number of correct answers: _____. This is your *raw score*.

Step B

Use the score conversion table below to look up your raw score. The number to the left is your *scale score*: _____.

Reading Scale Conversion Table

Scale Score	Raw Score	Scale Score	Raw Score	Scale Score	Raw Score
36	39-40	24	27	12	9-10
35	38	23	26	11	7-8
34	37	22	24-25	10	6
33	35-36	21	23	9	5
32	34	20	21-22	8	–
31	33	19	20	7	4
30	–	18	19	6	3
29	32	17	17-18	5	–
28	31	16	16	4	2
27	30	15	14-15	3	–
26	29	14	12-13	2	1
25	28	13	11	1	0

READING PRACTICE TEST 1 EXPLANATIONS

Passage I

1. **D**   This reasoning question asks what the *narrator thinks* about *air travel*. Look for the lead words *air travel* to find the window for the question. In line 2, the author describes air travel as *bittersweet magic*. In lines 20–21, he says that it is *cheating space* and *cheating time*. With these descriptions, the author implies that air travel is unnatural. Look for an answer that matches this idea. Eliminate (A) because no comparison with other modes of travel is made, and because the author mentions some uncomfortable aspects of his flight. Eliminate (B) since the author describes air travel as *magic*. Eliminate (C) because, while the author does mention uncomfortable aspects of flying, he is still taking the flight for the convenience of getting from the west coast to the east coast quickly. Keep (D) because it matches the text from the passage. The correct answer is (D).

2. **H**   This reference question asks what is NOT established about the *narrator* in the *first three paragraphs*. When a question asks what is NOT mentioned in the passage, eliminate answers that are mentioned. In the first three paragraphs, the narrator makes several references to being on an airplane flight, including, *I try to decipher which city glimmers below from the size of its grid of light, as well as my perception of how long I have been flying*, in lines 9–11. Eliminate (F). In lines 1–2, the narrator states *that air travel allows* him *to fall asleep on the west coast and wake up on the east coast* indicating that he is indeed traveling east. Eliminate (G). In lines 11–12, the narrator asks the following questions: *Could that be Denver? Have I already napped a third of the flight?* The narrator clearly did NOT depart from Denver, so keep (H). Choice (J) is also supported by lines 9–11. Eliminate (J). The correct answer is (H).

3. **B**   This reasoning question asks about the *point of view from which the passage is told*. Because this is a general question, it should be done after all the specific questions. Look for the Golden Thread. The passage describes the experiences of someone who has moved out of his parents' house, returns to visit them, and muses about the changes that take place as time passes. Choice (A) is incorrect since the passage never mentions a vacation, and in line 35, the narrator states that he *moved away*. Eliminate (A). Keep (B) because it matches the passage. Although a *coma* is mentioned in lines 65–67, it is in reference to a *physicist* in an *in-flight* movie, not the narrator. Eliminate (C). Choice (D) is incorrect— the narrator's new home is in Southern California. Eliminate (D). The correct answer is (B).

4. **F**   This reference question asks which thing is *relatively new* to the narrator's *parents' house*. Work backward and use lead words from the answers to find the window for this question. In line 53, the narrator states that there are *trinkets on the wall* he doesn't *recognize*, so keep (F). Although the *fridge*, *brown Lexus*, and *bird-feeders* are mentioned in lines 55, 34, and 59, respectively, they are not described as new. Eliminate (G), (H), and (J). The correct answer is (F).

5. **D**   This reference question asks which answer does NOT appear in *recurring references* in the passage. When a question asks what is NOT mentioned in the passage, eliminate answers that are mentioned. The narrator mentions *unsteady slumber* in line 5 and *having trouble sleeping* in line 13. Eliminate

(A). In line 17, *flocks of birds* are mentioned, and in lines 58–60, the narrator describes *grackles that scare the goldfinches away from the bird-feeders*. Eliminate (B). The narrator describes gazing *out the window at the twinkling lights of the towns and cities below* in lines 7–8, and trying *to decipher which city glimmers below from the size of its grid of light* in lines 9–10. Eliminate (C). Although a *dance studio* is mentioned in line 46, there is no mention of dancing, so keep (D). The correct answer is (D).

6. **G** This reference question asks which *habit of his parents* the narrator finds *most upsetting*. Look for the lead words *my parents* to find the window for the question. In line 57, the narrator introduces *the mundane routines of* his *parents*. In lines 63–64, the narrator uses the phrase *most depressingly* to describe the way his parents *often fall asleep in front of the television, mouths gaping*. The phrase *most depressingly* suggests that the narrator finds the way his parents fall asleep to be their most upsetting habit. Look for an answer that matches this idea. Although the narrator mentions in line 32 that his father *now drives a different car*, no habit of buying new cars is ever described. Eliminate (F). Keep (G) because it matches the text from the passage. Although the narrator describes the *television they watch at night* as *uninspired* in lines 61–62, this isn't the *most upsetting* habit. Eliminate (H). Choice (J) can be eliminated because it is never discussed as a habit that upsets the narrator. The correct answer is (G).

7. **B** This reference question asks why the *coma victim has a sense of time as a relative phenomenon*. Look for the lead words *coma* and *time as a relative phenomenon* to find the window for the question. In lines 66–67, the *coma* victim is described as a *physicist*, and line 74 says, *As a physicist, he knew that time is a relative phenomenon*. Therefore, the coma victim has a sense of time as a relative phenomenon because he is a physicist. Look for an answer that matches this idea. Although lines 66–67 indicate the coma victim spent *ten years in a coma*, this doesn't answer the question that was asked. Eliminate (A). Keep (B) because it matches the text from the passage. There's nothing in the passage about *a side effect* or *medical treatment*. Eliminate (C). Although line 71 references the coma victim's *research…prior to his coma*, no information is given as to what that research involved. Eliminate (D). The correct answer is (B).

8. **J** This reference question asks which answer is NOT *part of the present* in the narrator's *hometown*. When a question asks what is NOT mentioned in the passage, eliminate answers that are mentioned. In lines 46–47, the narrator notes that the *old dance studio…seems to have finally closed*. Eliminate (F). The narrator observes, in lines 42–45, that *the performance stage…is now up-and-running, according to the marquee listing its upcoming shows*. Eliminate (G). In lines 45–46, the narrator remarks that *The Olde Towne Tavern is apparently now called Summit Station*. Eliminate (H). The narrator explains, in lines 48–50, that a *cluster of shops…famously burned to the ground* in the past but presently *has open doors and cars gliding in and out of the parking lot*. Keep (J). The correct answer is (J).

9. **C** This reasoning question asks about a *characteristic* of the *narrator's hometown* that is suggested by the details in the passage. Work backward and use lead words from the answers to find the window for this question. After remarking in line 27 that he *knows* [he's] *back home*, the narrator goes on to state in lines 27–29 that *there's no trace of palm trees, flat stretches*, or *perpendicular city streets*. Eliminate (A), (B), and (D). In lines 26–27, the narrator states that *as soon as* [he] *sees the dense stands of oak* he *knows* he is *back home*. Keep (C). The correct answer is (C).

10. **F**   This reasoning question asks what the author is most likely referring to when he *refers to science as* *"that rock of immutable truths."* Read a window around the line reference. The narrator refers to science as *that rock of immutable truths* as a way to emphasize the physicist's sense of bewilderment—before his coma, he had believed scientific truth to be unchanging but awoke to find his life's work obsolete. Look for an answer that matches the idea that scientific truth is unchanging. Keep (F) because it matches the text from the passage. Eliminate (G) because there is no support for the statement that the physicist is unable to comprehend the scientific advances. Choices (H) and (J) can be eliminated since both refer to the time he spent in a coma, not before. The correct answer is (F).

Passage II

11. **A**   This reasoning question asks what the author is trying to emphasize about the *Mayan men* with the statement *the men of the village were deeply suspicious.* Read a window around the line reference. The paragraph says that when the *representatives…first reached out to the women…the men…were deeply suspicious* and *the women were extremely shy, avoiding almost all eye contact with the strangers.* The text goes on to say that ultimately *the women agreed to the idea* and later delivered their orders *with great pride.* Remember, the question asks about the men, not the women, so the correct answer should indicate that the men were uncomfortable with the idea of the team employing the village's women. Look for an answer that matches this idea. Keep (A) because it matches the text from the passage. Eliminate (B) because there is no evidence that the men believed the representatives were lying. No other visitors are mentioned, so eliminate (C). There is no information about the men's perception of the women's talents, so eliminate (D). The correct answer is (A).

12. **F**   This reasoning question asks how the author perceives *MayaWorks.* Because this is a general question, it should be done after all the specific questions about the passage. Look for the Golden Thread. The answers to the specific questions for this passage indicate that the author has a positive perception of the organization. Look for an answer that matches this idea. Keep (F) because it matches the text from the passage. Although (G) has a positive tone regarding the perception of the organization, there are no *other countries* mentioned in Passage A. Eliminate (G). Eliminate (H) and (J) because they don't match the positive tone of the passage. The correct answer is (F).

13. **C**   This vocabulary in context question asks what the word *observers* means in line 29. Go back to the text, find the word *observers,* and cross it out. Carefully read the surrounding text to determine another word that would fit in the blank based on the context. The text discusses the wares created by the women of the village, including *religious items* such as *stoles for Christian priests* and *yarmulkes, or kippahs, for Jewish observers.* Therefore, *observers* could be replaced with "practitioners" (people who practice a faith). Look for an answer that matches this idea. Eliminate (A) because *experimenters* does not match "practitioners." Choice (B), *onlookers,* does not match "practitioners." This is a Words Out of Context trap answer based on another meaning of *observers.* Eliminate (B). Keep (C) because *believers* matches "practitioners." Choice (D) can be eliminated because *photographers* does not match "practitioners." The correct answer is (C).

14. **H**   This reference question asks which *product* is most likely to be *made by MayaWorks artists*. Look for the lead words *product* and *made by MayaWorks artists* to find the window for the question in Passage A. The third paragraph of Passage A describes the *finished products* and *wares created by MayaWorks artisans*, which include a variety of items *woven* from *yarn: placemats, napkins, pouches, Beanies, and footbags…*as well as *stoles…and yarmulkes*. Look for an answer that is consistent with items hand-made by weaving. Although a shirt could be handmade, the passage does not mention any products that are *screen-printed*. Eliminate (F). Choice (G) can be eliminated because no *sequined* products are mentioned in Passage A. Keep (H) because it matches the text from the passage. Choice (J) can be eliminated because *silverware* is not mentioned in Passage A. The correct answer is (H).

15. **B**   This reasoning question asks about the *main function* of the final paragraph of Passage A. Carefully read the last paragraph of Passage A to determine its main function. The author mainly discusses the *microcredit loans* MayaWorks provides, which allow villages to *upgrade weaving equipment, install water pumps…, and buy crops*. The author goes on to say that *100% of their microcredit loans have been paid back in full and on time*. Look for an answer that is consistent with these ideas. Choice (A) can be eliminated because the paragraph does not exist to spell out the *terms* of various loans. Keep (B) because it matches the text from the passage: the microcredit loans are an *outside investment*. Choice (C) can be eliminated because the paragraph focuses on the loans, not the *earnings*. Although the author specifies that *100% of the microcredit loans have been paid back in full and on time*, the function of the paragraph is not to establish the trustworthiness of the villagers. Eliminate (D). The correct answer is (B).

16. **G**   This reference question asks which issue related to *market prices* the author of Passage B criticizes. Work backward and use lead words from the answers to find the window for this question. Choice (F) can be eliminated because there's no mention of *buyers from outside local villages* in Passage B. In the fourth paragraph of Passage B, the author explains that a *minimum price floor for fair trade coffee is set,… at least $0.20 more than* market price, and that floor is *designed to rise when the market price…rises*. However, sometimes market price is higher than the fair-trade price, so it's more beneficial for the producers to sell their beans at market prices. Therefore, the minimum price floors aren't working the way they should. Keep (G). In lines 56–57, the author notes that *ensuring that smaller producers have access to international markets* is a *benefit*, not an issue of which to be critical. Eliminate (H). Although the author of Passage B references *higher-quality beans* in the fourth paragraph of Passage B, she is not critical of the quality. Eliminate (J). The correct answer is (G).

17. **D**   This vocabulary in context question asks what the word *offset* means in line 92. Go back to the text, find the word *offset,* and cross it out. Carefully read the surrounding text to determine another word that would fit in the blank based on the context. The author of Passage B uses the word to refer to the imbalance of the costs of becoming *fair-trade certified* and the money brought in for the sale of fair-trade beans. If the money coming in does not *offset* the costs of becoming certified, the money isn't enough to cover the costs. Look for an answer that matches this idea. Choice (A) can be eliminated because the costs aren't being *displaced*. Eliminate (B) because the point is that the costs are causing the producers to lose profits rather than gain them. Eliminate (C) because the costs are not being *shifted* anywhere. Keep (D) because it matches the text from the passage. The correct answer is (D).

18. **H** This reasoning question asks for a *difference in the purposes of the two passages*. Because this question asks about both passages, it should be done after the questions that ask about each passage individually. Consider the Golden Thread of both passages. Choice (F) can be eliminated because Passage A does not *critique a fair-trade arrangement*. Eliminate (G) because Passage B does not provide *an alternative to fair-trade systems*. Keep (H) because Passage A discusses MayaWorks, *one fair-trade organization*, and Passage B critiques several aspects of fair-trade systems, including *price floors*. Choice (J) can be eliminated because Passage A discusses MayaWorks in action, not in *development as an organization*, and while Passage B offers critiques of fair trade, it also mentions positive aspects of fair trade, so it does not argue for *doing away with fair trade*. The correct answer is (H).

19. **B** This reference question asks which topic Passage A provides *more information* about compared to Passage B. Because this question asks about both passages, it should be done after the questions that ask about each passage individually. Eliminate any answer choices that misrepresent either passage. Eliminate (A) because Passage A does not discuss how fair-trade organizations *choose the products they will buy*. Keep (B) because Passage A discusses *microcredit loans* and how they are used to build up communities, whereas Passage B does not. Choice (C) can be eliminated because Passage A is generally positive, with no discussion about *critical reactions* to the organization. Although *minimum prices* are mentioned in Passage B, they are not mentioned in Passage A. Eliminate (D). The correct answer is (B).

20. **H** This reference question asks which practice both passages *speak positively of*. Because this question asks about both passages, it should be done after the questions that ask about each passage individually. Eliminate any answer choices that misrepresent either passage. Eliminate (F) because Passage B does not mention *encouraging artisans' innovation*. Choice (G) can be eliminated because Passage A never discusses guaranteeing *a fair price*. Passage A describes how one fair trade organization helps *Mayan artisans who would otherwise have little commercial outlet for their talents*, and Passage B mentions *ensuring that smaller producers have access to international markets* as *one benefit attributed to fair trade*. Keep (H). Choice (J) might initially look good, but Passage A discusses the individuals helping their communities, not the *economic well-being* of *their cooperatives*. Eliminate (J). The correct answer is (H).

Passage III

21. **A** This reasoning question asks why the author mentions *Automobile Monthly and his mechanical bent*. Look for the lead words *Automobile Monthly* and *mechanical bent* to find the window for the question. In lines 54–67, the author discusses the interests he had pursued *years before* he *began to pursue music in earnest*, which *eventually* took *a "back seat"* to a new, greater, and this time lasting, passion for music. In this discussion, the author reveals that his *real focus* at one time *was on cars* and that he *eagerly devoured articles* on cars and *effortlessly* committed *that information to memory*. Look for an answer choice that indicates the author was once as devoted to cars as he eventually became to music. Keep (A) because it matches the text from the passage. The author indicates that his infatuation with cars changed over time and was ultimately overtaken by his interest in music. Eliminate (B). Choice (C)

can be eliminated because the passage never describes the author's playing style, so there is no support for calling it *mechanical*. Eliminate (D) because the author explains his love of cars came before his love of music; this answer makes it seem as though they were in competition and his love of cars was winning. The correct answer is (A).

22. **H** This reference question asks about the way the author *characterizes his upbringing* in the first paragraph. Carefully read the first paragraph to determine how the author characterizes his upbringing. In lines 7–10, the author says that as *rewarding as this existence was, it was somehow unfulfilling*; his *youthful imagination…often cast about for other, greater pursuits to occupy it*. Look for an answer that matches this text from the passage. Eliminate (F) because the passage does not state that the author usually worked with his brother. Eliminate (G) because the passage makes it seem like the author's upbringing made *the thought of embarking on a music career* beyond his *wildest imagination*. Keep (H) because it matches the text from the passage. Although the author describes his upbringing as *unfulfilling*, he does not mention it invariably resulting in his parents' approval. Eliminate (J). The correct answer is (H).

23. **C** This reference question asks which thing was mostly likely *the first to engage the author's passionate interest*. Work backward and use lead words from the answers to find the window for this question. The third paragraph, lines 44–67, explains that the author's obsession with cars took place *years before* he *began to pursue music*. Furthermore, the end of that paragraph refers to his even earlier, *previous infatuations with archery, and before that dinosaurs*. This means that dinosaurs were his earliest interest. Eliminate (A), (B), and (D) because those interests did not engage the author's passionate interest first. The correct answer is (C).

24. **F** This reasoning question asks what the statement in lines 39–43 is *most likely intended to suggest*. Read a window around the line reference. In this window, the author summarizes his delight with how effectively the music replicates the sensory and emotional experience of a thunderstorm. Look for an answer that matches this idea. Keep (F) because it matches the text from the passage. Eliminate (G) because the passage does not suggest that movies mislead the audience, only that they often do not replicate the experience of the thunderstorm as well as this music does. Eliminate (H) because the author is not concerned with changing the character of new reports; he is only pointing out how well music can communicate. Although the author suggests that it is not easy to replicate a thunderstorm, the purpose of his statement is to make a point about music's ability to convey a rich experience similar to thunderstorms. Eliminate (J). The correct answer is (F).

25. **A** This reference question asks what the *lepidopterist netting butterflies* represents. Look for the lead words *lepidopterist netting butterflies* to find the window for the question. In the second paragraph, the author recounts the early experiences in his youth that led him to have an interest in music. He describes the thrill he took in learning Latin, Greek, Yiddish, German, Spanish, and Italian and, in lines 22–23, compares the eagerness with which he learned them to *the energy of a lepidopterist netting butterflies*. Look for an answer that matches this text from the passage. Keep (A) because it matches the text from the passage. Eliminate (B), (C), and (D) because the author uses the phrase to describe his youth, not his present self, Ms. Fenchurch, or anything music-related, respectively. The correct answer is (A).

26. **J**   This reference question asks for the *images* that lines 34–39 present. Read a window around the line reference. Lines 34–36 describe chaos in the thunder and lightning stage, followed by resolution and relaxation in lines 37–38 when *the music eases, hope and reason are restored, and soothing notes help the listener forget the chaos.* Look for an answer that matches this text from the passage. Eliminate (F) because there is no support in the passage for jealousy or resentment. Although storms are sometimes described as "angry," they are not described as *hateful.* Eliminate (G). Choice (H) can be eliminated because *love* is not a strong match for anything described in the text from the passage. Keep (J) because it matches the text. The correct answer is (J).

27. **C**   This reference question asks about *Ms. Fenchurch's teaching*, which includes *playing notes in a particular order.* Read a window around the line reference. The lesson Ms. Fenchurch imparts to the author, in lines 81–83, is that music is more than just the notes on the page; *it's about expression and perhaps more important, communication.* Find an answer that matches this text from the passage. Eliminate (A) because the *speed* at which the notes are played is not discussed. Choice (B) can be eliminated because it does not provide an accurate summary of Ms. Fenchurch's teaching in the last paragraph. Keep (C) because it matches the text from the passage. Eliminate (D) because Ms. Fenchurch places greater emphasis on *communication.* The correct answer is (C).

28. **J**   This reference question asks which answer *does NOT reasonably describe a transition presented by the author.* When a question asks what is NOT mentioned in the passage, eliminate answers that are mentioned. Read a window around the line reference. Lines 27–34 portray a calm lightness darkening into a cloudy apprehension and ultimately becoming a howling, thrilling, and frightening sensory overload. Eliminate (F), (G), and (H) because they all match up with something in lines 27–34 and are in correct chronological order. Keep (J) because it describes the transition in reverse, so it does NOT describe a transition in the passage. The correct answer is (J).

29. **A**   This reasoning question asks about the main purpose of the last paragraph, so carefully read the paragraph to determine its objective. The last paragraph begins, in line 68, with the author's rhetorical question: *So what made the difference?* The author reveals, in lines 69–77, that what made his love for music *continue to burn where other passions had fizzled* was a *"who,"* Ms. Fenchurch. The author, in lines 78–83, then outlines the influence Ms. Fenchurch had on his life and musical development. Find an answer choice that matches this idea. Keep (A) because it matches the text from the passage. Eliminate (B) because the author does not provide an *anecdote,* and there are no details relating to Ms. Fenchurch's *conducting style.* Although there are some character traits mentioned about Ms. Fenchurch, there is little *detailed background information*, and even if there were, the purpose of the paragraph is to explain the influence Ms. Fenchurch had on the author's life and musical development. Eliminate (C). Choice (D) can be eliminated because the paragraph does not mention the effect music has on Ms. Fenchurch. Rather, the paragraph mentions the influence Ms. Fenchurch had on the author's love of music. The correct answer is (A).

30. **J**   This reasoning question asks about the point of view of the author. Because this is a general question, it should be done after all the specific questions. Look for the Golden Thread. Phrases such as *sense of wonder* in line 3 and *unforeseen path* in line 15 indicate that the author is surprised by his career choice.

Furthermore, throughout the passage, there are references to people, events, and subject matter that influenced the author's interest in music. Find an answer that matches this idea. Choice (F) can be eliminated because the passage is not linear; it moves back and forth in time. Additionally, the passage does not list momentous events in the author's career, but more momentous influences on the author. Eliminate (G) because the passage does not delve into any specifics regarding *Mozart* and *Handel*, and the description of *The Tempest* is presented without comparison to any other piece of music. Choice (H) can be eliminated because the passage as whole is not persuasive in nature. The author is relating personal reflections, not advocating a certain course of action. Keep (J) because it matches the text from the passage. The correct answer is (J).

Passage IV

31. **D** This reference question asks about the *courtship rituals of seahorses*. Look for the lead words *courtship rituals* to find the window for the question. *Seahorses' courtship rituals* can be found on line 22 in the second paragraph of the passage. The author notes, in lines 31–32, that *other males continue… snapping their heads at each other*, not at females. Eliminate (A). Although the passage mentions, in lines 28–29, the fact that seahorses *typically camouflage themselves among the sea grasses*, this does not refer to their courtship rituals. In lines 26–27, the author states that during courtship the seahorses *dress up* in *a whole array of vivid colors*. Eliminate (B). Choice (C) can be eliminated because it refers to mating/birthing, not courtship. In lines 29–30, the author indicates that *courtship typically lasts about two weeks, during which the female and her potential mate will meet once a day*. This supports (D). The correct answer is (D).

32. **F** This reference question asks what *hinders* the *seahorse's swimming ability*. Look for the lead words *swimming ability* to find the window for the question. In lines 7–9, the passage states that the seahorse's *equine head and tapered body shape are a great disadvantage when it comes to* its *swimming ability*. Look for an answer that matches this text from the passage. Keep (F) because it matches the passage. Eliminate (G) because, as noted in lines 10–11, the seahorse *lacks the caudal, or "tail" fin*. Choice (H) can be eliminated because the passage mentions, in lines 9–10, that the seahorse *manages to maneuver about by fluttering its dorsal fin*. So, the dorsal fin is what gives the seahorse what little swimming ability it has. Although the passage mentions that *the seahorse lacks teeth* in lines 15–16, it does not link this to swimming ability. Eliminate (J). The correct answer is (F).

33. **B** This reference question asks about information that resolves *scientists' confusion as to why male seahorses both compete for mates and give birth*. Look for the lead word *scientists* to find the window for the question. In lines 61–65, the author indicates that the scientists' confusion relates to *Bateman's principle*, which *holds that whichever sex expends less energy in the reproductive process should be the sex that spends more energy competing for a mate*. It may then seem confusing to scientists that males both compete for mates and give birth. However, the author continues the discussion in lines 65–72, by discussing *A study conducted by Pierre Robinson*, which shows that females do in fact expend more energy in the reproductive process than do males. Thus, males should be the ones competing for mates after all. Look for an answer that

matches this idea. Although a female's *ovipositor* is a detail involved in the mechanics of males giving birth, it does not resolve the confusion surrounding why the males also compete for mates. Eliminate (A). Keep (B) because it matches the text from the passage. The monogamy of seahorses is explained by efficient birthing cycles, but it does not itself explain why males give birth yet compete for mates. Eliminate (C). Choice (D) can be eliminated because the length of time spent competing for mates still does not explain why males give birth yet complete for mates. The correct answer is (B).

34. **J**   This reference question asks about one of the main ideas in the passage. Because this is a general question, it should be done after all the specific questions. Look for the Golden Thread. The correct answer should address something about the seahorse's unusual mating habits. Look for an answer that matches this idea. Although the first paragraph of the passage explains that the seahorse manages some mobility, it still portrays the seahorse as a poor swimmer. Eliminate (F). Choice (G) can be eliminated because the fifth paragraph of the passage mentions *Pierre Robinson*'s research as offering a potentially viable explanation for why male seahorses are responsible for birth. Although the third paragraph of the passage indicates that the male seahorse has a *brood pouch*, this is not a main idea of the passage. Eliminate (H). The last paragraph of the passage begins by explaining that seahorses *have the distinction of being one of a very small number of monogamous species*. Keep (J) because it matches the text from the passage. The correct answer is (J).

35. **A**   This vocabulary in context question asks what the word *signature* means in line 13. Go back to the text, find the word *signature*, and cross it out. Carefully read the surrounding text to determine another word that would fit in the blank based on the context of the passage. In line 3, the passage mentions the seahorse's *remarkable appearance*, and in line 7, the passage mentions the seahorse's *distinctive equine head*. The mention of its *signature* prehensile tail is another indication that this feature is associated primarily with seahorses. Look for an answer that matches this idea. Keep (A) because it matches the text from the passage. Although the tail is useful, that is not what *signature* conveys. Eliminate (B). Choice (C) is a trap answer based on the equivalent meanings of *autograph* and *signature*. Eliminate (C). Choice (D) is also a trap answer because of its association to one's signature; however, it makes no sense to call a seahorse's tail *legally obligated*. Eliminate (D). The correct answer is (A).

36. **F**   This reasoning question asks for the main purpose of the fourth paragraph, so carefully read the paragraph to determine its objective. The fourth paragraph provides details of *fertilization*, *hatching*, and giving *birth*. Look for an answer that matches this text from the passage. Keep (F) because it matches the text. Choices (G) and (H) can be eliminated since *capillaries* and the *number of fry*, respectively, are mentioned only in passing. There is no mention in the paragraph about *the amount of salinity seahorse eggs can tolerate*. Eliminate (J). The correct answer is (F).

37. **B**   This reference question asks about an advantage of *the monogamy of seahorse mates*. Look for the lead word *monogamy* to find the window for the question. In lines 81–82, the author explains that *a stable monogamous couple can develop an efficient birthing cycle in which* the male *incubates one clutch of eggs while the female begins generating the next*. Therefore, when the males give birth to one clutch of eggs, the females are almost ready with the next clutch. Look for an answer that matches this

idea. Although the passage mentions the transition from low to high *salinity*, it does not describe this as a benefit of monogamy. Eliminate (A). Keep (B) because it matches the text from the passage. Eliminate (C) because the transition from *fertilization to incubation* takes place in and only relates to the gestation stage within the male's brood pouch. Choice (D) can be eliminated because the initial transition from *courtship to mating* is when a female would actually select her mate. Monogamy has meaning only once a mate has been selected. The correct answer is (B).

38. **H** This vocabulary in context question asks what the word *lost* means in line 80. Go back to the text, find the word *lost*, and cross it out. Carefully read the surrounding text to determine another word that would fit in the blank based on the context of the passage. According to lines 77–80, if the female can't find a *trustworthy male partner* to receive her eggs, *they will be expelled into the ocean*, which is essentially throwing them away. Therefore, the months spent growing the eggs will be wasted. Look for an answer that matches this idea. Choices (F), (G), and (J) are synonyms for *lost*, but none are consistent with the context of the passage. Keep (H) because it matches the text from the passage. The correct answer is (H).

39. **D** This reference question asks which aspect of *a male seahorse's pregnancy provides the best evidence that the seahorse species conforms to the idea behind Bateman's Principle*. Look for the lead words *Bateman's Principle* to find the window for the question. In lines 56–72, the author explains the paradox scientists see in the seahorse species, which is that males both give birth and compete for mates. According to *Bateman's Principle*, in lines 61–64, the sex that expends more energy in the reproductive process should not be the sex that competes for mates. The author reports, in lines 65–72, that *Pierre Robinson* found that male seahorses' increased *oxygen intake* during pregnancy does not qualify males as the sex that expends more energy in the reproductive process. Hence, seahorses conform to *Bateman's Principle*. Look for an answer that matches this idea. Choices (A), (B), and (C) can be eliminated because, although they refer to aspects of the seahorse's reproductive process, they do not relate to *Bateman's Principle*, which focuses on energy expenditure. Keep (D) because it matches the text from the passage. The correct answer is (D).

40. **G** This reference question asks why *the brood pouch becomes increasingly saline* for *young seahorses*. Look for the lead words *brood pouch* and *increasingly saline* to find the window for the question. In lines 46–55, the author explains that the *brood pouch…regulates a low-salinity environment* initially, but *becomes increasingly saline to help acclimate the young seahorses to the salt water* of the ocean that awaits them. Look for an answer that matches this text from the passage. Eliminate (F) because there is no support in the passage for *premature hatching*. Keep (G) because it matches the text from the passage. Choice (H) can be eliminated because nothing suggests that the *capillary network* extracts salt. Eliminate (J) because the passage does not suggest other mammals have exposure to salt. The correct answer is (G).

Chapter 11
Reading
Practice Test 2

READING TEST

35 Minutes—40 Questions

DIRECTIONS: There are four passages in this test. Each passage is followed by several questions. After reading each passage, choose the best answer to each question and blacken the corresponding oval on your answer document. You may refer to the passages as often as necessary.

Passage I

PROSE FICTION: This passage is adapted from the novel *The Smell of Fresh Muffins* by Woody Jessup (©1985 by Woody Jessup).

The narrator is going to help his grandfather paint a room in the narrator's house. Garth is a friend of the narrator's grandfather.

Garth should be here any minute. I'm kind of glad, actually, that Grandpa sent his buddy to pick us up. Daddy always runs late because he tries to squeeze in one extra thing at the last minute, and Grandpa tends to misjudge how slowly he drives
5 nowadays. Garth has only picked us up a couple times before, but each time he was here at 2:17 on the nose.

Garth seems to see his schedule as various-sized blocks of activities that must be inserted into the correct-sized slot of time. Grandpa says that since Garth's wife died, Garth has
10 married his schedule. He says people use a routine to distract themselves from their life. Grandpa seems to know human nature pretty well, so I believe him.

We see Garth's tan Oldsmobile pull slowly into the parking lot. His car is a good match for his personality: boring but reliable.
15 Garth doesn't joke too much with people besides Grandpa. He was in the Marines for many years in the fifties. His posture and his way of speaking to people are both perfectly upright.

"Hey, kids. How was school?" Garth asks as we start piling into the back seat. "You know, one of you can sit up front."

20 Sis and I exchange a look with each other, hiding our feelings of reluctance. I remind her, with my eyes, that last time I rode up front, and she silently accepts her fate.

We start to drive off towards our house, where my Grandpa is currently re-painting our living room.

25 "You two ever done any painting?" Garth asks. We shake our heads. "It's like icing a cupcake. Does your mom ever let you do that? I mean, did she?"

"Sometimes." Clara chimes in. "She normally gave us one or two to play with, but she knew we couldn't make 'em as
30 pretty as she could, with that little swirl thing on top."

"Ah, of course." Garth grins. "Well, that swirl is what painting is all about. If you start with too little icing, you smear it out thin to cover the whole top of the cupcake, but you can still see the cake peeking through, right?"

35 We nod. He continues, "But if you start with a good dollop, more than you really need, you can swoosh it around with one clever twist of your wrist. The extra stuff just comes off onto your knife...or your paintbrush if you're painting."

"Maybe I need smarter wrists," Clara sighs skeptically.

40 We park a block down from our house so that Daddy won't see Garth's car when he gets home from work. Grandpa wanted the painted room to be a surprise.

As soon as we step in our kitchen door, we can smell the paint from the living room. Grandpa is wearing paint-covered
45 overalls, but the paint stains are dry, and none of them are the bright sky color that Clara picked for the living room.

"Hey, Sam. Hey, Clara. Grab yourself a brush and a smock before I steal all the good spots for myself!" Grandpa chuckles. We assume he will not let us up on a ladder, so he must be
50 counting on us to work on the bottom three feet of the wall.

Sis and I grab two new brushes that Grandpa must have just bought at the store. It seems a crime to dip them into the paint the first time and forever ruin their purity.

"Don't be afraid to give it some elbow grease, now." Grandpa
55 encourages, letting us watch him as he applies thick strokes of paint to the wall.

We begin working in our own areas, creating splotchy islands of blue.

Grandpa pauses from his work to watch our technique. He
60 grins. "Fun, isn't it?"

"What if Daddy's disappointed he didn't get to do this himself?" I ask.

"Disappointed I did him a favor? If I know Arthur, he'll be happy to have avoided the manual labor. He'll just be dis-
65 appointed he didn't get to see his kids finally covering up the awful beige wall that came with the house."

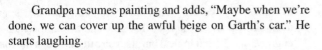
Grandpa resumes painting and adds, "Maybe when we're done, we can cover up the awful beige on Garth's car." He starts laughing.

70 Garth seems not to mind or notice. He is concentrating on painting the corner without getting any stray streaks on the ceiling.

Grandpa notices Garth's serious expression and says, "He even paints like a Marine." Another chuckle. Garth does not look away from his corner but adds, "and your Grandpa likes
75 talking more than working—just like a civilian." Sis and I are accustomed to their jovial back-and-forth.

I feel sad to hear Grandpa say we will cover up the wall that came with the house. That is the color we grew up with. That is the color of the living room with Mom still in it. I don't
80 want to cover up our memories, even though they make us sad now. But covering up is different from removing. We will put a layer of sky blue on the surface so that we feel invigorated, but we will know that Mom's layer is always protected underneath.

1. Which of the following statements regarding the idea for painting the room is best supported by the passage?

   A. While Clara was reluctant to do it, Grandpa ultimately convinced her it was okay.
   B. Garth suggested the idea to Grandpa, who then told the narrator and her sister.
   C. Clara envisioned the idea, and Garth helped provide some of the supplies.
   D. Although Grandpa planned the activity, Clara was involved in the decision making.

2. As presented in the passage, the exchange between the narrator and his sister when Garth comes to pick them up can best be described as:

   F. an expression of frustration due to the curiosity the narrator and his sister felt regarding Garth's unusual tardiness.
   G. a situation that is initially confusing to the narrator until his sister reminds him about the project to repaint the living room.
   H. a favorite game that the narrator plays with his sister to determine which person gets the honor of sitting in front.
   J. a nonverbal conversation that allows the narrator and his sister to determine which of them receives an unfavorable consequence.

3. Based on the passage, Garth and Grandpa can be reasonably said to share all of the following characteristics EXCEPT:

   A. painting experience.
   B. good posture.
   C. the ability to drive.
   D. willingness to poke fun.

4. Clara's reference to having "smarter wrists" (line 39) primarily serves to suggest her:

   F. remaining doubt about equaling her mother's skills.
   G. growing excitement regarding learning how to paint.
   H. deepening confusion about how painting relates to cupcakes.
   J. increasing concern that people see her as intelligent.

5. Viewed in the context of the passage, Grandpa's grin (lines 59–60) most nearly reflects a feeling of:

   A. irony.
   B. intense relaxation.
   C. mild satisfaction.
   D. harsh disapproval.

6. The narrator's statement "His car is a good match for his personality" (line 14) most nearly means that in the narrator's opinion, Garth is:

   F. too conservative in his choice of cars.
   G. highly dependable, but not very flashy.
   H. more upright than many Oldsmobile drivers.
   J. too concerned with how others see him.

7. Garth clearly recommends that the children apply both paint and icing in which of the following ways?

   A. Gently
   B. Respectfully
   C. Conservatively
   D. Confidently

8. In the second paragraph, the main conclusion the narrator reaches is that:

   F. Garth considers tardiness a character flaw.
   G. Garth is extremely talented at organizing his schedule.
   H. people can use a routine to avoid focusing on something painful.
   J. Grandpa is a very keen observer of human behavior.

9. In terms of the development of the narrator as a character, the last paragraph primarily serves to:

   A. add to the reader's understanding of his guilt.
   B. explain his relationship to his mother.
   C. describe his underlying emotional conflict.
   D. portray the strained relationship he has with Grandpa.

10. It can most reasonably be inferred that Arthur is the name of:

   F. Garth and Grandpa's friend.
   G. the narrator.
   H. the narrator's father.
   J. the neighbor who lent them the ladder.

Passage II

SOCIAL SCIENCE: Passage A is an excerpt from the article "Electric Cars Face Power Outage" by Justin Sabo (© 2010 by Justin Sabo). Passage B is adapted from "Why is the Market for Hybrid Electric Vehicles (HEVs) Moving Slowly?" by Rahmani, Djamel and Loureiro, Maria L. Published March 21, 2018.

Passage A by Justin Sabo

So why are there hardly any purely electric vehicles on the road today? In 1996, General Motors released the EV1, the first fully electric vehicle designed and released by a major auto manufacturer. GM entered this unfamiliar territory bravely but
5 reluctantly, motivated by emissions-control legislation enacted by the California Air Resources Board (CARB). This could not possibly have been good news for American automakers. Many believed that electric vehicles were not commercially viable. It would be very expensive to research, develop, and market a
10 new type of car, and with consumer demand for such cars a big unknown, the companies feared stiff economic losses would result from the new regulations. GM was pessimistic its EV1 could be a viable commodity, but it felt that the best way to force CARB to undo the mandate was to play ball: they would
15 bring an electric car to the market and let everyone watch it fail.

Previous electric vehicle prototypes from major automakers had consisted of converting existing gasoline models, a process neither elegant nor inexpensive. The EV1, however, was designed from the start as an electric car, and lightness and
20 efficiency were incorporated throughout the design. The cars were only available to be leased, because GM wanted to be able to reclaim them if necessary. Ultimately, GM reclaimed all the EV1's it had leased, intending to destroy them. EV1 owners were livid that their prized possessions were going to become
25 scrap metal. They offered GM "no-risk" purchasing terms, essentially begging GM to let them buy the car while exempting GM from being accountable for any future maintenance or repair issues. They were denied.

Why? Skepticism brewed regarding GM's deeper motives
30 for canceling the EV1 program. Alleged pressure from the oil industry helped coax CARB into repealing their electric-car mandate. Others pointed to the fiscal losses GM would suffer if electric cars became popular.

Other researchers portrayed a different story. Dr. Kenneth
35 Train of UC Berkeley presented a study which claimed Americans would only be interested in buying an electric car if it were priced at least $28,000 less than a comparable gasoline-fueled car. This study was frequently touted by automakers who hoped to prove that the electric car was not a financially viable product.

40 Whether the electric car can transcend consumers' distrust of the unfamiliar and the auto and oil industries' reluctance to change is unknown. What is certain is the fact that a new technology poses challenges that go well beyond mechanical engineering. Technological hurdles can often come in the form
45 of political, economic, and social obstacles.

Passage B by Djamel Rahmani and Maria L. Loureiro

Up to now, despite the best efforts of certain sectors, electric vehicles (EVs) and hybrid electric vehicles (HEVs) simply have not made the splash in the global market that many were expecting. On paper, HEVs in particular should be popular:
50 they don't have battery problems, they don't suffer from a lack of infrastructures, and they benefit from public incentives in many countries. Yet drivers have avoided switching from diesel and gasoline vehicles to electric ones. The reason isn't clear. Is price to blame? Perhaps it's other misconceptions about hybrid
55 vehicles that are preventing consumers from making the jump.

A recent survey of those in the market for a new automobile found that nearly half of those surveyed perceived HEVs to be cleaner than gasoline or diesel cars. Three out of ten drivers believed that HEVs have lower running costs than conventional
60 cars. However, many of the drivers surveyed also perceived them to be more expensive, slower, and less powerful than conventional cars. In addition, some drivers do not exactly know what HEVs were: although they said they had negative perceptions of the HEVs, they also preferred cheaper cars with
65 low fuel consumption, implying that fuel economy may be an attractive reason to buy HEVs. Similarly, low CO_2 emissions increase the utility derived from a car, and are another reason to encourage drivers to buy HEVs.

Another study found that drivers are willing to pay a pre-
70 mium close to $2000 to change from conventional automobiles to HEVs, but that amount is significantly lower than the current market price markup for HEVs. In order to boost sales, economic incentives for the consumer must be clearly articulated, and marketing campaigns must be designed to provide accurate
75 information on HEVs.

Another potential solution is to promote the use of HEVs for taxis and public transport, and to encourage the public authorities to replace their conventional cars with HEVs. This may help to further promote the image of HEVs, and to reduce
80 the current distrust towards this alternative fuel technology.

This set of findings may be relevant in order to adopt appropriate and effective strategies in the future aimed at reducing road transport, greenhouse gas emissions, and their contribution to climate change. Future research should look deeper at the role
85 of economic incentives under different scenarios, characterized in many occasions by strong cultural differences, risk aversion, and myopic time preferences.

Questions 11–14 ask about Passage A.

11. The author primarily portrays the efforts of GM to design an electric car as:

A. resulting from overconfidence in consumer enthusiasm for electric vehicles.

B. directed more at perfecting the marketing than at perfecting the science.

C. intended to showcase GM's superiority over its competitors.

D. motivated in part by a desire to fail.

12. The statement in lines 7–8 most likely represents the view of all of the following groups EXCEPT:

F. the executives at GM who commissioned the design of the EV1.

G. the members of the California Air Resources Board who issued the mandate.

H. the other American automakers at the time the CARB mandate was issued.

J. Dr. Kenneth Train and his research team at UC Berkeley.

13. The author most likely intends his answer to the question posed in line 29 to be:

A. definitive; he believes the real reasons are plain to see.

B. incomplete; he is convinced that CARB had some unknown involvement.

C. genuine; he has no guesses about GM's motives for the denial.

D. speculative; he thinks that plausible explanations have been put forth.

14. It can reasonably be inferred from the last paragraph of Passage A that the author thinks that any forthcoming electric vehicle will:

F. face challenges larger than simple design.

G. be embraced by most automakers.

H. overcome the skepticism of consumers.

J. succeed if sold at a lower price.

Questions 15–17 ask about Passage B.

15. The main idea of the first paragraph of Passage B (lines 46–55) is that

A. HEV purchases may be influenced by unaccounted factors.

B. HEV makers must learn to compete with the makers of diesel and gasoline vehicles.

C. HEVs are cheaper and more reliable than EVs are.

D. researchers question how consumers evaluate the risks of HEVS.

16. In the context of the passage, the authors of Passage B most likely use the statistics in the second paragraph (lines 56–68) in order to:

F. establish fuel economy as the most attractive quality of HEVs.

G. emphasize the complexities of sampling driver perceptions.

H. support a paradox introduced in the previous paragraph.

J. criticize how HEVs are perceived by the public.

17. According to Passage B, one reason for low sales of HEVs is that:

A. neither public transport nor public officials themselves make much use of HEVs.

B. HEV maintenance costs are too prohibitive for most casual consumers.

C. consumers are not usually willing to pay more for environmental gains.

D. the cost of switching to an HEV outweighs perceived benefits.

Questions 18–20 ask about both passages.

18. The authors of both passages would most likely agree that:

F. EVs and HEV sales are unlikely to improve in the future.

G. consumers will pay more to switch to an alternative vehicle.

H. traditional automakers would profit from investing in HEV technology.

J. Europeans are willing to pay more for alternative fuels than are their American counterparts.

19. Which of the following best describes a difference between the two passages?

A. Passage A criticizes traditional automakers like GM for their role in shaping public opinion, whereas Passage B excuses them.

B. Passage A focuses on providing context, whereas Passage B is primarily concerned with research.

C. Both passages are pessimistic about the future of EVs, whereas Passage B is less cautionary about possibilities for HEVs.

D. Passage A provides a history of electric vehicles, whereas Passage B describes the technology used in new electric cars.

20. In explaining obstacles preventing the widespread use of electric vehicles, both passage authors refer to:

F. public misconceptions about electric cars.

G. lack of support from car manufacturers.

H. challenges converting gasoline engines to electric ones.

J. expensive marketing campaigns.

Passage III

HUMANITIES: The following passage is adapted from the essay "The Torres Revolution" by Greg Spearman (©2001 by Greg Spearman).

The question of who invented the guitar may forever remain a mystery. However, the father of the modern classical guitar is generally regarded as Antonio Torres Jurado, a carpenter from Sevilla, Spain, who began making guitars as a hobby in
5 the 1850's and ultimately created the design that practically all classical guitar makers use to the present day. By refining the craft of guitar-making, Torres expanded the dynamic and tonal range of the instrument, allowing the guitar to go beyond its traditional, supporting role and into the spotlight as a featured
10 concert solo instrument.

Early guitars had four pairs of strings—the word "guitar" itself being a translation from a Persian word meaning "four strings." During the Renaissance, instruments resembling the modern guitar had begun to appear throughout Europe. One
15 of these, the lute, became the standard stringed instrument across most of Europe, but in Spain there was more variation in developing forms of the guitar. A plucked version called the *vihuela* was popular in aristocratic society, while a strummed instrument referred to as the *guitarra latina* was used by com-
20 moners. Once a fifth string was ultimately added to the latter, the *guitarra latina* became the national preference and rendered the *vihuela* obsolete.

As the 17th century progressed, Spanish guitars, widely adored by monarchs, noblemen, and common folk alike, spread
25 throughout the rest of Europe and began to displace the once-popular lute. Along the way a sixth string was added to the design. The 18th century saw the more "prestigious" music of harpsichords, pianos, and violins come to the fore, while the guitar was relegated back to the informal gatherings of com-
30 mon folk. Eventually, however, the virtuosity of such Spanish guitarists as Ferdinand Sor rekindled the public's respect and admiration for guitar music. Esteemed composers such as Haydn and Schubert began writing guitar music, but while the performances of the Spanish guitar masters were wildly popular,
35 the acoustic and structural limitations of the guitar continued to present a problem when playing in large concert halls—a problem that Andres Torres meant to solve.

One of the guitar's chief limitations that Andres Torres tackled was its feeble sound output. Torres enlarged the body
40 of the guitar, particularly the "bouts" (rounded parts) in the soundbox, significantly increasing its volume and giving the guitar its familiar hourglass shape. Because the guitar also had to compete with the impressive polyphony (the number of notes that can be played at one time) of the piano, Torres also
45 reduced the width of the fretboard, making it easier for guitar-ists to reach many notes at once and allowing them to perform music with a complexity comparable to that of pieces played on keyboard instruments.

The genius of Torres's design, however, was the way he
50 re-engineered the internal structure of the instrument. Because the strings on a guitar must be wound tightly to produce enough tension to vibrate at the correct pitch, they constantly pull on the neck of the guitar, essentially trying to snap it in two. The arch of the neck counters some of this force, but the majority
55 is absorbed by wooden braces inside the instrument. Torres did not invent the idea of fan-bracing, which refers to pieces of wood laid out diagonally inside the body to distribute both tension and sound waves, but he did perfect it. He increased the number of braces from three to seven, and organized them
60 in a symmetric pattern allowing the vibrations of the guitar to be evenly distributed within the soundbox.

The effectiveness and elegance of Torres's design was immediately apparent in the improved tone and volume of the instrument, and ultimately revealed by the fact that his design
65 has remained virtually unchanged in over 150 years. Torres guitars were extremely rare and highly-sought by musicians in the 19th century. One aspiring guitarist of the time, Francisco Tarrega, traveled to Sevilla in the hopes of buying one of Torres's famous guitars. Although Torres initially intended to sell Tarrega
70 one of the stock guitars he had available, he reconsidered once he heard Tarrega play. Deeply impressed, Torres instead gave Tarrega a guitar he had made for himself several years before.

Just as Torres revolutionized the design of classical guitars, so would Tarrega eventually become recognized as the singular
75 authority on classical guitar playing techniques. Tarrega had grown up playing both guitar and piano, the latter being recog-nized as the more useful compositional tool, while the guitar was regarded as merely a functional accompaniment to a singer or a larger ensemble. Once Tarrega beheld the beauty and range
80 of expression of the Torres guitar, he committed himself fully to exploring its compositional palette.

Tarrega, who studied at the Madrid Conservatory, rose to great prominence, not only playing original pieces but also trans-lating the great piano works of such composers as Beethoven
85 and Chopin for guitar. He became a global ambassador for the guitar, introducing and refining many of the techniques that classical guitarists worldwide now consider essential, including how to position the guitar on one's knee and optimal fingering and plucking techniques for the left and right hand.

21. Based on the passage, the author would most likely agree that both Torres and Tarrega were:

   A. not fully appreciated for their musical genius until after their deaths.
   B. local sensations whose reputation never reached the global fame of other composers.
   C. extremely influential contributors to the evolution of classical guitar playing.
   D. very talented instrument makers who gained much fame for their talents.

22. As it is used in line 49, the phrase *the genius of Torres's design* most nearly refers to the:

F. innovative idea that classical guitars could be the center-piece of a performance, rather than merely an accompaniment.

G. improved tonal quality and volume resulting from the number and positioning of wooden braces within the soundbox.

H. invention of an arched neck, which counters the effects of the tension caused by the tightly wound strings.

J. expansion of the width of the guitar, in order to accommodate a sixth string and allow for more polyphony.

23. Which of the following statements best describes how the second paragraph (lines 11–22) relates to the first paragraph?

A. It provides supporting details concerning Torres's innovative idea to use a fifth string.

B. It compares the modern guitar to its earlier relatives, such as the lute and *vihuela*.

C. It moves the discussion to a period that predates the innovator described in the first paragraph.

D. It counterbalances the argument in the first paragraph by providing details that suggest early guitars were superior in many ways to later guitars.

24. As it is used in line 81, the phrase *compositional palette* most nearly means:

F. artistic potential.

G. colorful components.

H. volume output.

J. physical features.

25. For purposes of the passage, the significance of Spanish guitarists such as Ferdinand Sor is that they:

A. were reluctant to accept modifications to the traditional design of the guitar.

B. gave Torres suggestions about his design.

C. were among the most talented lute players in Europe at the time.

D. helped develop and sustain interest in the guitar as a reputable instrument.

26. Which of the following questions is NOT answered by the passage?

F. What is the meaning of an instrument's polyphony?

G. When was the beginning and the ending of the Renaissance?

H. Who is the father of the modern guitar?

J. What were some of the earlier forms of the guitar?

27. According to the passage, the *vihuela* was a Renaissance version of the guitar that:

A. was ultimately overtaken in national popularity by another type of guitar.

B. became the Spanish aristocrats' version of the lute.

C. initially came to fame through the notoriety of Ferdinand Sor.

D. was one of Torres's earlier models before he perfected his fan-bracing design.

28. According to the passage, the Torres guitar was better suited than previous versions of the guitar to:

F. Beethoven's works.

G. being a featured instrument.

H. five strings.

J. folk music.

29. According to the passage, the popularity of Spanish-style guitars during the 18th century was:

A. increasing due to the simultaneous decline in popularity of the lute.

B. aided by the growing popularity of other instruments that complemented the guitar's sound.

C. hindered by common folk's inability to master fingering and plucking techniques.

D. diminished by the perception that it was not as refined as other contemporary instruments.

30. It can most reasonably be inferred that which of the following was a direct expression of respect for Tarrega's playing abilities?

F. The manner in which Torres determined which guitar he would sell to Tarrega

G. The translation of Beethoven's and Chopin's works from piano to guitar

H. The eventual end to the popularity of the *guitarra latina*

J. The way Haydn and Schubert began composing music specifically for guitar

Passage IV

NATURAL SCIENCE: The following passage is adapted from the article "Heavyweights of the Sea" by Carmen Grandola (©2001 by Carmen Grandola).

The earth's oceans possess an incredible variety of life, ranging from nearly microscopic plankton to the blue whale, the largest animal on the planet. In the world of fish, the mola sunfish and the whale shark are the two biggest varieties. The
5 mola is the biggest bony fish, whereas the whale shark, which is a cartilaginous fish, is simply the biggest fish there is. While most ocean-dwellers spend their days balancing their position on the food chain as both predators and prey, these titanic swimmers have little to worry about from predators. Instead, they must
10 focus on finding enough food to sustain the massive amounts of nutrients needed to support their bulky bodies.

Truly one of the most unusual-looking products of evolution's creative hand, the mola sunfish resembles a giant fish head with a tail. Most fish have long bodies, with fins in the
15 middle roughly dividing their length in two. Rather than having a caudal (tail) fin, like most fish, the mola looks like a fish that has been chopped just past the halfway point, with a rounded clavus joining its dorsal (top) and anal (bottom) fins. The mola uses its clavus to steer its rather awkwardly-shaped body
20 through the water. Its body has a very narrow cross-section—it is basically a flattened oval with a head at the front, and very high dorsal and anal fins at the back. In fact, the mola's height is often equal to its length, which is unusual in fish, which are typically elongated. Mola means "millstone" in Latin, and these
25 fish live up to their name, growing to 10–20 ft. in length and height and weighing in at an average of 2,000 lbs.

The mola's diet is extremely varied but nutrient-poor, consisting mainly of jellyfish, but also comb jellies, squid, and eel grasses. In order to consume enough daily nutrients, the mola
30 must be a voracious eater and be willing to travel through a wide range of oceanic depths—from surface to floor in some areas—in search of their food. After ascending from cooler waters, the mola will float on its side at the ocean's surface in order to warm itself through solar energy. Molas have a beaked
35 mouth that does not totally close, so they chew their food in several stages, breaking down each mouthful into smaller chunks before spitting them out and then going to work on the more bite-sized pieces.

The whale shark, another giant of the sea, grows to sizes
40 that dwarf the maximum size of a bony fish. Some have been measured at over 40 ft. in length and over 75,000 lbs. in weight. This leviathan, like the mola, mostly frequents tropical and warm-temperate waters. The whale shark possesses over 300 rows of teeth, but it does not use them in the same manner as
45 most other sharks. The whale shark is one of only a handful of filter-feeding sharks. This means rather than using powerful teeth and jaws to rip apart large prey, the whale shark eats tiny, nearly microscopic food such as zooplankton, krill, and macro-algae. The whale shark "hunts" by opening its mouth

50 and sucking in a huge mouthful of ocean water. It then closes its mouth and expels the water through its gills, at which point gill rakers act as sieves, separating the tiny, sometimes millimeter-wide, life forms from the water. Once all the water is expelled, the food is swallowed.

55 When you're one of the biggest species in your neighborhood, you probably don't have to worry about getting picked on much. This is certainly true of the whale shark, which has no natural predators and can easily live 70–100 years in the ocean. Its biggest health risk comes through exposure to
60 humans. The whale shark does much of its feeding near the surface of the water, where it has been known to accidentally bump into boats. Both animal and vessel can end up severely damaged in these exchanges. The other hazard humans create for whale sharks is pollution in the water. As the whale
65 shark filter feeds, it sometimes takes in garbage and nautical debris such as oars.

The mola, on the other hand, has a few challenges. Its thick skin is covered in a dense layer of mucus, which is host to a vast array of parasites. To try and rid itself of these uninvited
70 guests, the mola will often float on its side near the surface of the water, inviting gulls and other birds to feast on the parasites. Similarly, the mola will sometimes launch its considerable bulk up to ten feet out of the water before crashing back down in an effort to dislodge some of the parasites. With its habit of
75 floating near the surface, the mola, like the whale shark, often runs the risk of being hit by boats. Finally, smaller molas are sometimes subject to attack by sea lions.

31. The author's attitude regarding molas and whale sharks can best be described as one of:

A. conviction that human interference will ultimately jeopardize each species.

B. resentment towards their need to eat so much other marine life on a daily basis.

C. impartiality in considering the perils of their environment compared to other fish.

D. interest in how their grandiose size affects their habits and survival.

32. It can reasonably be concluded from the passage that the mola temporarily expels its food when eating due to the fact that it:

F. is a bony fish rather than a cartilaginous one.

G. possesses a mouth that cannot completely close.

H. hunts on the ocean floor but eats at the surface.

J. is normally floating on its side near the surface.

33. According to the passage, the most significant difference between the predatory threats facing the whale shark and the mola is that the whale shark:

    A. does not compete for the same food as its predators do, while the mola competes for the same food its predators do.

    B. is unaffected by its proximity to humans, while the mola is sometimes endangered by humans.

    C. faces few genuine environmental threats but must contend with the nuisance of parasites.

    D. is less likely to be attacked by another ocean-dwelling species than is the mola.

34. It can most reasonably be inferred from the passage that nautical vessels pose a threat to both the mola and the whale shark primarily because these vessels:

    F. can sometimes unsuspectingly collide with fish.

    G. stir up a violent wake that disrupts the ocean currents.

    H. jettison large debris overboard which can land on fish.

    J. deplete the fish's supply of prey through over-fishing.

35. The passage indicates that the quantity of food a fish must eat is primarily determined by the:

    A. mass of the fish's body.

    B. depth at which the fish hunts.

    C. type of gill rakers it has.

    D. number of its teeth and size of its mouth.

36. The passage supports the idea that all of the following are included in the diet of the mola EXCEPT:

    F. comb jellies.

    G. zooplankton.

    H. eel grasses.

    J. squid.

37. The main purpose of the last two paragraphs is to:

    A. provide additional support for the earlier claim that the mola and the whale shark are two of the biggest creatures inhabiting the ocean.

    B. convey to the reader to the ironic fact that such large species of fish can be vulnerable to miniature threats such as parasites.

    C. summarize the types of threats, or lack thereof, present in the environments of the mola and whale shark.

    D. demonstrate the fact that even the biggest fish in the sea have to worry about being preyed upon by something.

38. According to the passage, the gill rakers a whale shark has are primarily intended to:

    F. spit out partially chewed food.

    G. rip apart the whale shark's large prey.

    H. bridge together its 300 rows of teeth.

    J. filter out food from a mouthful of water.

39. According to the passage, the Latin-derived name for the mola refers to the:

    A. atypical rounded clavus of the mola.

    B. mola's distinctive half-fish shape.

    C. voracious eating the mola's diet requires.

    D. mola's enormous size and weight.

40. The main purpose of the passage is to:

    F. offer support for the notion that the mola is pound-for-pound a better hunter than is the whale shark.

    G. provide a general overview of the habitats, eating habits, and survival challenges relating to two of the biggest species of fish.

    H. increase awareness for the fragile status of mola and whale shark populations and encourage conservationists to intervene.

    J. suggest that the unlikely traits possessed by the mola and the whale shark do not have clear evolutionary answers.

END OF TEST
STOP! DO NOT TURN THE PAGE UNTIL TOLD TO DO SO.
DO NOT RETURN TO A PREVIOUS TEST.

Chapter 12
Reading
Practice Test 2
Answers and
Explanations

READING PRACTICE TEST 2 ANSWERS

1.	D		21.	C
2.	J		22.	G
3.	B		23.	C
4.	F		24.	F
5.	C		25.	D
6.	G		26.	G
7.	D		27.	A
8.	H		28.	G
9.	C		29.	D
10.	H		30.	F
11.	D		31.	D
12.	G		32.	G
13.	D		33.	D
14.	F		34.	F
15.	A		35.	A
16.	H		36.	G
17.	D		37.	C
18.	G		38.	J
19.	B		39.	D
20.	F		40.	G

SCORE YOUR PRACTICE TEST

Step A

Count the number of correct answers: _____. This is your ***raw score***.

Step B

Use the score conversion table below to look up your raw score. The number to the left is your ***scale score***: _____.

Reading Scale Conversion Table

Scale Score	Raw Score	Scale Score	Raw Score	Scale Score	Raw Score
36	39-40	24	27	12	9-10
35	38	23	26	11	7-8
34	37	22	24-25	10	6
33	35-36	21	23	9	5
32	34	20	21-22	8	–
31	33	19	20	7	4
30	–	18	19	6	3
29	32	17	17-18	5	–
28	31	16	16	4	2
27	30	15	14-15	3	–
26	29	14	12-13	2	1
25	28	13	11	1	0

READING PRACTICE TEST 2 EXPLANATIONS

Passage I

1. **D** This reference question asks which statement about *painting the room* is most consistent with the text. As there is no good lead word in this question, work the question later. In lines 45–46, the passage states that *Clara picked* the paint color. Choice (A) mentions Clara's reluctance to paint, which is not stated in the text. Eliminate (A). Choice (B) states that *Garth suggests the idea to Grandpa*, and while Garth is involved in the painting process, the text never explicitly states that painting was Garth's idea. Eliminate (B). Choice (C) states that *Clara envisioned the idea*, which seems to match the text of lines 45–46, which state that Clara picked the color. Keep (C). Choice (D) states that *Clara was involved in the decision making*, which matches the text of lines 45–46 as well. Choice (C) could be true, but based on the text, we do not know for sure that *Clara envisioned the idea*, just that she picked out the color. Eliminate (C). Choice (D) must be true based on the text as picking the color is being *involved in the decision making*. The correct answer is (D).

2. **J** This reference question asks which description of *the exchange between the narrator and his sister* most closely matches the text. Look for the lead word *sister* to find the window for the question. Lines 20–21 state that that the narrator and his sister *exchange a look with each other, hiding our feelings of reluctance*. Nothing in this window relates to *Garth's unusual tardiness*, so eliminate (F). Eliminate (G) because nothing in the window states that the exchange is *a situation that is initially confusing*. Choice (H) states that the exchange is about *which person gets the honor of sitting in front*. But the text states that the narrator's sister is *accepting her fate* when she sits in the front. Eliminate (H). As the exchange is through looks, it is *nonverbal*, and having to sit in the front seat is certainly seen as *an unfavorable consequence*. Keep (J). The correct answer is (J).

3. **B** This reference question asks which characteristic *Garth and Grandpa* do not *share*. Be sure to notice that this is an EXCEPT question. Work backward and use lead words from the answers to find the window for this question. Throughout lines 25–39, Garth discusses painting with the siblings, showing that he has previous *painting experience*. In lines 44–45, Grandpa is described as *wearing paint-covered overalls, but the paint stains are dry*, showing that he has painted at some point in the past. Eliminate (A), as both Garth and Grandpa have *painting experience*. In lines 16–17, the text states that Garth's *posture and his way of speaking are both perfectly upright*. However, Grandpa's posture is never mentioned. Keep (B), since *good posture* is not said to be shared. In lines 13–14, the text states that *we see Garth's tan Oldsmobile pull slowly into the parking lot* with Garth driving. In lines 4–5, the passage states that *Grandpa tends to misjudge how slowly he drives nowadays*, which tells that Grandpa also drives. Eliminate (C) because both have *the ability to drive*. In line 76, Grandpa and Garth's interaction is described as *their jovial back and forth*. Eliminate (D). The correct answer is (B).

4. **F**   This reasoning question asks why Clara referred to having *smarter wrists*. Read a window around the line reference. Earlier in the passage, in lines 29–30, Clara states that she *couldn't make 'em as pretty as* her mother *could*. Garth explains how to make cupcakes as pretty as her mother does *with one clever twist of your wrist*. Clara responds by saying that she *needs smarter wrists*, clearly doubting that she can ice a cupcake as Garth describes. Keep (F) because Clara having doubts *about equaling her mother's skills* matches the text. Choice (G) states that the narrator is feeling *growing excitement*, which is not stated in the window. Eliminate (G). Eliminate (H) because it states that Clara feels *confusion*, which is not supported by the passage. Eliminate (J) because it states that Clara feels *increasing concern*, which is not supported by the text in this window. The correct answer is (F).

5. **C**   This reasoning question asks what feeling *Grandpa's grin* reflects in the context of the passage as a whole. Read a window around the line reference. In line 60, right after Grandpa's grin is mentioned, Grandpa says *fun, isn't it?* which shows that Grandpa is definitely feeling positive about the situation. Eliminate (A) and (D) because they are not positive enough to reflect Grandpa's feelings. Choice (B) is *intense relaxation*. Grandpa is never shown to relax within this window, so eliminate (B). Choice (C) is *mild satisfaction*, which is positive enough to match the text from the passage. The correct answer is (C).

6. **G**   This reference question asks the narrator's opinion of Garth given his statement about the car. Read a window around the line reference. In line 14, the passage states that Garth's personality is *boring but reliable*. Choice (F) states that Garth is *too conservative in his choice of cars*. While this could seem to match *boring*, nothing in the text supports the idea that the narrator thinks that Garth is *too conservative*. Eliminate (F). Choice (G) states that Garth is *highly dependable* which matches *reliable* from the passage. It also states that he is *not very flashy* which matches the idea of *boring*. Keep (G). Choice (H) states that Garth is *more uptight than many Oldsmobile drivers*. Garth is not compared to other drivers within this window, so eliminate (H). Choice (J) states that Garth is *too concerned with how others see him*. Within this window, Garth does not show any concern for how others see him. Eliminate (J). The correct answer is (G).

7. **D**   This reasoning question asks in what way Garth *recommends that the children apply both paint and icing*. Look for the lead word *icing* to find the window for the question. In lines 35–37, Garth says *if you start with a good dollop, more than you really need, you can swoosh it around with one clever twist of your wrist*. Look for an answer that matches this text from the passage. Eliminate (A) because *gently* is too tentative to match Garth's recommendations. Eliminate (B) because *respectfully* is also too tentative. Choice (C) is *conservatively*, which is the opposite of what is in the text. Eliminate (C). *Clever twist of your wrist* matches *confidently*, so keep (D). The correct answer is (D).

8. **H**   This reasoning question asks what conclusion the narrator reaches in the second paragraph. Carefully read the second paragraph, which states that the narrator believes Grandpa when he says that *people use a routine to distract themselves from their life*. Look for an answer choice that matches this text from the passage.. While the second paragraph does state that Garth *has married his schedule*, his opinions on tardiness in others are not stated. Eliminate (F). Choice (G) is a Right Answer, Wrong Question trap answer: although the text indicates that Garth organizes his schedule well, this is not

the main conclusion that the narrator reaches. Eliminate (G). Keep (H) because it matches the text from the passage. Choice (J) states that *Grandpa is a keen observer of human behavior*. This seems like an attractive answer, as it closely matches the text of the last sentence of the paragraph, but the question asks about the main conclusion the narrator makes in this paragraph. This paragraph is about Garth, not Grandpa. Eliminate (J). The correct answer is (H).

9. **C**   This reasoning question asks how the last paragraph serves in the *development of the narrator as a character*. Carefully read the last paragraph. The narrator is *sad* that *we will cover up the wall*, but knows that *covering up is different than removing*. While the narrator is certainly sad in the last paragraph, there is nothing supporting a feeling of *guilt*. Eliminate (A). Though the last paragraph discusses the narrator's *mother*, their *relationship* is never explored. Eliminate (B). The narrator's *underlying emotional conflict* between moving on and holding on to his mother's memory matches the text from the passage. Keep (C). Throughout the text, the narrator's relationship with his Grandpa is generally described positively, which does not match *strained*. Eliminate (D). The correct answer is (C).

10. **H**   This reference question asks who Arthur most likely is. Look for the lead word *Arthur* to find the window for the question. He is mentioned in line 63. In lines 61–62, the narrator asks *what if Daddy's disappointed he didn't get to do this himself?* *Arthur* is *Daddy*, the narrator's father. Eliminate (F), (G), and (J) because they do not match this text from the passage. Choice (H) correctly matches the text. The correct answer is (H).

Passage II

11. **D**   This reference question asks how the author *portrays the efforts of GM to design an electric car*. Because this is a general question, it should be done after all of the specific questions. Look for the Golden Thread. In this case, GM was not particularly interested in designing an electric car because they *believed that electric vehicles were not commercially viable*. Choice (A) is the opposite of the Golden Thread, so eliminate (A). No mention of GM's *marketing* campaigns is made in this passage, so eliminate (B). No *competitors* are mentioned, so eliminate (C). Keep (D) because it matches the text from the passage. The correct answer is (D).

12. **G**   This reference question asks who was NOT included in the groups represented in lines 7–8. Read a window around the line reference. When the question asks what is NOT mentioned, eliminate answers that are mentioned. The *many* in line 7 refers to the *American automakers* in the previous sentence. As *GM* is an *American automaker*, eliminate (F). The *California Air Resources Board who issued the mandate* is a government agency, not an automaker, so keep (G). Choice (H) is *the other American automakers*, so eliminate (H). Choice (J) is *Dr. Kenneth Train and his research team at UC Berkley*. Use the doctor's name as a lead word to find his name in lines 34–35. In lines 38–39, the passage states that Train's *study was frequently touted by automakers*, showing that Dr. Train is a member of the group mentioned in the question. Eliminate (J). The correct answer is (G).

13. **D** This reasoning question asks about the answer to the author's question in line 29. Read a window around the line reference. The author is asking why GM wouldn't allow EV1 owners to keep their cars, despite the fact that the owners begged GM to let them buy the cars. The author goes on throughout lines 29–33 to say that skepticism brewed, there was *alleged pressure from the oil industry,* and that *others pointed to the fiscal losses GM would suffer.* Look for an answer that matches this text from the passage. Eliminate (A) because there's no *definitive* answer in the paragraph, just possibilities. Eliminate (B) because the author does not indicate that CARB was involved in an unknown way. Eliminate (C) because the author mentions several possibilities throughout the paragraph. Choice (D) matches both the author's lack of certainty and the multiple possible explanations explored in the paragraph. The correct answer is (D).

14. **F** This reasoning question asks what the author thinks must be true about any forthcoming electric vehicle. Carefully read the final paragraph of Passage A to determine what the author is saying. In lines 42–44, the author states that *a new technology poses challenges that go well beyond mechanical engineering.* Eliminate any answers that aren't consistent with this text from the passage. Choice (F) paraphrases the lines above, so keep it. Choice (G) can be eliminated because there is no evidence that they will be *embraced by automakers.* Choice (H) can be eliminated because the author clearly states it is unknown if that distrust can be *overcome.* There is no mention of changing *prices* in the last paragraph, so eliminate (J). The correct answer is (F).

15. **A** This reasoning question asks about the main idea of the first paragraph of Passage B. Carefully read the paragraph to determine the main idea. The paragraph discusses the surprisingly low sales of electric vehicles even when it seems like they should sell well. Choice (A) matches the main idea, so keep it. Eliminate (B) because the paragraph is not about *learning to compete,* but about why EVs sell more poorly than would be expected. Choice (C) can be eliminated because the authors are not comparing HEVs and EVs. Eliminate (D) as risk evaluation is not mentioned in the first paragraph. The correct answer is (A).

16. **H** This reasoning question asks why the authors of the passage *most likely use the statistics in the second paragraph* of Passage B. Carefully read the paragraph and determine what role the statistics play in the context of the passage. The statistics show that consumers have conflicting opinions on electric vehicles: consumers agree that HEVs are cleaner than gasoline engines but also think they are expensive and slower, stating that they prefer cars with better fuel economy. Look for an answer choice that is consistent with this idea. Although the drivers want fuel-efficient cars, their attitudes toward HEVs do not reflect that. Eliminate (F). Choice (G) refers to *the complexities of sampling perceptions,* which does not match the text from the passage. Eliminate (G). Choice (H) is consistent with the text, so keep (H). Eliminate (J) because there is no criticism in this paragraph. The correct answer is (H).

17. **D** This reference question asks why HEV sales are so low, according to Passage B. There is not a good lead word in this question, so work the question later. In lines 53–55, two possible reasons are presented: *price* and *other misconceptions.* Choice (A) refers to neither money nor misconceptions, so eliminate (A). Choice (B) does mention price, but *maintenance costs* are never mentioned in this passage. Eliminate (B). Choice (C) might initially look attractive, but it can be eliminated because the passage never explicitly deals with *environmental gains.* Keep (D) because it matches the text from the passage. The correct answer is (D).

18. **G** This reference question asks for the idea that *the authors of both passages would most likely agree* with. Because this question asks about both passages, it should be done after the questions that ask about each passage individually. Eliminate any answer choices that misrepresent either passage. The author of Passage A does not make any predictions about the *future sales* of electric vehicles, so eliminate (F). Both passages indicate that *consumers will pay more*: Passage A does so in lines 35–38 and Passage B in lines 69–70. Keep (G). Although it might seem logical, there is no mention in either passage about future *profit* for automakers. Eliminate (H). There is no mention of the differences between Europeans' and Americans' fuel-purchasing habits, so eliminate (J). The correct answer is (G).

19. **B** This reference question asks which answer *best describes a difference between the two passages*. Because this question asks about both passages, it should be done after the questions that ask about each passage individually. Consider the Golden Thread of both passages. Though Passage A states that GM shaped *public opinion*, Passage B does not mention GM, much less excuse them. Eliminate (A). Choice (B) is consistent with Passage A, which provides context for the introduction and perception of the electric vehicle. It is also consistent with Passage B, as the authors refer to *research*. Keep (B). Choice (C) can eliminated because Passage A does not discuss HEVs. Eliminate (D) because Passage A is not a *history of electric vehicles*, though it does provide a history of one single electric vehicle. The correct answer is (B).

20. **F** This reference question asks which obstacle *preventing the widespread use of electric vehicles* is referred to by both passages. Because this question asks about both passages, it should be done after the questions that ask about each passage individually. Eliminate any answer choices that misrepresent either passage. Both passages discuss *public misconceptions about electric cars*, so keep (F). While (G) is well supported by Passage A, Passage B does not address how much *support* is given by *car manufacturers*. Eliminate (G). Passage A discusses the conversion from *gasoline* to *electric*, but Passage B does not. Eliminate (H). Eliminate (J) because there is no mention of *expensive marketing campaigns* in Passage A. The correct answer is (F).

Passage III

21. **C** This reference question asks what the author most likely believes about both Torres and Tarrega. There is not a good lead word in this question, so work the question later. In line 2, the author credits Torres as *the father of the modern classical guitar,* and in lines 74–75, the author refers to Tarrega *as the singular authority on classical guitar playing techniques.* Choice (A) is unsupported because there is nothing in the passage that relates to being appreciated more *after death*. Eliminate (B) because the passage does not compare the degree of *global fame* between *composers*. Keep (C) because it matches the text from the passage. Eliminate (D) because Tarrega was famous for guitar playing techniques, not for making guitars. The correct answer is (C).

22. **G** This vocabulary in context question asks what the phrase *the genius of Torres' design* refers to. Read a window around the line reference. In the fifth paragraph, the author states that *the genius of Torres's design* is *the way he re-engineered the internal structure* of the guitar. The paragraph does not discuss the role of the guitar for solo playing or accompaniment, so eliminate (F). The *number and positioning of wooden braces within the soundbox* relates to the guitar's internal structure, so keep (G). The passage does not say that Torres invented *an arched neck*, so eliminate (H). The passage does not state that Torres expanded the *width of the guitar*, so eliminate (J). The correct answer is (G).

23. **C** This reasoning question asks which statement best describes the relationship between the first two paragraphs. Carefully read the first two paragraphs to find their relationship. The first paragraph establishes Torres as the *father of the modern classical guitar*, and the second paragraph provides information on the emergence of early guitar forms. Look for an answer choice that matches this idea. Eliminate (A) because the text does not indicate that Torres added a *fifth string*. Eliminate (B) because the second paragraph does not mention the *modern guitar*. Keep (C) because it matches the text from the passage. Eliminate (D) because the second paragraph does not compare *early guitars* to *later guitars*. The correct answer is (C).

24. **F** This vocabulary in context question asks what the phrase *compositional palette* means in line 81. Go back to the text, find the phrase *compositional palette*, and cross it out. Carefully read the surrounding text to determine another phrase that would fit in the blank based on context. The text says that *once Tarrega beheld the beauty and range of expression of the Torres guitar*, he sought to explore its *compositional palette*. Therefore, Tarrega was inspired by the many things that the Torres guitar could do, so the phrase should mean something like "musical possibilities." Keep (F) because it matches the text from the passage. Choice (G) is a Words Out of Context trap answer: the word *palette* can also refer to color, but this meaning is not supported by the text. Eliminate (G). Choice (H) does not match the text from the passage, so eliminate it. Choice (J) does not match the text, so eliminate it. The correct answer is (F).

25. **D** This reasoning question asks for the *significance of Spanish guitarists* like *Ferdinand Sor*. Look for the lead words *Ferdinand Sor* to find the window for the question. Lines 30–32 state that *such Spanish guitarists as Ferdinand Sor rekindled the public's respect and admiration for guitar music*. There is nothing supporting their reluctance to consider new designs; in fact, the passage explains that the limitations of the traditional design frustrated them. Eliminate (A). There is nothing in the window that states that the musicians had contact with *Torres* during his *design* process. Eliminate (B). The musicians discussed in the window are guitar players, not *lute* players. Eliminate (C). Choice (D) matches the text from the passage, so keep (D). The correct answer is (D).

26. **G** This reference question asks which question is not answered by the passage. Work backward and use lead words from the answers to find the window for this question. Look for the lead word *polyphony*. Lines 43–44 define *polyphony*, so eliminate (F). Look for the lead word *Renaissance*, which can be found in line 13. No dates are given for the *Renaissance*, so keep (G). Look for the lead words *father of the modern guitar*, which can be found in line 2. The passage says that *Torres* is the *father of the modern classical guitar*, so eliminate (H). Look for the lead word *earlier forms of guitar*, which can be found in line 11. Throughout paragraph 2, several *earlier forms of guitar* are mentioned, so eliminate (J). The correct answer is (G).

27. **A**   This reference question asks about the *vihuela*. Look for the lead word *vihuela* to find the window for the question. Line 18 introduces the *vihuela*, and lines 21–22 state that *the guitarra latina became the national preference and rendered the vihuela obsolete*. Choice (A) matches the text from the passage, so keep (A). Eliminate (B) because the passage does not indicate that the *vihuela* was intended to be a *version of the lute*. Eliminate (C) because there is no mention that *Ferdinand Sor* played or popularized the *vihuela*. Eliminate (D) because the passage never mentions *Torres* as having any involvement with the *vihuela*. The correct answer is (A).

28. **G**   This reference question asks what Torres' version of the guitar is better suited to than previous versions. Work backward and use lead words from the answers to find the window for this question. Look for the lead word *Beethoven*, which can be found in line 84. There is no mention of previous versions of the guitar in this paragraph, so eliminate (F). Look for the lead words *featured instrument*, which can be found in lines 9–10. These lines state that the *Torres* guitar pushed the guitar *into the spotlight as a featured concert solo instrument*, so keep (G). Look for the lead words *fifth string*, which can be found in line 20. As this part of the text is describing the evolution of the guitar before Torres, eliminate (H). Look for the lead words *folk music*. Lines 28–30 say that *the guitar was relegated back to the informal gatherings of common folk*. However, Torres is not mentioned here, so eliminate (J). The correct answer is (G).

29. **D**   This reference question asks what the passage states about *the popularity of Spanish-style guitars during the 18th century*. Look for the lead words *18th century* to find the window for the question. Lines 27–29 state that as *more "prestigious"* instruments rose in popularity, the guitar was *relegated* back to being a *folk* instrument. Eliminate (A) because it does not match the text from the passage. Eliminate (B) because the passage states that the *growing popularity of other instruments* hurt the guitar's popularity. Eliminate (C) because the passage never discusses whether *common folk* could master playing *techniques*. Keep (D) because it matches the text from the passage. The correct answer is (D).

30. **F**   This reasoning question asks which answer choice correctly expresses respect for Tarrega's playing abilities. There is no good lead word in this question, so work this question later. Lines 69–71 state that *Torres initially intended to sell Tarrega one of the stock guitars* but that he *reconsidered once he heard Tarrega play*. Therefore, Torres showed respect to Tarrega's playing ability when he decided on a guitar to sell him. Look for an answer choice that matches this idea. Keep (F) because it matches the text from the passage. Eliminate (G) because it does not mention *Torres*. Eliminate (H) because it does not mention either of the men. Eliminate (J) because it does not mention *Torres*. The correct answer is (F).

Passage IV

31. **D** This reasoning question asks for *the author's attitude* toward *molas and whale sharks*. Because this is a general question, it should be done after all the specific questions. Look for the Golden Thread. In lines 3–4, the author remarks that *the mola sunfish and the whale shark are the two biggest varieties.* Throughout the rest of the passage, the author shows how such massive beings are able to survive. Eliminate (A) because, although the author mentions each species potentially being harmed by proximity to humans, these dangers are not described as species-threatening. Eliminate (B) because nowhere is the author's tone or language resentful. Eliminate (C) because the author suggests in the first paragraph that the mola and whale shark have much less to worry about in terms of predators than do other fish. Keep (D) because it matches the text from the passage. The correct answer is (D).

32. **G** This reference question asks why the mola expels its food while eating. Look for the lead words *mola* and *food* to find the window for the question. Lines 34–38 say that the mola spits food out while eating. The reason for this is that *molas have a beaked mouth that does not totally close.* Eliminate (F) since the passage does not discuss eating habits as a function of being *bony* or *cartilaginous.* Choice (G) matches the text from the passage, so keep it. Eliminate (H) because the passage does not indicate that the mola eats only at the *surface.* Eliminate (J) since the passage indicates that the mola only floats on its side to warm up. The correct answer is (G).

33. **D** This reasoning question asks for the difference between *the predatory threats facing the whale shark and the mola.* Look for the lead word *predator* to find the window for this question. In lines 57–58, the author states that the whale shark *has no natural predators.* In lines 76–77, the author states that *smaller molas are sometimes subject to attack by sea lions.* So, the molas have at least one predator and the whale shark has none. Eliminate (A) because the whale shark has no predators. Eliminate (B) because the passage indicates that both species are sometimes adversely affected by contact with *humans.* Eliminate (C) because the passage only speaks of molas being bothered by *parasites.* Keep (D) because it matches the text from the passage. The correct answer is (D).

34. **F** This reference question asks for the main threat that nautical vessels pose to both animals. Since *boats* are *nautical vessels,* use both as lead words to find the window for the question. Lines 60–62 say that the *whale shark...has been known to accidentally bump into boats.* Lines 75–76 say that *the mola, like the whale shark, often runs the risk of being hit by boats.* Choice (F) matches the text from the passage, so keep (F). Eliminate (G) because *wakes* are not mentioned in the passage. Eliminate (H) because *nautical debris* is said to be a hazard only for the whale shark's filter feeding, not a threat to both species. Eliminate (J) because *overfishing* is not mentioned. The correct answer is (F).

35. **A** This reference question asks what determines how much food a fish must eat. There is no good lead word for this question, so work this question later. Lines 9–11 state that molas and whale sharks *must focus on finding enough food to sustain the massive amounts of nutrients needed to support their bulky bodies.* Keep (A) because it matches the text from the passage. Eliminate (B) because the passage never connects ocean *depth* and food requirements. Eliminate (C) because *gill rakers* relate to how the whale shark eats, not the quantity that any fish eats. Eliminate (D) because the passage does not connect *teeth* or *mouth* size with dietary needs. The correct answer is (A).

36. **G**   This reference question asks which of the answer choices is not included *in the diet of the mola*. When a question asks what is NOT mentioned in the passage, eliminate answers that are mentioned. Look for the lead word *diet of a mola* to find the window for the question. Lines 27–29 say that the *mola's diet* consists of *jellyfish, comb jellies, squid, and eel grasses*. Eliminate (F), (H), and (J) because each of these is in lines 27–30. *Zooplankton* are not mentioned as part of the mola's diet, so keep (G). The correct answer is (G).

37. **C**   This reasoning question asks for purpose of the last two paragraphs, so carefully read them to determine their objective. Lines 55–57 state that big fish are rarely picked on. The paragraphs then go into detail about the dangers faced by each fish, which are not very numerous or threatening in nature. Eliminate (A) because, although some details in these paragraphs reinforce the large size of the two species, the purpose of the paragraphs is to discuss potential threats. Eliminate (B) because it relates only to the mola, and these paragraphs do not convey irony. Keep (C) because it matches the text from the passage. Eliminate (D) because the whale shark has no natural predators, so this answer couldn't apply to the second-to-last paragraph. The correct answer is (C).

38. **J**   This reference question asks about the primary purpose of the gill rakers of a whale shark. Look for the lead words *gill rakers* to find the window for the question. Lines 52–53 indicate that the gill rakers function by *separating the tiny...life forms*, which are food, *from the water*. Eliminate (F) because the mola, not the whale shark, *spits out partially chewed food*. Eliminate (G) because the whale shark does not *rip apart* prey. Eliminate (H) because the *gill rakers* are not mentioned in connection with the whale shark's *teeth*. Keep (J) because it matches the text from the passage. The correct answer is (J).

39. **D**   This reference question asks what *the Latin-derived name for the mola refers to*. Look for the lead word *Latin* to find the window for the question. Lines 24–26 say that mola *means "millstone" in Latin*, and it proceeds to discuss the mola's impressive size. Look for an answer choice that matches this idea. Eliminate (A), (B), and (C) because, though they are details mentioned about the mola, they are not related to the massive size that the mola's Latin name denotes. Keep (D) because it matches the text from the passage. The correct answer is (D).

40. **G**   This reasoning question asks for the main purpose of the passage. Because this is a general question, it should be done after all the specific questions. Look for the Golden Thread. The passage describes two types of very large fish. Eliminate (F) because the two fish are rarely compared and never in terms of their hunting abilities. Keep (G) because it matches the text from the passage. Eliminate (H) because, though the passage does discuss what threats are present in the environment of each fish, it does not say that either species is threatened. Eliminate (J) because, although the author refers to evolution in one passing remark, his discussion of the two fish is not based on how they evolved. The correct answer is (G).

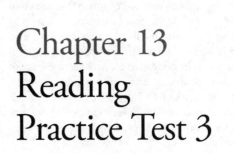

Chapter 13
Reading
Practice Test 3

READING TEST

35 Minutes—40 Questions

DIRECTIONS: There are four passages in this test. Each passage is followed by several questions. After reading each passage, choose the best answer to each question and blacken the corresponding oval on your answer document. You may refer to the passages as often as necessary.

Passage I

PROSE FICTION: This passage is an excerpt from the short story "Whimpering Wanderlust" by Gretchen Mueller (© 1955 by Gretchen Mueller).

Jacob Mathinson accepted, almost too early in his life, that he would never be a world-famous architect. His grandmother had instilled an indelible streak of humility in Jacob as a boy, telling him that he was special to her, but that the rest of the world
5 was under no obligation to feel the same way. He attended Mount St. Mary's College, not because it had a renowned architectural program, but because he was able to get a partial scholarship by playing on the school's tennis team. Jacob did not want to admit it, especially years later, but his decision may have also
10 been swayed by his desire to follow Erin Crawford, his high school crush, wherever she decided to go. Architecture was not his first calling, and, hence, his ambition towards ascending in the field extended only so far as his desire to walk through the streets of, say, Prague one day, a fetching girl on his arm,
15 commenting on the array of Baroque, Renaissance, and even Cubist masterpieces along the Old Town Square.

Growing up in Gettysburg, Pennsylvania, Jacob, an average though not exceptional student, was not exactly exposed to a climate of forward thinking. The local economy was a tradi-
20 tional, if unimaginative, one. Most of the infrastructure had been built during the Reconstruction to support the railroad industry. In the summer of 1919, when Jacob was born, the town seemed frozen in the late 19th century, with bootblack, locksmith, and apothecary shops that seemed more at home in pre-industrial
25 times. This lack of innovation deepened Jacob's disinterest in personal or academic enterprise. His impression was that there was little of interest to be discovered outside of Gettysburg, save a patchwork of towns as predictable as the repeating pattern of black and white tiles on a checkerboard.

30 During his junior year in high school, Jacob worked as a tour guide on one of the double-decker buses that shuttled tourists, Civil War enthusiasts mostly, around the perimeter of Gettysburg. Fancying himself as cutting quite a figure in his clean, pressed uniform, it was his great hope that one day Erin
35 Crawford might take the tour and see him in action. He even went so far as to give her a voucher for a free ride, but as each tour began, he would heave a lonesome sigh, crestfallen that she with her sweet lilac fragrance had not whisked past him as the customers loaded on to the bus.

40 Nonetheless, Jacob enjoyed the job, partly because it was easy—it consisted of reading a script of noteworthy details about the Gettysburg Battlefield—but mostly because it allowed for personal embellishment, since the tour included some of the area's historic buildings as well. Jacob spent months explain-
45 ing to his customers that the sloping roof on the Dobbin House Tavern is a pristine example of Celtic style architecture, and that the Shriver House Museum is one of the oldest standing pre-colonial buildings in America. Although for months he described these buildings of architectural interest, it wasn't
50 until he left that job that he actually began to think about them, notice them, and allow the buildings to "speak" to him in an aesthetic conversation.

The following summer, Jacob worked with his uncle, a residential plumber. Jacob enjoyed seeing homes in the in-
55 termediate stages of construction, half-naked, their internal structure exposed. Jacob found great satisfaction in the task of finding the most efficient and cohesive way to intertwine the circulatory system of plumbing into the skeletal structure of each house's wooden framework. Again, he found a way to
60 incorporate visions of Erin into his work, imagining that Erin's parents would get a flooded basement, and he and his uncle would arrive heroically, save the day, and leave her parents thinking, "that Jacob is a great boy." (Jacob's fascination with the science and art of building blossomed in his freshman
65 year at Mount St. Mary's, as did his fascination with the many young women also attending the school. Perhaps their attentions provided much-needed distraction from the difficulties he was having in his pursuit of Erin.)

He had not accounted for Mount St. Mary's size relative
70 to his high school and the difficulty of "accidentally" running into someone in the halls. Throughout the first semester, Erin might as well have been a ghost to Jacob, who tried his very best to make her acquaintance, but to no avail. Many years later, already married to Martha, a seamstress from Gettysburg, Jacob
75 would daydream about the single time he and Erin had some-thing resembling a date. With a resigned sigh, he remembered his hands trembling, even while jammed into the pockets of his pressed Ogilvy's slacks; and the curious nature of her fragrance that seemed floral from a distance but minty up close; and the
80 musical sound her shoes made on the cobblestone road leading to the assembly hall; and the way she seemed to be fearlessly striding toward an unknown future while he was just trying to acclimate to the present.

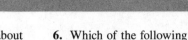

1. The passage supports all of the following statements about Jacob's job as a tour guide EXCEPT that:

    A. he observed many buildings with their skeletal structures exposed.
    B. there were some prepared remarks that Jacob was to read.
    C. the tour catered to certain people with a common interest.
    D. he wore what he considered to be a flattering uniform.

2. One of the main ideas of the second paragraph (lines 17–29) is that:

    F. due to the nature of Gettysburg, Jacob did not have much desire to travel elsewhere.
    G. Jacob imagined a better architectural plan for the town's older buildings.
    H. it was hard for Jacob to find a job with mainly pre-industrial types of merchants.
    J. Jacob lacked motivation for his studies because he planned to work for the railroad.

3. The events in the passage are described primarily from the point of view of a narrator who presents the:

    A. actions and thoughts of both Jacob and Erin.
    B. the inner emotions and thoughts of only Jacob.
    C. actions and thoughts of all the characters discussed.
    D. dialogue of all the characters, which suggests their thoughts.

4. According to the passage, all of the following were aspects of Jacob's job with his uncle EXCEPT:

    F. seeing unfinished construction.
    G. impressing Erin's parents.
    H. daydreaming while he worked.
    J. finding efficient paths for plumbing.

5. According to the passage, Jacob's ambition toward becoming an architect included a desire to:

    A. point out interesting architecture to a girl.
    B. find a new way to utilize plumbing.
    C. redesign the Dobbin House roof.
    D. enroll at a renowned architectural school.

6. Which of the following questions is NOT answered by the passage?

    F. What factors influenced Jacob's choice to go to Mount St. Mary's College?
    G. Did Erin ever use her voucher for a free tour with Jacob?
    H. How many people went to Jacob's high school?
    J. What effect did the old infrastructure of Gettysburg have on Jacob?

7. The passage indicates that compared to when Jacob worked as a tour guide, after he stopped working there he found the buildings of Gettysburg:

    A. less fascinating.
    B. more fascinating.
    C. less historically noteworthy.
    D. more historically noteworthy.

8. The passage indicates that Jacob's primary response to the events described in the last paragraph is:

    F. remorse that he and Erin were largely disconnected.
    G. anger concerning the excessive size of Mount St. Mary's.
    H. gratitude for ultimately meeting and marrying Martha.
    J. contentment regarding the fact that he got to date Erin.

9. That Jacob had an indelible streak of humility was:

    A. a quality shared by most people who grew up in a working class community like that of Gettysburg.
    B. a consequence of accepting that he would probably never be a world-famous architect.
    C. an effect of Jacob's grandmother's words of caution regarding the unbiased impressions of the rest of the world.
    D. a character trait that evolved through years of pursuing but never obtaining Erin's affection.

10. In the passage, the statement that Erin was fearlessly striding toward an unknown future (lines 81–82) is best described as the opinion of:

    F. the author of the passage, but not the opinion of Jacob.
    G. Jacob as he struggled to "accidentally" run in to Erin at Mount St. Mary's.
    H. Erin, who has little interest in Jacob because he has no urge to leave Gettysburg.
    J. Jacob as he reflects on the one date he had with Erin.

Passage II

SOCIAL SCIENCE: This passage is excerpted from the article "The Irresistible Force" by Angela Suspak. (© 2008 by Luminary)

The author is reviewing the biographical book *The Long Walk Home* by Grace Jergensen.

During the summer of 1892, a reputable black store owner was lynched in Memphis, Tennessee. This outraged many local citizens, but Ida B. Wells felt compelled to take action and write a letter decrying the horrific act in the local press. However, as a
5 black woman, her race and identity posed formidable obstacles. The volatility of her message, combined with the pervasive chauvinism of the times, made her "a hushed voice in the race debate," according to Grace Jergensen, who writes a biography of Wells, entitled *The Long Walk Home*. Wells, taking matters
10 into her own hands, joined a fledgling black newspaper called *The Free Speech and Headlight* as co-owner and editor.

Writing under the pseudonym of "Iola," Wells lashed out against the intolerance and brutality of racially-motivated lynchings. She vilified the perpetrators of the crime, while also
15 chastising the white community at large for virtually condoning these actions by its inaction. With her incendiary rhetoric, Wells became a hero in the civil rights community and a potential target for violence. Jergensen details the difficulties Wells underwent shortly after her article was published. While at an
20 editing convention in New York, Wells learned that she had become a despised figure in Memphis, and the target of death threats. Considering the imminent danger she would face if she returned home, "Wells had to decide whether she would rather be a nomad or a martyr."

25 Wells was not used to backing down from a challenge, though. She was born just months before the Emancipation Proclamation declared an end to slavery. She grew up with the mindset of equal rights for all, despite being exposed to the deeply ingrained and intractable racial divisions in the South.
30 Her parents perished when she was only 18 during a bout of yellow fever that plagued her hometown of Holly Springs, Mississippi. Wells, the oldest of eight siblings, was thrust into the role of caretaker. Wells's Aunt Georgine recalls that "Ida saw herself now as the grown-up and wanted to be strong. She
35 did all her crying in private so the little ones wouldn't see her." Jergensen reflects that Wells learned early on "that she was in charge of protecting her brothers and sisters, and that feeling extended later in life to her figurative brothers and sisters in the struggle for racial and gender equality."

40 Wells went to Rust College to become a teacher, and her ability to mold the thought processes of others made her a persuasive orator and writer. Jergensen compares Wells's debating style to that of Socrates, who used shrewdly-worded questions and statements to lead his opponent from his original
45 sense of certainty into a state of doubt about the correctness of his convictions. Similarly, Wells frequently started her essays and speeches with general questions about morality, fairness,

and human rights, baiting her opposition into admitting certain core principles before challenging them to reconcile these
50 fundamental rights with the unfair and discriminatory laws and practices they endorsed.

After a public speaking tour of England, Wells made a home for herself in Chicago, where she met the man who would eventually become her husband, Ferdinand Barnett. Together, they
55 raised two sons and two daughters, though later in life, Wells would bemoan the fact that she felt as though the responsibility of raising and supporting the four children became her primary concern, while her husband became engrossed in a political bid to become a Circuit Court judge.

60 Domestic life didn't spell the end of Wells's struggle against inequality, however—during her time in Chicago, she founded the nation's first civic organization for black women. It was initially called the Women's Era Club, though it would later be renamed the Ida B. Wells Club. In 1895, her book
65 *A Red Record* was published, documenting the history of racially-motivated lynchings in America. Although the book succeeded in motivating an audience of progressive thinkers, race-related riots and violence continued virtually unabated into the early 20th century.

70 Jergensen conveys a clear appreciation for the deep reserves of patience on which Wells was repeatedly forced to draw in order to maintain her devotion to both family and society, despite often being castigated or ignored by both. By retracing Wells's "long walk home" from the grueling aftermath of her
75 parents' death, through her exile from Memphis, to her eventual involvement in creating the NAACP (National Association for the Advancement of Colored People), Jergensen leaves the reader feeling exhausted, expending such vast amounts of sympathy for the injustices Wells faces. As portrayed by Jergensen, Wells is a
80 protagonist who nobly walks a self-chosen path of monumental toil, with rewards few and far between. One such reward must have been the passage of women's suffrage in 1920 with the 19th Amendment which Wells, then a grandmother, was finally able to see first-hand.

11. In the statement in lines 36–39 Jergensen most strongly stresses:

A. a consistent propensity Wells had to take care of those in need of help.
B. the way Wells's family persuaded her to take part in the civil rights struggle.
C. the lessons of equality that Wells learned by acting like a parent to her siblings.
D. a powerful metaphor Wells would later use in many of her incendiary speeches.

12. As portrayed in the passage, the reaction of Wells to her parents dying from a bout of yellow fever is best described as:

    F. sad and frightened.

    G. mournful but resilient.

    H. relieved and emboldened.

    J. brave but hopeless.

13. The passage's author most strongly implies that Wells's relationship with her husband:

    A. began a decline in her activism as she turned her focus to starting a family.

    B. was the most lasting consequence of her public speaking tour in England.

    C. did not halt her efforts in the struggle for equality.

    D. was the main reason behind her starting the Ida B. Wells Club.

14. Lines 6–9 most nearly mean that Wells:

    F. faced the problem of audiences reluctant to hear what she had to say.

    G. spoke too softly for many people to take her ideas seriously.

    H. did not believe that people would discredit her because of her race or gender.

    J. had to create a pen name in order to have her newspaper articles be read by the mainstream.

15. According to the passage, who disapproved of the ideas described in lines 12–16?

    A. Wells herself

    B. Jergensen

    C. Some people in Memphis

    D. The civil rights community

16. Another reviewer of Jergensen's book sums up Wells in this way:

> A tireless and outspoken advocate of equality, Ida B. Wells did not shy away from making controversial demands of her audience...sometimes jeopardizing her own safety, always reminding her listeners that equality was in accord with their fundamental sense of fairness.

How does this account of Wells compare to that of the passage's author?

    F. This account portrays Wells's demands as fair, whereas the passage's author remains less convinced.

    G. This account emphasizes the danger Wells put herself in, whereas the passage's author does not mention this.

    H. Both provide a comparably unflattering portrayal of Wells's goals and tactics.

    J. Both provide a comparably flattering portrayal of Wells's goals and tactics.

17. For the passage's author, lines 81–84 mainly support her earlier point that:

    A. Wells did manage to see some of her goals realized in her lifetime.

    B. family was an essential factor in motivating Wells's struggle.

    C. significant changes happen in society with each new generation.

    D. Wells became much wiser and more thankful in her old age.

18. According to the passage, Jergensen believes that Wells had a style of debating similar to that of Socrates because Wells:

    F. had a strong sense of certainty about her philosophical convictions.

    G. did not advance her own agenda but only wanted to understand her opponent.

    H. understood that clever oration can only do so much to further a cause.

    J. used points of agreement to show her opponents problems with their points of view.

19. The passage's author characterizes the book *A Red Record* most nearly as:

    A. a good effort that was troubled by philosophical inconsistencies.

    B. unusually radical compared to other books from the same era.

    C. impressively broad in the scope of social issues it tackled.

    D. mainly effective at inspiring its like-minded readers.

20. The passage most strongly suggests that Wells approached her life as a:

    F. bleak marathon.

    G. determined struggle.

    H. confusing journey.

    J. constant triumph.

Passage III

HUMANITIES: Passage A is adapted from the novel *Southern Charmed Life* by Robert Anderson (© 1978 by Robert Anderson). Passage B is an excerpt from a 1986 interview with B.B. King (Library of Congress, 1986).

Passage A by Robert Anderson

Feeling particularly fearless for a ten year old, Sis asked B.B. why he likes playing sad music. B.B. gave a rich chuckle and decided he had to look Kathy Mae in the eyes for this one. He shifted his guitar to the side and turned his husky frame as
5 far as he could, until his marbled, twinkling brown eyes could look straight into hers.

"Honey, the music isn't sad. Life is sad...sometimes. And the Blues is just how you get through it. It's hard for a young 'un to hear the Blues right because you haven't been through
10 enough pain of livin' yet." My Uncle was smiling, looking in the rear-view mirror at Sis, trying to judge her reaction. She seemed to be partly insulted by the implication that she would not be able to "get" the Blues.

"Have you ever cried yourself to sleep?" B.B. asked. Sis
15 tightened her lips in resentment. "Don't be shy. We all have. Didn't you feel better when you woke up?" Sis tentatively agreed.

B.B. explained, "It's because the pain is distant when you wake up. The Blues is how I cry myself to sleep. It puts a dream in between me and the pain, just like a thick frosted window
20 pane that muffles it and makes it fuzzy to see." Sis and I turned to each other, finding this pearl of wisdom difficult to digest and resigning to the fact that some things were not meant for kids.

Years later, I would find a deep appreciation for B.B.'s music. Whenever I hear him play, I can't help but to imagine
25 a waterfall—the pressure of the falling water was the weight of the pain. The mournful verses he sung made me think of the space behind the waterfall, a calm place of imprisonment, where a thundering curtain of water is all you see in front of you. And when he started his guitar solo, it was like I turned
30 into a bird that flew out through the waterfall. The heavy water pounded my light, buoyant frame down as I passed through it, but, once through, I was able to feel the freedom of lift, the droplets of water rolling off my wings as I soared up towards the clouds, and the waterfall was only something beautiful to
35 behold in the distance.

Passage B by B.B. King

I used to play a place in Twist, Arkansas. Still there, Twist, Arkansas. They used to have a little nightclub there that we played quite often. They used to take something looked like a big garbage pail and set it in the middle of the floor, half fill
40 it with kerosene, and would light that fuel and that's what we used for heat. This particular night, two guys started to fighting and one of 'em knocked the other one over on this container. When they did, it spilled on the floor.

Now it was already burning, so when it spilled, it looked
45 like a river of fire. Everybody ran for the front door including yours truly, but then I realized that I'd left my guitar inside. I went back for it. The building was a wooden building and it was burning so fast when I got my guitar, it started to collapse around me. So I almost lost my life trying to save the guitar.
50 Well the next morning we found that these two guys was fighting about a lady. I never did meet the lady, but I learned that her name was Lucille so I named my guitar Lucille to remind me not to do a thing like that again.

The early years when I was starting, blues player, you wasn't
55 always welcome in a lot of the other places. People usually have preconceived ideas about blues music. They always feel that it's depressing and that it's just something that a guy sit out on a stool, grab a guitar, and just start singing or mumbling or whatever. Hard times don't necessarily mean being poor all the
60 time. I've known people that was a part of a family and always feel that the family likes everybody else but them. That hurts and that's as deep a hurt as you can possibly get. I've known people that would have problems with their love life. This is kind of how blues began, out of feeling misused, feeling like
65 they had nobody to turn to.

I don't like to feel that I owe anything. I like to feel that I pay my own way, no free lunch. When people give me all these great compliments, I thank them, but still go back to my room and practice. A lot of times I say to myself, "I wished I
70 could be worthy of all the compliments that people give me sometimes." I'm not inventing anything that's going to stop cancer or muscular dystrophy or anything, but I like to feel that my time and talent is always there for the people that need it. When someone do say something negative, most times I think
75 about it, but it don't bother me that much.

Questions 21–24 ask about Passage A.

21. In Passage A, King uses the simile in lines 19–20 to convey the ability of the Blues to:

A. get the most emotion out of a musical instrument.
B. dull the sharpness of suffering.
C. transform complex feelings into simple ones.
D. help people relax and get to sleep.

22. As it is used in line 21, the word *digest* most nearly means:

F. understand.
G. stomach.
H. memorize.
J. study.

23. It is most reasonable to infer from Passage A that King believes a true appreciation of the Blues comes primarily from:

A. an upbringing similar to King's in Mississippi.
B. watching it performed live by musicians.
C. experiencing the struggles of life.
D. having deeply held religious beliefs.

24. The narrator compares the feeling created by King's guitar solos to the feeling of:

F. "a thick frosted window pane" (lines 19–20).
G. "the space behind the waterfall" (line 27).
H. "a thundering curtain of water" (line 28).
J. "a bird that flew out through the waterfall" (line 30).

Questions 25–27 ask about Passage B.

25. According to Passage B, King most likely references the nightclub fire in order to emphasize:

A. how little his life was worth living without his treasured guitar.
B. that his guitar gained him entry to such nightclubs despite widespread prejudice.
C. his peaceable nature and overall aversion to violence.
D. how a single decision could have a lasting impact.

26. As it is used in line 64, the word *misused* most nearly means:

F. clinically depressed.
G. ill-treated.
H. outraged.
J. misled.

27. In Passage B, King indicates that he:

A. feels humbled by the encouragement he receives from strangers.
B. regrets reentering the burning building to save his guitar.
C. believes his talents are only appreciated by those who are broken-hearted.
D. once aspired to become a medical doctor.

Questions 28–30 ask about both passages.

28. Which of the following best describes a difference in the two passages?

F. Passage A relies heavily on figurative language to communicate the narrator's ideas, while Passage B uses a more straightforward style of expression.
G. Passage A highlights King's sense of humor, while Passage B explains his love of storytelling.
H. Passage A is primarily about King's career path, while Passage B is more focused on his home life.
J. Passage A praises King's kindness and humble character, while Passage B critiques choices he had made in the past.

29. The narrator of Passage A would most likely respond to King's statement in Passage B (lines 74–75) with:

A. envy.
B. esteem.
C. mistrust.
D. pity.

30. Both passages suggest that:

F. music can heal sickness.
G. anyone can play the Blues.
H. pain is a part of living.
J. most people are prejudiced.

Passage IV

NATURAL SCIENCE: The following is adapted from the article "Seeking an Intelligent Definition of Intelligence" by Clark Matthews (© 2010 by Clark Matthews).

Cognitive psychologists who study humans and other animals are perpetually attempting to understand the type and extent of intelligence possessed by their subjects. Hindering their efforts is the ongoing debate about how we should define
5 such a nebulous concept as 'intelligence' in the first place. A scatter-hoarder species of squirrel would probably define intelligence as the ability to remember and re-locate the thousands of caches of food it has burrowed in hiding places throughout its environment. A dog, on the other hand, may emphasize its
10 ability to trace the source of objects in its environment based on the direction of the air current containing that smell.

There is a risk of bias in how we define intelligence because each species has evolved very specialized abilities based on its unique environmental niche and the techniques
15 and strategies that niche requires for survival. If we use our concepts of human capacities to define intelligence, we may be creating a standard that other animals couldn't hope to meet. Conversely, if we only mean by intelligence "the most highly refined capacities of that species" we make intelligence something
20 that can only be compared within a species, not across species.

One definition of intelligence holds that it is "a wide range of abilities relating to learning from one's environment and experience, and combining that learning with abstract reasoning to solve problems." Scientists frequently begin assessing
25 an animal's intelligence based on its susceptibility to classical or operant conditioning. Both methods involve pairing either a stimuli or a behavior with certain consequences, and waiting to see if a subject learns to associate the two and act accordingly. The faster the animal appears to absorb and act on the
30 association, the faster we believe it has 'learned' it. This gives us one supposedly objective means of comparing intelligent behavior across species.

The other primary evidence of an animal's intelligence is its ability to solve novel and/or complex problems. A spider
35 that spins a web to solve the problem of trapping insects for food is not considered to be displaying intelligence because the problem (food gathering) and behavior (spinning webs) are both embedded in the evolutionary history of a spider's habitat. An elephant that picks a lock at the zoo is thought to be acting

40 intelligently, since elephants do not pick locks in their native habitat and hence have no instinctive knowledge of how do undo them. The veined octopus is seen as a tool-user, scouring the ocean for coconut shells, which it proceeds to bring back to its homestead for the sake of building shelter. Although many
45 other animals, such as crabs and ants will take shelter using nearby objects, animal psychologists consider the long-term planning involved in the veined octopus's behavior as better evidence that it can conceptualize a goal and then act on it.

As if defining intelligence weren't tricky enough, measur-
50 ing intelligence is also a tenuous task. Ultimately, scientists can only observe an animal's behavior. So how can they ascertain if the animal is just behaving instinctively or if it is actually conceptualizing, thinking abstractly, and aware of its problem solving process? Because understanding is a private experience,
55 observing an animal's external behavior and hoping to infer its level of understanding is always a guessing game.

Both "intelligent" behavior and "unintelligent" behavior can be deceiving. Irene Pepperberg's famous subject, the parrot Alex, showcased a variety of impressive problem solving and
60 communication abilities that suggested an internal awareness and capacity for intelligence was present. For instance, Alex correctly called a "key" a "key," no matter what size, color, or orientation a certain key was. This suggests Alex had grouped the individual keys used to train him into a general category that
65 could be applied to novel stimuli. However, sometimes Alex gave wrong answers to a task he had completed successfully many times before. This was interpreted as Alex's boredom and frustration at repeating a task he had already mastered. Although the behavior looked unintelligent, experimenters
70 believed it was not due to a lack of understanding. Conversely, there is also the perpetual concern of the Clever Hans Effect, in which seemingly intelligent behavior is not believed to be the result of genuine understanding. The name comes from a horse named Clever Hans who was paraded around Europe in
75 the early 20th century, supposedly a marvel of animal intelligence. Hans could indicate the correct solution to arithmetic problems by tapping his hoof the appropriate number of times. Ultimately, though, scientists realized that Hans was getting the answer by reading nonverbal clues from his trainer. The trainer
80 would unknowingly tense up as the correct number of taps was getting nearer, which signaled to Hans when it was time to stop tapping. So although Hans exhibited behavior that seemed indicative of underlying intelligence, scientists do not believe he was actually solving the problems conceptually in his mind.

31. The main function of the second paragraph (lines 12–20) in relation to the passage as a whole is to:

- **A.** explain the human bias that is the focus of the rest of the passage.
- **B.** advance the argument that intelligence should be defined in human terms.
- **C.** show how certain types of definitions have undesirable consequences.
- **D.** provide background information about the evolutionary niches of species.

32. According to the passage, what is the primary problem with defining intelligence as "the most highly refined capacities" of a given species?

- **F.** It would be a standard that no species could hope to meet.
- **G.** It would not take into account each species' unique environmental niche.
- **H.** It would too closely mimic our concepts of human intelligence.
- **J.** It would not be a standard we could use to compare one species to another.

33. According to the passage, all of the following behaviors seem to be intelligent EXCEPT:

- **A.** a spider solving the problem of trapping insects by spinning a web.
- **B.** an elephant picking a lock at the zoo.
- **C.** a veined octopus finding coconut shells for its shelter.
- **D.** a parrot identifying keys of various shapes and sizes.

34. According to the passage, scientists often start their assessment of an animal's intelligence by:

- **F.** analyzing its ability to solve new and complex problems.
- **G.** identifying the most highly refined capacities of that species.
- **H.** stimulating the animal and observing its behavior.
- **J.** seeing how much information the animal can absorb.

35. Suppose beavers typically gather sticks from the forest floor and take them to a stream to construct a dam. One beaver that cannot find enough sticks on the ground begins to strip bark from dying trees. Based on the passage, the author would most likely describe the behavior of this beaver as:

- **A.** intelligent if the lack of sticks is a novel problem.
- **B.** unintelligent if there was long-term planning.
- **C.** impressive and the result of operant conditioning.
- **D.** deceptive and illustrating the Clever Hans effect.

36. The passage indicates that the shelters of the veined octopus differ from those of crabs and ants in that the octopus shelters:

- **F.** are more likely to be constructed from nearby objects.
- **G.** are made of much sturdier materials than are crab and ant shelters.
- **H.** have more architectural interest than those of the crabs and ants.
- **J.** seem more to be the result of a long-term plan.

37. The primary purpose of the passage is to:

- **A.** define intelligence as it applies to non-human species.
- **B.** explore some of the challenges, both conceptual and practical, involved in assessing intelligence.
- **C.** identify the criteria used to discriminate between intelligent and unintelligent behavior.
- **D.** compare and contrast how intelligence appears within human species versus how it appears in non-human species.

38. The author mentions the behavior of the parrot Alex in the last paragraph primarily to:

- **F.** demonstrate that poor performance does not necessarily indicate poor comprehension.
- **G.** illustrate the meaning of intelligent behavior as applied to parrots.
- **H.** highlight an animal believed to be unintelligent which nonetheless acted intelligently.
- **J.** supply proof that animals can indeed learn the meaning of a concept.

39. As it is used in line 54, the word *private* most nearly means:

- **A.** internal.
- **B.** secretive.
- **C.** subtle.
- **D.** shy.

40. In the context of the passage, the phrase "can be deceiving" (line 58) most nearly suggests that an animal's behavior:

- **F.** often is intended to trick other animals in its environment.
- **G.** is the hardest thing about an animal to measure in a scientific way.
- **H.** will fool observers who are not trained to know better.
- **J.** does not always serve as a reliable indicator of that animal's mental activities.

END OF TEST
STOP! DO NOT TURN THE PAGE UNTIL TOLD TO DO SO.
DO NOT RETURN TO A PREVIOUS TEST.

Chapter 14
Reading
Practice Test 3
Answers and
Explanations

READING PRACTICE TEST 3 ANSWERS

1.	A	21.	B
2.	F	22.	F
3.	B	23.	C
4.	G	24.	J
5.	A	25.	D
6.	H	26.	G
7.	B	27.	A
8.	F	28.	F
9.	C	29.	B
10.	J	30.	H
11.	A	31.	C
12.	G	32.	J
13.	C	33.	A
14.	F	34.	H
15.	C	35.	A
16.	J	36.	J
17.	A	37.	B
18.	J	38.	F
19.	D	39.	A
20.	G	40.	J

SCORE YOUR PRACTICE TEST

Step A
Count the number of correct answers: _____. This is your *raw score*.

Step B
Use the score conversion table below to look up your raw score. The number to the left is your *scale score*: _____.

Reading Scale Conversion Table

Scale Score	Raw Score	Scale Score	Raw Score	Scale Score	Raw Score
36	39-40	24	27	12	9-10
35	38	23	26	11	7-8
34	37	22	24-25	10	6
33	35-36	21	23	9	5
32	34	20	21-22	8	–
31	33	19	20	7	4
30	–	18	19	6	3
29	32	17	17-18	5	–
28	31	16	16	4	2
27	30	15	14-15	3	–
26	29	14	12-13	2	1
25	28	13	11	1	0

READING PRACTICE TEST 3 EXPLANATIONS

Passage I

1. **A** This reference question asks which statement about *Jacob's job as a tour guide* is NOT supported by the passage. When a question asks what is NOT mentioned in the passage, eliminate answers that are mentioned. Lines 30–68 discuss Jacob's job as a tour guide. Choice (A) states that Jacob saw *buildings with their skeletal structures exposed*, but the passage doesn't indicate that the underlying structure of any of the buildings is visible. Keep (A). Lines 40–42 indicate that Jacob's job involved *reading a script*. This supports (B), so eliminate it. Lines 30–33 indicate that the tourists on Jacob's tour were *Civil War enthusiasts mostly*. This supports (C), so eliminate it. Choice (D) is supported by the phrase *Fancying himself as cutting quite a figure in his clean, pressed uniform* (lines 33–34), so eliminate (D). The correct answer is (A).

2. **F** This reasoning question asks for a main idea of the *second paragraph*. Read the second paragraph as the window. The first few sentences of the second paragraph establish that Gettysburg is a town that is stuck in the past. Jacob is affected by the *lack of innovation* and gets the impression that *there was little of interest to be discovered outside Gettysburg*. Keep (F) because the impression Jacob was left with could mean he would not feel any desire to travel. Eliminate (G) and (H) because the paragraph does not discuss an *architectural plan* or Jacob's employment with *pre-industrial types of merchants*. While the *railroad* is brought up in the paragraph, eliminate (J) because it doesn't talk about Jacob planning on working there. The correct answer is (F).

3. **B** This reasoning question asks about the *point of view* of the narrator. Because this is a general question, it should be done after all the specific questions. Look for the Golden Thread. The passage narrates *Jacob's* thoughts. The passage does not narrate the thoughts of *Erin* or other *characters*, so eliminate (A), (C), and (D). Keep (B) because it matches the text from the passage. The correct answer is (B).

4. **G** This reference question asks which was NOT an aspect of *Jacob's job with his uncle*. When a question asks what is NOT mentioned in the passage, eliminate answers that are mentioned. Look for the lead word *uncle* to find the window for the question. Lines 53–54 state that *Jacob worked with his uncle, a residential plumber*. The rest of the paragraph discusses that work. Eliminate (F) because lines 54–56 say that *Jacob enjoyed seeing homes in the intermediate stages of construction*. Keep (G) because the paragraph does not indicate that Jacob's job involved *impressing Erin's parents*; rather, he dreamt about this idea. Eliminate (H) because it is supported by lines 73–75. Eliminate (J) because it is supported by lines 56–59. The correct answer is (G).

5. **A** This reference question asks about *Jacob's ambition toward becoming an architect*. Look for the lead word *architect* to find the window for the question. Lines 12–13 say that Jacob's *ambition towards ascending in the field* was to impress a girl by describing architectural features in *Prague*. Choice (A) matches this idea, so keep it. Eliminate (B) because the passage never mentions Jacob devising *a new way to utilize plumbing*. Eliminate (C) because the passage never mentions a desire to *redesign the Dobbin House roof*. Eliminate (D) because lines 6–7 state that Jacob went to Mount St. Mary's, *not because it had a renowned architectural program*. The correct answer is (A).

6. **H**   This reference question asks which answer choice is NOT answered in the passage. When a question asks what is NOT mentioned in the passage, eliminate answers that are mentioned. Work backward and use lead words from the answers to find the window for this question. Eliminate (F) because the question is answered in line 7: *he was able to get a partial scholarship*. Eliminate (G) because the question is answered in lines 36–39. Keep (H) because the passage does not indicate *how many people went to Jacob's high school*. Eliminate (J) because the question is answered in lines 25–26: *this lack of innovation deepened Jacob's disinterest in personal or academic enterprise*. The correct answer is (H).

7. **B**   This reference question asks what Jacob thought of the *buildings in Gettysburg* once he *stopped working as a tour guide*. Look for the lead words *Gettysburg* and *buildings* to find the window for the question. The fourth paragraph mentions buildings in Gettysburg. Lines 48–52 state that it wasn't *until he left that job* that Jacob started thinking more about the buildings. Eliminate (A) because it is the opposite of what the passage indicates. Keep (B) because it matches the text from the passage. Eliminate (C) and (D) because the passage doesn't draw any comparison between how *historically noteworthy* Jacob thought the buildings were during and after his job as a tour guide. The correct answer is (B).

8. **F**   This reference question asks about *Jacob's primary response to the events described in the last paragraph*. Read the last paragraph as the window. The paragraph states (line 76) that Jacob recalls the memory of a date with Erin *with a resigned sigh*. Choice (F) says that Jacob feels *remorse* over his disconnect with Erin. This matches *resigned sigh*, so keep (F). Eliminate (G) because the passage does not indicate that Jacob was angry about the *size of Mount St. Mary's*. Eliminate (H) because the passage does not express his *gratitude* for marrying *Martha*. Eliminate (J) because *contentment* does not match *resigned sigh*. The correct answer is (F).

9. **C**   This reasoning question asks about Jacob's *indelible streak of humility*. Look for the lead words *indelible streak of humility* to find the window for the question. The phrase is used in lines 2–5: Jacob's grandmother instilled this humility in him by telling him that *the rest of the world was under no obligation* to think he was *special*. Eliminate (A) because the passage never suggests humility is a trait of the *working class*. Eliminate (B) because Jacob's humility is the *consequence* of his feeling that he won't be famous. Choice (C) matches the text from the passage, so keep it. Eliminate (D) because the passage never draws a connection between Jacob's pursuit of *Erin* and his humility. The correct answer is (C).

10. **J**   This reasoning question asks for the source of the opinion that *Erin was fearlessly striding toward an unknown future*. Read a window around the line reference to find the window for this question. This phrase is part of a sentence in which *Jacob* reminisces about *Erin*. Therefore, the opinion belongs to Jacob. Eliminate (F) because it contradicts the text from the passage. Eliminate (G) because, though the opinion belongs to Jacob, it does not concern his struggles locating *Erin* at college. Eliminate (H) because the lines are from Jacob's standpoint, not *Erin's*. Keep (J) because it matches the text from the passage. The correct answer is (J).

Passage II

11. **A**   This reasoning question asks what the statement in lines 36–39 *stresses*. Read a window around the line reference. This statement from Jergensen talks about the way Wells took care of her siblings and how she looked out for the rights of those experiencing racial inequality. Look for an answer choice that matches this idea. Keep (A) because it matches the text from the passage. The text in the window makes no reference to Wells being *persuaded* by her *family*, so eliminate (B). While the window states that Wells is a parental figure to her *siblings*, it does not indicate that she learned *lessons of equality* from this. Eliminate (C). Eliminate (D) because the window does not reference a *metaphor*. The correct answer is (A).

12. **G**   This reasoning question asks for a description of Wells' reaction to her parents' deaths. Look for the lead words *yellow fever* to find the window for the question. Lines 30–39 state that Wells felt the need to be strong for her siblings, yet mourned in private. The correct answer needs to state both of these factors. Eliminate (F) because, while Wells was sad due to her parents' deaths, the text does not indicate that she was frightened. Keep (G) because it matches the text from the passage. Eliminate (H) because the text supports the opposite of *relieved* and *emboldened*. Eliminate (J) because there is no evidence that Wells felt *hopeless*, even though there is support that she was *brave*. The correct answer is (G).

13. **C**   This reasoning question asks what the narrator implies about the relationship between *Wells* and *her husband*. Look for the lead words *Wells* and *husband* to find the window for the question. Lines 60–61 suggest that Wells' domestic life didn't spell the end of her struggle against inequality. The passage also describes Wells' continued activism after marriage. Eliminate (A) because it contradicts the text from the passage. Eliminate (B) because Wells met her husband in *Chicago*, not *England*. Choice (C) is supported by the text, so keep it. Eliminate (D) because there is no connection between her husband and the *Ida B. Wells Club*. The correct answer is (C).

14. **F**   This reference question asks for the meaning of lines 6–9. Read a window around the line reference. Lines 7–8 portray Wells as a *hushed voice in the race debate*. Keep (F) because it matches the text from the passage. Eliminate (G) because the phrase *hushed voice* is metaphorical, not literal. Eliminate (H) because it contradicts the text from the passage. While the passage does state that Wells created a pen name, it does not state this was done for a *mainstream newspaper*. Eliminate (J). The correct answer is (F).

15. **C**   This reference question asks *who disapproved of the ideas described in lines 12–16*. Read a window around the line reference. In this window, the passage states that Wells became *a despised figure in Memphis* (line 21). Eliminate (A) and (B), as the text implies that a group of people despised Wells. Keep (C) because it matches the text from the passage. Eliminate (D) because line 17 states that Wells *became a hero in the civil rights community*. The correct answer is (C).

16. **J**   This reasoning question asks for a comparison between two accounts of Wells. Because this is a general question, it should be done after all the specific questions. Look for the Golden Thread. The passage portrays Wells in a positive light, detailing her boldness and persuasive tactics. The reviewer's account portrays Wells as *a tireless and outspoken advocate of equality*. Eliminate (F) because the passage does not question Wells' *fairness*. Eliminate (G) because the passage does state that Wells put herself in *danger* to complete her objectives. Eliminate (H) because both Jergensen and the reviewer consistently paint Wells positively. Keep (J) because it matches the text from the passage. The correct answer is (J).

17. **A**   This reference question asks which earlier statement is supported in lines 81–84. Read a window around the line reference. The author mentions Wells' issues with only occasional rewards for what she does and uses women's suffrage in 1920 as an example of a reward. Keep (A) because it matches the text from the passage. Eliminate (B) because the passage never states that *family* motivated Wells' struggle. Eliminate (C) because the passage never suggests that each generation brings *significant change* to *society*. Eliminate (D) because the passage does not state that Wells *became much wiser and more thankful in her older age*. The correct answer is (A).

18. **J**   This reference question asks why *Wells* was similar to *Socrates* in her *style of debating*. Look for the lead word *Socrates* to find the window for the question. Lines 43–46 state that Socrates *used shrewdly-worded questions and statements to lead his opponent from his original sense of certainty into a state of doubt about the correctness of his convictions*. Likewise, the author states that Wells asks questions to bait others to question their morality and fairness. Eliminate (F) because the text does not mention *philosophical convictions*. Eliminate (G) because the passage states that Wells would ask questions in order to *advance her agenda*. Eliminate (H) because the text indicates that Socrates and Wells based their debating strategies on *clever oration*. Keep (J) because it matches the text from the passage. The correct answer is (J).

19. **D**   This reference question asks *how the author characterizes the book A Red Record*. Look for the lead words *A Red Record* to find the window for the question. Lines 66–69 state that the book motivated an audience of *progressive thinkers*, while the practical measures of the problem it addressed did not improve. Eliminate (A) because the window does not mention *philosophical inconsistencies*. The text does not call the book *unusually radical*, so eliminate (B). Eliminate (C) because the book focuses on the history of lynching in America, not a broad *scope of social issues*. Keep (D) because it matches the text from the passage. The correct answer is (D).

20. **G**   This reasoning question asks about the way in which *Wells approached her life*. Because this is a general question, it should be done after all the specific questions. Look for the Golden Thread. The passage, overall, describes Wells' strength and the positive outcomes of her activism. Eliminate (F) and (H) because both are negative. Keep (G) because it reflects Wells' perseverance. Eliminate (J) because the passage does not suggest that Wells constantly triumphed. The correct answer is (G).

Passage III

21. **B**   This reasoning question asks what ability of the Blues is conveyed by the simile in lines 19–20. Read a window around the line reference. King says the Blues *puts a dream between [him] and the pain, like a thick frosted windowpane.* The simile shows that the Blues has the ability to dull sadness and hurt. Eliminate any answers that are not consistent with that idea. Eliminate (A) because the simile is about a style of music, not a particular instrument. Choice (B) is a paraphrase of the text from the passage, so keep it. Eliminate (C) because there's no indication that the Blues is *transforming* emotions, but rather muffling or dulling them. Although King does refer to sleeping, he is not discussing the Blues's ability to help anyone sleep. Eliminate (D). The correct answer is (B).

22. **F**   This vocabulary in context question asks what the word *digest* means in line 21. Go back to the text, find the word *digest,* and cross it out. Carefully read the surrounding text to determine another word that would fit in the blank based on the context of the passage. After King compares the Blues to a frosted window, the author and her sister *turned to each other,* deciding some things weren't *meant for kids* after they found his *pearl of wisdom difficult to digest.* The word in context should mean something similar to "grapple with" or "accept." Eliminate anything inconsistent with this idea. Keep (F), which matches the text from the passage. Eliminate (G) because, although *stomach* might be an attractive answer initially, they are not physically digesting anything. Eliminate (H) and (J) because neither *memorize* nor *study* match the text from the passage. The correct answer is (F).

23. **C**   This reasoning question asks what can be inferred about where *King believes a true appreciation for the Blues comes from.* Look for the lead words *appreciation* and *Blues* to find the window for the question. In his conversation with Sis, he says that it's hard for *a young 'un to hear the Blues right because [they] haven't been through enough pain of livin' yet.* Therefore, those who appreciate the Blues *have* been through the pain of living. Eliminate any answers that aren't consistent with that idea. Eliminate (A) because King never refers specifically to his own *upbringing.* Eliminate (B) because the window does not mention watching the Blues performed by *live musicians.* Choice (C) is a paraphrase of the text, so keep (C). Eliminate (D) because King never discusses *religious beliefs.* The correct answer is (C).

24. **J**   This reference question asks what feeling cited by the narrator compares to the *feeling created by King's guitar.* Look for the lead words *King's guitar* to find the window for the question. Notice that each answer choice provides a specific line reference, so read carefully around each line reference to determine whether it refers to King's guitar solo or something else. Eliminate (F) because the *thick glass pane* refers to the way that the Blues muffles pain, not King's guitar solo. Choice (G) might initially look promising because the author is talking about listening to King play, but the *space behind the waterfall* is in reference to the *mournful verses.* Eliminate (G). Eliminate (H) because the *thundering curtain of water* is part of a metaphor describing the mournful verses. The author describes the guitar solo starting and how his heart feels like *a bird that flew out of the waterfall.* This is consistent with (J). The correct answer is (J).

25. **D**   This reference question asks what King most likely means to emphasize when he discusses the *nightclub fire*. Look for the lead words *nightclub fire* to find the window for the question. In the second paragraph of Passage B, King talks about the event, how the fire started and how he almost died running back into the club for his guitar. Later, he mentions that he named his guitar Lucille after the woman who two men were fighting over when they started the fire, *to remind [him] not to do a thing like that again*. Eliminate any answer choices that aren't consistent with that text from the passage. Choice (A) can be eliminated because there's no evidence that King thought his life was worth less than his guitar. Eliminate (B) because the passage does not mention *prejudice*. Eliminate (C) because King tells the story to explain the lesson he learned, not to describe his own nature. Keep (D) because it is consistent with the text from the passage. The correct answer is (D).

26. **G**   This vocabulary in context question asks what the word *misused* means in line 64. Go back to the text, find the word *misused,* and cross it out. Carefully read the surrounding text to determine another word that would fit in the blank based on the context of the passage. King refers to people who feel rejected by *family* or who face *problems with their love lives.* He goes on to say that's how the Blues began, *out of feeling misused,* so the word must mean something like "hurt" or "treated badly." Eliminate (F) and (H), because neither *clinically-depressed* nor *outraged* is consistent with "hurt" or "treated badly." Choice (G) matches the text from the passage, so keep it. Choice (J) can be eliminated because there's no evidence that the people were *misled,* simply that they were *hurt.* The correct answer is (G).

27. **A**   This reference question asks what King indicates in Passage B. There is no good lead word in this question, so work the question later. Eliminate any answer choices that aren't supported by the passage. Choice (A) is supported by King's statement in lines 67–69 that when people give him compliments, he thanks them but still goes back to his room to practice. Keep (A). Eliminate (B) because, although King certainly learned a lesson from the fire, there is no evidence that he *regrets reentering the building.* Eliminate (C) because, although those who are broken-hearted may appreciate the Blues, there's no indication that *only* the broken-hearted like it. Eliminate (D) because, though King mentions *cancer or muscular dystrophy,* there is no mention of his aspirations *to become a medical doctor.* The correct answer is (A).

28. **F**   This reasoning question asks which of the following best describes a difference between the two passages. Because this question asks about both passages, it should be done after the questions that ask about each passage individually. Consider the Golden Thread of both passages. Keep (F) because Passage A uses a great deal of *figurative language*, while Passage B is more *straightforward.* Eliminate (G) because Passage A does not highlight *King's sense of humor.* Eliminate (H) because Passage A does not primarily focus on King's *career path.* Eliminate (J) because Passage A focuses more on King's music than on his *kindness and humble character.* The correct answer is (F).

29. **B**   This reasoning question asks how the narrator of Passage A would most likely respond to the statement in Passage B on lines 74–75. Read a window around the line reference. In lines 74–75, King states, *When someone do say something negative, most times I think about it, but it don't bother me that much.* The author of Passage A feels *deep appreciation* for King and his music. Therefore, the author would likely think favorably of King's statement. Eliminate (A), (C), and (D) because each of these is negative. *Esteem* is consistent with *deep appreciation*, so keep (B). The correct answer is (B).

30. **H**   This reasoning question asks for an idea that both passages suggest. Because this question asks about both passages, it should be done after the questions that ask about each passage individually. Consider the Golden Thread of both passages. Although Passage A mentions the Blues helping with pain, there is no mention of the music's ability to *heal sickness*. Eliminate (F). Eliminate (G) because there is no discussion about who can or can't play the Blues. Keep (H): in line 7 of Passage A, King says, *Life is sad... sometimes.* In lines 60–65 of Passage B, King talks about the kinds of *hard times* that people go through. Eliminate (J) because there is no discussion of *prejudice* in Passage A. The correct answer is (H).

PASSAGE IV

31. **C**   This reasoning question asks about the function of the *second paragraph*. Read the second paragraph as the window. The paragraph explains that defining intelligence in human terms might create a standard that other species can't meet. Therefore, we can't compare intelligence between species. Eliminate (A) because the *rest of the passage* does not focus on *human bias*. Eliminate (B) because it contradicts the text from the passage. Choice (C) is supported by the paragraph, so keep it. Eliminate (D) because this paragraph does not *provide background information* about *evolutionary niches*. The correct answer is (C).

32. **J**   This reference question asks for the *primary problem with defining intelligence as "the most highly refined capacities"* of a given species. Look for the lead words *"the most highly refined capacities"* to find the window for the question. Lines 17–20 state that the definition makes *intelligence something that can only be compared within a species, not across species*. Look for an answer choice that matches this text from the passage. Eliminate (F) because the text does not indicate that the problem relates to an unmeetable *standard*. Eliminate (G) because the text does not indicate that the problem relates to *environmental niches*. Eliminate (H) because the text from the passage does not mention *human intelligence*. Keep (J) because it matches the text. The correct answer is (J).

33. **A**   This reference question asks which behavior is NOT intelligent, according to the passage. Work backward and use lead words from the answers to find the window for this question. Look for the lead word *spider*, which can be found in line 34. Lines 35–36 state that a spider that spins a web *is not considered to be displaying intelligence*, so keep (A). Look for the lead word *elephant*. Lines 39–40 state that *an elephant that picks a lock at the zoo is...acting intelligently*. Eliminate (B). Look for the lead words *veined octopus*. Lines 42–44 state that the veined octopus is intelligent because of its actions, so eliminate (C). Look for the lead word *parrot*. Lines 61–65 present Alex the parrot's ability to identify and group objects as intelligent. Eliminate (D). The correct answer is (A).

34. **H**   This reference question asks how *scientists often start their assessment of an animal's intelligence*. Look for the lead words *scientists* and *assessment* to find the window for the question. Lines 24–26 say that *scientists frequently begin assessing an animal's intelligence based on its susceptibility to classical or operant conditioning*. This method involves *pairing either a stimuli or a behavior with certain consequences, and waiting to see if a subject learns to...act accordingly*. Look for an answer choice that matches this text from the passage.

Eliminate (F) because the idea of *solving new and complex problems* does not match the text. Eliminate (G) because the text does not indicate that scientists first *identify the most highly refined capabilities* of a species. Keep (H) because it is a paraphrase of the text from the passage. Eliminate (J) because the passage never mentions testing an animal's capacity to absorb *information*. The correct answer is (H).

35. **A** This reasoning question asks how the author of the passage would most likely describe the *behavior* of the *beaver*. Because this is a general question, it should be done after all the specific questions. Look for the Golden Thread. The passage discusses the definition of intelligence in animals, and the beginning of the fourth paragraph states that one of the primary sources of evidence for intelligence is the ability to solve novel problems. Keep (A) because the beaver in the example solves the stick problem by using bark—a solution to a novel problem. Eliminate (B) because *long-term planning* is a trait of something being intelligent, not *unintelligent*. Eliminate (C) because there is no indication that the behavior is *the result of operant conditioning*. Eliminate (D) because the *Clever Hans effect* would prove a lack of intelligence, if true. The correct answer is (A).

36. **J** This reference question asks how *the shelters of the veined octopus differ from those of crabs and ants*. Look for the lead word *veined octopus* to find the window for the question. Lines 44–48 discuss the long-term planning abilities of the veined octopus, stating that the octopus's behavior is *better evidence that it can conceptualize a goal and then act on it*. Eliminate (F) because it applies to crab and ant shelters. Eliminate (G) because sturdiness is not mentioned in the passage. Eliminate (H) because *architectural interest* does not appear in the passage. Keep (J) because it matches the text from the passage. The correct answer is (J).

37. **B** This reasoning question asks for the *primary purpose of the passage*. Because this is a general question, it should be done after all the specific questions. Look for the Golden Thread. The passage begins by discussing the difficulties of defining intelligence across species, then moves to the challenges of measuring intelligence. Eliminate (A) because the passage does not offer one clear definition of intelligence. Keep (B) it matches the text from the passage. Eliminate (C) because, while the passage does bring up *intelligent and unintelligent behavior*, it does not specify criteria for them. Choice (D) is incorrect because the passage is not organized around a comparison between *human* and *non-human species*. The correct answer is (B).

38. **F** This reasoning question asks why the author mentions *the behavior of the parrot Alex in the last paragraph*. Read the last paragraph as the window. Lines 57–58 state, *Both "intelligent" and "unintelligent" behavior can be deceiving.* Alex often performed tasks well, but sometimes gave wrong answers. Lines 69–70 state, *Although the [wrong] behavior looked unintelligent...it was not due to a lack of understanding.* Keep (F) because it matches the text from the passage. Eliminate (G) because the purpose of the paragraph is not to *illustrate the meaning of intelligent behavior as applied to parrots*. Eliminate (H) because it contradicts the text from the passage. Eliminate (J) because it does not match the text. The correct answer is (F).

39. **A**   This vocabulary in context question asks what the word *private* means in line 54. Go back to the text, find the word *private,* and cross it out. Carefully read the surrounding text to determine another word that would fit in the blank based on the context of the passage. The text says that *understanding is a private experience*, so the word must mean something like "personal." *Internal* matches "personal," so keep (A). *Secretive* is a trap answer based on another meaning of *private* that is not supported by the text. Eliminate (B). Neither *subtle* nor *shy* matches "personal," so eliminate (C) and (D). The correct answer is (A).

40. **J**   This reasoning question asks what the phrase *can be deceiving* suggests about *animal behavior*. Read a window around the line reference. Lines 57–58 precede a discussion of a parrot who behaved unintelligently despite researchers believing it knew how to behave intelligently, and a horse who behaved intelligently but ultimately seemed to not have an intelligent grasp of its behavior. Therefore, the phrase *can be deceiving* suggests that an animal's behavior does not necessarily demonstrate whether or not the animal is intelligent. Eliminate (F) because the examples provided do not suggest that the animals intended to *trick* others. Eliminate (G) because the phrase does not indicate that animal behavior is *the hardest thing...to measure in a scientific way*. Eliminate (H) because the passage does not indicate that an animal's behavior may *fool observers*. Keep (J) because it matches the text from the passage. The correct answer is (J).

Chapter 15
Reading
Practice Test 4

READING TEST

35 Minutes—40 Questions

DIRECTIONS: There are four passages in this test. Each passage is followed by several questions. After reading each passage, choose the best answer to each question and blacken the corresponding oval on your answer document. You may refer to the passages as often as necessary.

Passage I

PROSE FICTION: This passage is adapted from the novel *Birds of Paradise* by Minnie Foroozan (©2002 by Minnie Foroozan).

As a young woman, Ani Kealoha had never dreamt of someday owning a hotel on her native island of O'ahu, but—as she would happily tell any of the hotel guests and staff at her 120-room "home away from home"—her outgoing and car-
5 ing nature, along with a strong work ethic and natural ability for organization, had practically made it her destiny. Ani had grown up in a small but happy family of limited means. Most days, Ani would help her parents with their market stall on King Kekaulike Street, where they served increasing numbers
10 of tourists and military personnel. If she ever had aspirations of wealth, it was just to have enough money to visit the faraway places these visitors would talk about—Los Angeles, Sydney, or even New York. They captured her imagination and filled her with a desire for adventure.

15 In the years before statehood, once her sisters were old enough to assume some of her duties at the market, Ani Kealoha's desire to help her family and teenage sense of adventure led her to find other work as well. Hawaii's grow-ing and near year-round influx of tourists allowed ample
20 opportunity for someone of her character. She was a skillful musician and naturally graceful; she would play ukulele and dance to the *hapa-haole* music for the frequent tourist hula shows, eventually acting as "manager" for several groups of musicians and dancers. Ani "The Fearless" would walk from
25 hotel to hotel, asking to see the manager and, more often than not, convincing him that he should invite her group to perform. It was during these frequent visits that she became familiar with the already world-famous Moana Hotel. During one of her visits, she learned of, and was eventually offered,
30 an opening for a staff position at the hotel, and she accepted without hesitation.

Although she started there as a chambermaid, Kealoha recalled her time at the Moana with nostalgia. The endless parade of visitors, from the obscure to the famous, never grew
35 tiresome for her, and her enthusiasm for her work soon saw her managing the entire housekeeping staff. After again proving her capability and resourcefulness as a manager, she was even-tually to manage all guest services for the hotel.

With the arrival of statehood in 1959, everything changed.
40 Now a citizen of the United States, she, like her sisters and many of her friends, was eager to take advantage of the new opportunities citizenship offered. While her sisters chose to go to university on the mainland, Ani's experience qualified her to be employed as a civilian for the Quartermaster Corps,
45 helping to organize and distribute supplies to American units and troops still stationed throughout the Pacific.

Gazing out of her office window, listening to the sound of the surf and the ocean breeze in the palms, she often thought of her time as a clerk in the Quartermaster Corps, where she met
50 Lt. James Santos, to whose company she had been assigned, and with whom she would gradually fall in love and then marry a year later. In the days just after their marriage, they lived on the Army base in a small but neat bungalow-style home. When Santos, now "Jimmy," was later promoted to Lieutenant Colonel,
55 Kealoha left her clerking position and spent her time turning their little bungalow into a home—cooking meals in their tiny kitchen, adding a rug here, curtains there, and the big purchase, a brand-new radio. Then one day, Jimmy came home with a surprise: a tiny, half-starved, brown puppy, apparently orphaned.
60 They nursed him back to health, and gave him the grand name Pua Pua Lena Lena—after the beloved dog of Hawaiian myth— which was almost immediately shortened to "Pup."

Thinking about evenings at home with Jimmy, listening to programs like *Hawaii Calls* and with Pup sitting and staring
65 at the radio (looking for all the world like the dog on the RCA Victor label), Kealoha would smile and think about the first time she met Jimmy. Born in the Philippines and raised in Tacoma, Jimmy was young for his rank, being only 24 years old at the time, and newly-arrived in Hawaii. He was slightly-built and
70 fair-skinned, which made him look even younger than he was. As such, he made a special effort to maintain what he felt was the "proper" military bearing. At their first meeting, when she had reported to his office, he was terse, but not rude, and called her "Ms. Kealoha." She could tell that he was trying to make
75 his voice sound deeper than it actually was.

Lieutenant Santos was a tireless worker, and seemed to always find a reason to be at or near her desk, but at the same time, he would seldom speak to her or even make eye contact. Kealoha thought perhaps he felt that she, as a civilian, needed
80 extra supervision, and she made an extra effort to demonstrate just how capable she was.

1. The events in the passage are described primarily from the point of view of a narrator who presents the:

   A. thoughts of Kealoha, her customers, and her family as conveyed in dialogue.
   B. inner thoughts and sentiments of Kealoha only.
   C. inner thoughts of Kealoha and Santos only.
   D. inner thoughts and emotions of all the people in Kealoha's life.

2. The passage supports all of the following statements about the Moana Hotel EXCEPT that:

   F. it was one of the better-known hotels on the island of O'ahu.
   G. Kealoha worked there as a chambermaid.
   H. it had more rooms than the hotel Kealoha currently owns.
   J. its guests included celebrities as well as people who were not as well-known.

3. Which of the following questions is NOT answered by the passage?

   A. What kind of business did Kealoha's parents own?
   B. How long did Santos live in the Philippines before moving to Tacoma?
   C. How did Pup react when Kealoha and Santos listened to the radio?
   D. Under what circumstances did Kealoha first become aware of Santos?

4. One of the main ideas of the second paragraph (lines 15–31) is that:

   F. as a young woman, Kealoha often changed jobs because she quickly grew bored at each position.
   G. Kealoha's work as a musical group manager earned her the nickname Ani "The Fearless."
   H. working many jobs at once, Kealoha lost the opportunity to spend holidays with her family.
   J. because of her abilities and outgoing nature, Kealoha held a variety of jobs as a young woman.

5. According to the passage, all of the following were aspects of Kealoha's time at the Moana Hotel EXCEPT:

   A. cooking meals in the kitchen.
   B. working there as a chambermaid.
   C. receiving a promotion for her efforts.
   D. seeing celebrities.

6. In the passage, the statement that Santos appeared even younger than he was is best described as the opinion of:

   F. Kealoha which she expresses to him in an effort to compliment him.
   G. Santos which he states to the men in his command in hopes that Kealoha will overhear.
   H. Kealoha which she forms while working at Quartermaster Corps.
   J. Kealoha which replaced her earlier impression of him that he reminded her of someone she once knew.

7. The passage indicates that Kealoha's primary response to the events described in the fourth paragraph (lines 39–46) is:

   A. sadness due to her sisters' departure.
   B. concern about the loss of her heritage.
   C. optimism gained from new opportunities.
   D. dismay over the increased number of troops.

8. According to the passage, as a young woman, Kealoha made goals for herself that included:

   F. opening her own market.
   G. owning a farm on a different island.
   H. going to university on the mainland.
   J. traveling to different cities.

9. The passage indicates that compared to her work at her parents' market, Kealoha's job at the Moana offered:

   A. longer hours.
   B. shorter hours.
   C. fewer opportunities for advancement.
   D. more opportunities for advancement.

10. That Santos felt self-conscious about his age was:

    F. a confession he shared with the men in his platoon to put them at ease with him.
    G. an insight Kealoha made based on the manner in which he spoke to her.
    H. a question Kealoha posed to him in the first private conversation the two shared.
    J. an opinion he held because he had been promoted so early in his career.

Passage II

SOCIAL SCIENCE: This passage is adapted from the article "A Mann for All Seasons" by Tiptan Held (©2007 by Brookvale).

Held is reviewing the biography *Lasting Vision* by Thomas Younger.

In 1837 the state of Massachusetts formed the first-of-its-kind State Board of Education, and the search began for someone to fill the role of First Secretary. Horace Mann, a state senator from Massachusetts, accepted the position, despite a successful
5 and promising political career and the lack of any demonstrated interest in public education prior to his appointment. He was supposedly drawn to the role solely because it offered a dependable salary, a perk not offered to state legislators. Whatever his motivation may have been, as Thomas Younger writes
10 in his new biography, "Once the reins of the school system were placed in the sure hands of Horace Mann, the landscape of education in Massachusetts, and indeed the United States, was to change forever." And so it proved: after accepting the position, Mann turned to his duties with an unexpected, almost
15 unbelievable zeal, foregoing all other interests, both political and private, in their pursuit.

Thus began the legacy of the man who would eventually become known as the "Father of American Public Education," a surprising epitaph for a man whose own education, at least
20 during his formative years, was not particularly exceptional. Mann was born in 1796 in Franklin, Massachusetts and was raised by his parents on their family farm. From the time he was ten years old until he was twenty, he never attended more than six weeks of school in any given year. Some years, he didn't
25 attend at all. However, his Yankee upbringing had taught him the value of hard work and self-reliance. With the support of a tutor and using the resources of the town library, he studied on his own. He enrolled at Brown University at the age of twenty and graduated three years later as class valedictorian.

30 Younger's biography paints a picture of Mann as one of the most visionary and energetic reformers of his time, as well as one of the most prolific. He had already reached the relatively advanced age of forty-one when he was named First Secretary of the Board of Education, making the quality and quantity of
35 his accomplishments even more impressive. In what Younger calls "an unprecedented and daringly progressive campaign," Mann implemented the "common school" model, in which children from all social classes attended the same school. He argued that the common school model benefited all of society
40 and insisted that the single most important responsibility of a

civilized state is the education of its citizens. In his description of Mann's reforms, Younger seems to invite a comparison to the similarly "radical" notions of abolition—a cause Mann would champion with equal fervor upon his election to the U.S. Senate
45 in 1848—and the Civil Rights movement almost a century later.

Mann's considerable dedication to reform was certainly impressive, all the more so considering the hardships he faced along the way, both public and private. Then, as now, education reform was a hotly-contested subject, and Mann encountered
50 resistance at nearly every turn, not only from the institutions he was trying to change but also from students, parents, and teachers. His stance on nonsectarian instruction angered many parents and various religious groups, just as his controversial proposal for the disuse of corporal punishment displeased a
55 group of schoolteachers in Boston. Mann also met with difficulty in his personal life; his grief over his first wife's death in 1832 never wholly left him. At about the same time, he inherited substantial debts left by his only brother. Despite these difficulties (or perhaps because of them), Mann's tireless
60 pursuit of his vision for change continued unabated, fueled by his singular passion and boundless energy.

Younger's well-structured narrative of Mann's life and works goes far beyond a simple recounting of his actions and achievements. By following him from his beginnings as
65 a self-educated young man, through his personal and professional travails and triumphs, to his eventually being named President of Antioch University, a larger story than that of a single individual emerges. Mann's crusade for public education becomes the story of reform itself, of drive and determination,
70 of struggle and sacrifice, and how the vision of one person, pursued relentlessly and with sufficient vigor, can spark change for an entire state, a nation, and indeed the world. Within a year of his appointment as Secretary of the Board of Education, Mann had visited every schoolhouse in the state to assess
75 personally the condition and quality of each. In 1838, Mann instituted the "normal" school system (a school whose primary purpose is to train high-school graduates to be teachers themselves, thereby establishing "norms") in Massachusetts and founded *The Common School Journal*, a publication in
80 which Mann, acting as sole editor, laid down his principles for public education. During his tenure, he also published a series of annual reports, which were circulated widely and influenced other school systems to adopt similar measures. It was this commitment not only to ideals but also to action,
85 Younger seems to tell us, that made Horace Mann an example for others who seek to effect social reform.

11. The passage's author most strongly implies that Mann's interest in public education:

   A. was the result of a lifelong passion for education reform.
   B. gradually lessened after his appointment as First Secretary of the Board of Education.
   C. began in earnest after his appointment as First Secretary of the Board of Education.
   D. ended abruptly after his wife's death in 1832.

12. According to the passage, who disapproved of the proposal described in lines 52–55?

   F. A group of Boston schoolteachers
   G. Younger
   H. Mann's parents
   J. Mann himself

13. As portrayed in the passage, Mann's reaction to the personal hardships he faced is best described as:

   A. angry and afraid.
   B. uncaring and selfish.
   C. surprised but confident.
   D. saddened but resolute.

14. In the statement in lines 10–13, Younger most strongly emphasizes:

   F. the significance and impact of Mann's leadership as First Secretary of the Board of Education.
   G. the folly of Mann's decision to give up a promising career in the legislature.
   H. how Mann's upbringing had prepared him perfectly for his new position.
   J. the contrast between the state education in Massachusetts and other places in the United States.

15. According to the passage, Younger believes Mann sets an example for others who seek social reform because Mann:

   A. never sought the approval of others for his efforts to reform public education.
   B. recognized that education reform can come about only through increased legislation.
   C. was relentless in the pursuit of his own education.
   D. was committed not only to his ideals but also to action.

16. The passage most strongly suggests that Mann felt the use of corporal punishment in education was:

   F. necessary.
   G. improper.
   H. motivational.
   J. justified.

17. Lines 35–38 most nearly mean that Mann:

   A. patterned his model for a new school system on one that existed elsewhere.
   B. cautiously instituted small reforms, one at a time, in order to achieve his goals.
   C. fearlessly challenged the accepted social norms of the period in his efforts to reform education.
   D. was more concerned with cost-saving measures than was his predecessor.

18. The passage's author characterizes Mann in the U.S. Senate most nearly as:

   F. boldly engaged in other important reforms affecting the nation.
   G. obsessively focused on the issue of education.
   H. surprisingly inconsistent in his voting record on education issues.
   J. amazingly articulate about the role of the state in educating its citizens.

19. For the passage's author, lines 72–75 mainly serve to support his earlier point that:

   A. Mann had left the state legislature in order to be able to travel more.
   B. there weren't enough schoolhouses in Massachusetts in the nineteenth century.
   C. Mann tirelessly pursued his goal of improving and reforming education.
   D. Mann was not effective at his job due to his extensive travel.

20. Another reviewer of Younger's book sums up Mann in this way:

   Perhaps the single most important figure in American education reform, Horace Mann devoted himself entirely to the cause of public education. Despite facing widespread criticism, Mann never wavered in his commitment to universal education, and the effects of his reforms can still be seen today.

   How does this account of Mann compare to that of the passage's author?

   F. This account emphasizes Mann's commitment to reform, while the passage's author debunks it.
   G. Both offer a similar and complimentary summary of Mann's work as a reformer.
   H. Both offer a similar and critical summary of Mann's work as a reformer.
   J. This account mentions Mann facing criticism, while the passage's author doesn't.

Passage III

HUMANITIES: This passage is adapted from the memoir *Sewing Circles* by Maria Erica Soreno (©2008 by Maria Erica Soreno).

Ingrid Bergman was a popular actress in Hollywood films of the 1940s and 1950s.

In the autumn of 1945, my older sister Ines and I lived with Tia Elena in her little house in Pasadena. There, working from her little shop on Paso Robles Street, Tia Elena had made quite a name for herself as a skilled *costurera*, sewing beautiful
5 dresses for the women in the surrounding neighborhoods. In fact, her work was of such quality that sometimes she would get special orders from some of the nearby film studios, where she had worked years previously.

It was one such order she had received from RKO Radio
10 Pictures that seemed particularly important to her: a gorgeous, flowing, beige crepe evening gown, so intricate that I knew it must be for something or someone special.

"It's the most beautiful dress you've ever done, *Tia*," I told her.

Tia Elena looked at me and smiled. "*Sì, hija,* and so it
15 should be—it's for the most beautiful woman in Hollywood. Would you and your sister like to meet her?"

Ines and I exchanged glances and said nothing, uncertain if our aunt was making a genuine offer.

The next day, however, with the just-finished gown pack-
20 aged carefully in a deceivingly plain white box, Tia Elena called to Ines and me to join her on the trip to the studio to deliver the dress. Excited, but still a little doubtful, Ines and I climbed into the car, Ines in the front and I in the back, holding the box, with its delicate contents, on my lap.

25 We arrived at the studio lot, met by a guard at the gate who smiled at Tia Elena and winked at my sister and me. "Welcome to RKO," he said and raised the gate to let us in. We parked the car and began walking towards one of the many buildings on the premises. Ines and I looked about in amazement at the
30 bustling studio lot—workers, costumed actors, cameramen, and hundreds of other people of every description were walking, running, standing, shouting, and laughing in a riot of noise and color. Tia Elena took the package from me. "Hold your sister's hand, Maria," she said, "We need to stay together."

35 Despite the chaos and the fact that many of the large buildings looked nearly identical, Tia Elena walked steadily onward, leading Ines and me up to one of the buildings, indistinguishable from the others apart from a large sign with the number 20 over the entrance. Inside was much the same as
40 outside—people everywhere, moving equipment, shouting directions, and generally appearing rushed. Apparently unfazed by all the activity, Tia Elena led us confidently through the maze of equipment and crowd of people until we arrived at a door with a star and the name "Ms. Bergman" on it.

45 After a quick, reassuring glance at my sister and me, Tia Elena knocked on the door, which was answered almost immediately by a woman so strikingly tall and beautiful that I could barely think to say anything. Tia Elena came to our rescue, however. "Ms. Bergman, these are my nieces, Ines and
50 Maria. I hope you don't mind visitors, but they were eager to hear your opinion about the dress."

Ms. Bergman smiled at us and crossed to where Tia was unfolding the dress for her. She gasped and exclaimed, "Oh, Elena—it's the most wonderful gown I've ever seen; I'm
55 afraid I'll never do it justice!" Tia Elena beamed with an artist's pride, but only replied modestly, "I'm so happy you like it, Ms. Bergman, but I could never have done it without help from Maria and Ines."

"Is that true, girls?" asked Ms. Bergman, and before we
60 could answer, said, "Well, your aunt is certainly lucky to have such helpful nieces. And please, enough of this 'Ms. Bergman' business; please call me Ingrid, and I'll call you Maria and Ines, just like friends should. Now, such expert work surely deserves a little reward." She took two photographs of herself
65 from a desk drawer and signed them. On mine she added, "For my friend, Maria," and then did likewise for Ines.

In my memory, our visit to the studio that day unfolds like a scene in my very own movie, full of spectacle and wonder and emotion. Ingrid was filming *Notorious* on the day of our
70 visit, and although I've seen all of her films, I still think of that particular film as "ours." Her masterful portrayal of the tragic character Alicia Huberman always makes me remember that day, if only because it stands in such stark contrast to the smiling, friendly, generous woman I met. She was to say, much
75 later, in an interview:

"I have no regrets. I wouldn't have lived my life the way I did if I was going to worry about what people were going to say."

I was only eleven when I met Ingrid Bergman and couldn't really understand the magnitude of her accomplishments, but as
80 I read those words now, spoken of a life lived on a stage, with successes and hardships alike in plain view for all to see, I can't help but recognize, and be inspired by, a truly independent spirit.

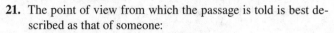

21. The point of view from which the passage is told is best described as that of someone:

    A. visiting a movie studio with her aunt and sister.

    B. wanting to become an actor like Bergman.

    C. trying to adjust to life in California.

    D. looking back warmly on meeting Bergman.

22. According to the passage, which of the following events occurred last chronologically?

    F. The narrator feels inspired by Bergman.

    G. The narrator and her sister receive photographs from Bergman.

    H. The narrator visits a movie studio.

    J. Tía Elena finishes the beautiful gown.

23. Through her description of her meeting with Bergman, the narrator portrays Bergman most nearly as:

    A. snobbish.

    B. rushed.

    C. friendly.

    D. regretful.

24. Based on the passage, the narrator's reaction to being first addressed by Bergman is one of:

    F. fright and silence.

    G. envy and jealousy.

    H. awe and speechlessness.

    J. excitement and doubt.

25. It is reasonable to infer that, following their first meeting with Bergman, the narrator and her sister:

    A. instantly understood the impact that meeting Bergman would have on their lives.

    B. were too busy helping their aunt with her work to think much about it.

    C. continued to see Bergman's movies in order to recapture fond memories of meeting Bergman.

    D. sold the rare autographed photos to a collector so they could afford beautiful dresses.

26. The narrator describes the building they visit at RKO as:

    F. "a riot of noise and color" (lines 32–33).

    G. "full of spectacle and wonder" (line 68).

    H. "indistinguishable from the others" (line 38).

    J. "strikingly tall and beautiful" (line 47).

27. As it is used in line 68, the word *spectacle* most nearly means:

    A. marvel.

    B. performance.

    C. demonstration.

    D. extravaganza.

28. The narrator makes the comparison in lines 73–74 to describe Bergman's:

    F. ability to act in almost any kind of movie.

    G. portrayal of a character completely different from herself.

    H. appeal to fans of all ages.

    J. dramatic reaction to meeting the narrator.

29. Based on the passage, how old was the narrator when she met Bergman?

    A. Twenty

    B. Sixteen

    C. Thirteen

    D. Eleven

30. It is most reasonable to infer from the passage that the narrator gains an appreciation of Bergman's accomplishments primarily as a result of:

    F. the way Bergman treated her when they met.

    G. the influence of her aunt and sister.

    H. her perspective as an adult.

    J. finally seeing Bergman wearing the dress Tía Elena had made.

Passage IV

SOCIAL SCIENCE: Passage A is adapted from *What is Life?* by Harrison George (© 2002 by Melman University Press). Passage B is adapted from "Planet, Dwarf Planet, or Celestial Body: Why Pluto is no Longer Considered to be a Planet" by Anne Goldberg-Baldwin.

Passage A by Harrison George

Few people have difficulty defining biology as "the study of life," which is a practical enough definition and certainly true. It may seem contradictory, then, that one of the most difficult and controversial issues biologists have to contend with
5 is defining what life really is. Since the time of Aristotle, there have been any number of definitions of life put forth, but as yet, there has been none that is accepted by all.

The very essence of a definition is to describe the complex in terms of the simple, but with a concept as vastly complex as
10 life itself, the use of simple terms can be problematic. Some of the more frequently-used conditions put forth for "alive-ness" are complexity, autonomy, self-reproduction, evolution, and metabolism, all of which are assuredly qualities possessed by entities we would recognize as "alive." However, is a for-
15 est fire, which self-reproduces and consumes fuel to produce energy (and therefore can be said to possess a "metabolism") alive? How about a computer virus that can evolve or mutate according to its "environment"?

Perhaps the answer eventually to be found in the quest for
20 a definition of life won't really be an answer at all, but rather a whole series of new questions—questions that will open up new areas of study and help scientists gain a broader understanding of life and its place in the universe. Remember that it wasn't so very long ago that scientists considered there to be only four
25 "elements" in the universe: fire, air, water, and earth. However, it was through efforts to gain a deeper understanding—to find a definition, if you will—of those four elements that scientists made monumental discoveries in physical and molecular chemistry. Scientists could finally define water, for example,
30 as a compound composed of two hydrogen atoms bonded to a single atom of oxygen. Now, such a straightforward and simple description of so esoteric a concept as life may be unrealistic, but that is a small matter. Perhaps in the end, rather than leading us to an answer, it will be the search itself that brings us
35 closest to understanding what it is to be "alive."

Passage B by Anne Goldberg-Baldwin

On August 24th, 2006, the International Astrological Union (IAU) issued a decree that effectively stripped Pluto of its planetary status from our solar system. While this debate surrounded Pluto, the true debate stems from the definition
40 of what constitutes a planet. Until the IAU's Resolution 5A, which defines the term, the definition of "planet" was deemed a fundamental assumption in the field of astronomy.

So what is a planet anyways? Why is a protoplanet not considered a planet? Why are others considered dwarf plan-
45 ets? What about asteroids and other objects in the galaxy and beyond? In simple terms, Resolution 5A defined a planet as a celestial body that orbits the sun, has enough mass to maintain a mostly circular orbit, and has cleared neighboring bodies from its orbital path.

50 Many celestial bodies fall short of this clearly defined term. Scientists debate what constitutes a "mostly circular orbit:" does it have to be a perfect circle? Most planets in our solar system do not have perfect circular orbits, but rather have slight variations that make the pathway an ellipse instead. Consider
55 Earth: there are times of the year in which the earth is closer to the sun and times when it is further away. Venus and Mercury have more elliptical patterns, and therefore experience more drastic differences in climate. Since Pluto is so much further away from the sun, isn't an increase in its orbit's elliptical shape
60 to be expected, if not amplified?

As for the other parameters, Pluto's mass is decidedly less than that of other planets (it is even smaller than Earth's moon), but it still is massive enough to maintain an orbit around the sun. However, how massive is massive enough to be a planet? One
65 reason to account for the anomaly of Pluto's orbit is its largest moon, Charon. Charon is approximately half the size of Pluto, which is significantly larger in ratio than other celestial bodies' moons. Due to the gravitational forces exerted on each other, some scientists have suggested that Pluto and Charon should
70 instead be treated as a dual orbiting system of celestial bodies, rather than the relationship of planet and moon.

While it is certainly true that Pluto does not follow the definition of "planet" by strictest standards, astronomers opposed to Resolutions 5A argue that the nomenclature defined is
75 confusing, if not misleading, and that not enough astronomers were given a vote. If the process were opened up to more astronomers to weigh in, would Pluto have remained under the planetary umbrella?

31. It can reasonably be inferred that the author of Passage A believes that compared with current efforts to define life, efforts to define the elements:

    A. definitely answered more questions.

    B. led to a less straightforward set of more complex qualities and conditions.

    C. were ultimately more satisfying.

    D. required greater cooperation among scientists.

32. Passage A suggests that searching for a definition of "life" will most likely:

    F. lead to confusion within the scientific community.

    G. be impossible given the history of contention on this question.

    H. lead scientists to broaden the definition to include viruses.

    J. spur new discoveries in the field of biology.

33. The author of Passage A describes the four elements of the universe in lines 23–25 primarily to:

    A. give an example of a more fruitful scientific pursuit.

    B. downplay concerns about the difficulty of defining life.

    C. draw a comparison with current questions about the nature of aliveness.

    D. introduce a less contentious precedent.

34. The author of Passage B mentions Earth and Venus (lines 54–58) primarily to:

    F. offer examples that raise questions about one aspect of Resolution 5A's definition of "planet."

    G. exemplify the types of celestial bodies that the author believes should be defined as planets.

    H. contrast true planets, which are closer to the sun, with dwarf planets such as Pluto, which are typically further away.

    J. provide additional examples of celestial bodies whose status as planets was once debated.

35. According to Passage B, astronomers who oppose Resolution 5A make which of the following claims?

    A. Resolution 5A clarified a confusing aspect of the definition of "planet."

    B. More astronomers should be made members of the International Astrological Union.

    C. The definition included in Resolution 5A may have been intended to mislead.

    D. Resolution 5A may not reflect the views of the majority of astronomers.

36. The author of Passage B indicates that some scientists believe Pluto and Charon should not be defined as planet and moon because:

    F. Pluto does not have enough mass to maintain a circular orbit by itself.

    G. Charon is too large to be categorized as a moon.

    H. such a definition requires a planet and moon to function as a dual orbiting system.

    J. the effect these celestial bodies have on one another makes another definition more appropriate.

37. The author of Passage B most directly suggests that, before 2006, the definition of "planet":

    A. was generally accepted by astronomers.

    B. was voted on by members of the International Astrological Union.

    C. stripped Pluto of its status as a planet.

    D. was a subject of long-standing debate in the field of astronomy.

38. Both passages support the idea that disagreement among scientists may:

    F. lead to simplistic definitions of complex concepts.

    G. be part of a process of answering questions about natural phenomena.

    H. cause rifts within scientific organizations.

    J. be more prevalent in the history of astronomy and biology than that of chemistry.

39. Compared with Passage B, Passage A is more concerned with:

    A. criticizing scientific controversy within the scientific community.

    B. outcome rather than process.

    C. narrower historical scope.

    D. opportunities for discovery.

40. Which of the following statements exemplifies a main similarity in the focus of the two passages?

    F. Both passages discuss questions that have sparked controversy within their respective fields.

    G. Both passages critique a lack of consensus concerning fundamental scientific principles.

    H. Both passages focus on moments of uncertainty with regard to scientific definitions that have since been definitively settled.

    J. Both passages discuss earth, though Passage A is focused on the element earth while Passage B focuses on the planet Earth.

END OF TEST
STOP! DO NOT TURN THE PAGE UNTIL TOLD TO DO SO.
DO NOT RETURN TO A PREVIOUS TEST.

Chapter 16
Reading
Practice Test 4
Answers and
Explanations

READING PRACTICE TEST 4 ANSWERS

1.	B	21.	D
2.	H	22.	F
3.	B	23.	C
4.	J	24.	H
5.	A	25.	C
6.	H	26.	H
7.	C	27.	A
8.	J	28.	G
9.	D	29.	D
10.	G	30.	H
11.	C	31.	A
12.	F	32.	J
13.	D	33.	C
14.	F	34.	F
15.	D	35.	D
16.	G	36.	J
17.	C	37.	A
18.	F	38.	G
19.	C	39.	D
20.	G	40.	F

SCORE YOUR PRACTICE TEST

Step A

Count the number of correct answers: _____. This is your *raw score*.

Step B

Use the score conversion table below to look up your raw score. The number to the left is your *scale score*: _____.

Reading Scale Conversion Table

Scale Score	Raw Score	Scale Score	Raw Score	Scale Score	Raw Score
36	39-40	24	27	12	9-10
35	38	23	26	11	7-8
34	37	22	24-25	10	6
33	35-36	21	23	9	5
32	34	20	21-22	8	–
31	33	19	20	7	4
30	–	18	19	6	3
29	32	17	17-18	5	–
28	31	16	16	4	2
27	30	15	14-15	3	–
26	29	14	12-13	2	1
25	28	13	11	1	0

READING PRACTICE TEST 4 EXPLANATIONS

Passage I

1. **B** This reasoning question asks about the point of the view of the narrator. Because this is a general question, it should be done after all the specific questions. Look for the Golden Thread. While a number of other people, including Kealoha's family, customers, and Santos, are all mentioned in the passage, they are all described from Kealoha's point of view, and only as she remembers them. Eliminate (A), (C), and (D) because none of these matches the Golden Thread. The correct answer is (B).

2. **H** This reference question asks for a statement about the *Moana Hotel* that is NOT supported by the passage. When a question asks what is NOT mentioned in the passage, eliminate answers that are mentioned. Look for the lead words *Moana Hotel* to find the window for the question. The Moana Hotel is described as *world-famous* in line 28, so eliminate (F). Lines 32–33 indicate that Kealoha worked at the hotel as a chambermaid; eliminate (G). Keep (H) because the passage does not discuss the number of *rooms* at the Moana. Line 34 states that the hotel hosted *an endless parade of visitors, from the obscure to the famous.* Eliminate (J). The correct answer is (H).

3. **B** This reference question asks for the question that is *NOT answered by the passage.* There is not a good lead word in this question, so work the question later. Eliminate (A) because line 8 indicates that Kealoha worked at her parents' *market stall.* Keep (B) because the passage does not indicate how long *Santos* lived in the *Philippines before moving to Tacoma.* Eliminate (C) because lines 64–65 indicate that, while Kealoha and Santos listened to radio programs, Pup was *sitting and staring at the radio.* Eliminate (D) because lines 49–50 state that Kealoha met Santos when she began working at the *Quartermaster Corps.* The correct answer is (B).

4. **J** This reasoning question asks about the main idea of *the second paragraph.* Read the second paragraph as the window. The paragraph lists the different jobs Kealoha held and relates them each to her personality. There is no evidence to support the fact that she grew *bored* with the jobs, so eliminate (F). The passage does mention her job as a *musical group manager*, but it is not the main idea of the paragraph. Eliminate (G). There is no mention of whether Kealoha *lost the opportunity to spend holidays with her family*, so eliminate (H). Keep (J) because it matches the text from the passage. The correct answer is (J).

5. **A** This reference question asks for a statement that was NOT an aspect of *Kealoha's time at the Moana Hotel.* When a question asks what is NOT mentioned in the passage, eliminate answers that are mentioned. Look for the lead words *Moana Hotel* to find the window for the question. The third paragraph mentions Kealoha working as a chambermaid, seeing famous people, and being promoted for her work, which supports (B), (C), and (D), respectively. Eliminate these answer choices. Keep (A) because the fifth paragraph mentions her *cooking meals in* a *tiny kitchen* at home, not at the Moana. The correct answer is (A).

6. **H** This reasoning question asks whose opinion is described by the statement that *Santos appeared even younger than he was.* Look for the lead words *Santos* and *younger* to find the window for the question. In lines 69–70, Kealoha thinks about the first time she met Santos and remembers that *he was*

slightly-built and fair-skinned, which made him look even younger than he was. Eliminate (F) since she thinks this thought instead of expressing it vocally. Eliminate (G) since this is Kealoha's thought, not Santos's. Keep (H) because it matches the text from the passage. Eliminate (J) because the thought describes the first time she meets Santos; therefore, she does not have an earlier impression of him. The correct answer is (H).

7. **C** This reference question asks about Kealoha's primary response to the events described in the fourth paragraph. Read the fourth paragraph as the window. Lines 41–42 describe Kealoha as *eager to take advantage of the new opportunities citizenship offered*. Although her *sisters* and *troops* are both mentioned, there is no evidence given for her feeling either *sadness* or *dismay*, respectively, related to these groups; eliminate (A) and (D). Eliminate (B) because there is no mention of a *concern about the loss of her heritage*. Keep (C) because it matches the text from the passage. The correct answer is (C).

8. **J** This reference question asks about Kealoha's *goals for herself* as a *young woman*. Look for the lead words *goals* and *young woman* to find the window for the question. Lines 1–2 state, *As a young woman, Ani Kealoha had never dreamt of someday owning a hotel.* Later in that paragraph, lines 11–13 describe Kealoha's aspirations *to have enough money to visit the faraway places these visitors would talk about— Los Angeles, Sydney, or even New York.* Look for an answer choice that matches this text from the passage. Eliminate (F) because, though Kealoha worked in her parents' *market*, there is no mention in the passage of her wanting to open one of her own. Eliminate (G) because there is no mention of her wanting to own a *farm*. Lines 42–43 indicate that Kealoha's sisters *chose to go to university on the mainland*, but Kealoha does not; eliminate (H). Keep (J) because it matches the text from the passage. The correct answer is (J).

9. **D** This reference question asks what *Kealoha's job at the Moana* offered *compared to her work at her parents' market*. Look for the lead words *market* and *Moana* to find the window for the question. Lines 7–14 state that Ani helped serve *tourists and military personnel*, and her *aspirations of wealth* only fueled dreams of traveling. The third paragraph states that Kealoha proved her *capability and resourcefulness* while at the Moana, ultimately earning several promotions. Eliminate (A) and (B) because the passage does not discuss the *hours* Kealoha worked. Kealoha is described in the third paragraph as having been promoted twice while at the Moana Hotel, and there is no evidence to show she was ever given added responsibility or higher pay while working for her parents, so eliminate (C). Keep (D) because the text indicates that Kealoha was promoted at the Moana. The correct answer is (D).

10. **G** This reference question asks about *Santos's* feeling of *self-consciousness* about his *age*. Look for the lead words *Santos* and *self-conscious* to find the window for the question. Lines 69–75 say that Santos looked *younger* than he was. *As such, he made special effort to maintain what he felt was the "proper" military bearing…He was terse, but not rude, and called her "Ms. Kealoha." She could tell that he was trying to make his voice sound deeper than it actually was.* Therefore, Kealoha infers that Santos is self-conscious about his age, based on how he acts toward her. Look for an answer choice that matches this text. Eliminate (F) and (H) because the passage does not say that Santos voiced concerns about his age. Keep (G) because it matches the text from the passage. Eliminate (J) because there is no evidence given for how Santos may have felt about being *promoted*. The correct answer is (G).

Passage II

11. **C** This reasoning question asks what the author implies about *Mann's interest in public education*. Look for the lead words *Mann* and *public education* to find the window for the question. Lines 4–6 say that Mann accepted the position of First Secretary of Education *despite...the lack of any demonstrated interest in public education prior to his appointment* and carried out his duties with *an almost unbelievable zeal*. Eliminate (A) and (B) because they contradict the text from the passage. Keep (C) because it matches the text. Eliminate (D) because lines 58–61 state that Mann continued his efforts for education reform after his wife's death. The correct answer is (C).

12. **F** This reference question asks who *disapproved of the proposal described in lines 52–55*. Read a window around the line reference. The *proposal* in lines 52–55 was for *the disuse of corporal punishment*, which *displeased a group of schoolteachers in Boston*. Keep (F) because it matches the text from the passage. Eliminate (G), (H), and (J) because there is no support in the passage that biographer *Younger, Mann's parents*, or *Mann himself* disapproved of Mann's proposal. The correct answer is (F).

13. **D** This reference question asks about the description of *Mann's reaction to the personal hardships he faced*. Look for the lead words *Mann* and *personal hardships* to find the window for the question. Lines 56–60 state that the grief Mann felt over the death of his first wife *never wholly left him*, and that he at about the same time, *inherited substantial debt*. Nonetheless, his *vision for change continued unabated*. There is no evidence in the passage that he felt either *angry* or *afraid*; eliminate (A). Similarly, Mann is never described as *uncaring* or *selfish*; in fact, he is consistently shown to be quite the opposite. Eliminate (B). While there is evidence that Mann was quite *confident*, nothing supports that he may have been *surprised* about either event; eliminate (C). Keep (D) because it matches the text from the passage. The correct answer is (D).

14. **F** This reasoning question asks what *Younger most strongly emphasizes* in lines 10–13. Read a window around the line reference. The passage states that Younger writes, *"Once the reins of the school system were placed in the sure hands of Horace Mann, the landscape of education in Massachusetts, and indeed the United States, was to change forever."* Keep (F) because it matches the text from the passage. Eliminate (G) because the passage does not emphasize the *folly* of his decision to accept the role. Eliminate (H) because the passage does not discuss how *Mann's upbringing* prepared him for the *new position*. These lines do not compare the *state education* in *Massachusetts* with that of *other places*, so eliminate (J). The correct answer is (F).

15. **D** This reasoning question asks why *Younger believes Mann sets an example for others who seek social reform*. Look for the lead words *social reform* to find the window for the question. In the last sentence of the passage, the author states that Mann was *an example for others who seek to effect social reform* because of his *commitment not only to ideals but also to action*. There is no mention in the passage of Mann *seeking approval*, so eliminate (A). While some of Mann's reforms involved legislation, there is no evidence that reform can come about *only* through increased legislation. Eliminate (B). While the passage mentions Mann's own education, this idea isn't what the author offers as *an example for others who seek social reform*. Eliminate (C). Keep (D) because it matches the text from the passage. The correct answer is (D).

16. **G** This reference question asks what the passage most strongly suggests about Mann's thoughts on *the use of corporal punishment in education*. Look for the lead words *corporal punishment in education* to find the window for the question. Lines 52–55 state that Mann advocated for *the disuse of corporal punishment*. Eliminate (F), as Mann did not deem it *necessary*. Keep (G), since *improper* matches the text from the passage. Eliminate (H) because the text does not match *motivational*. Eliminate (J) because Mann never describes corporal punishment as *justified*. The correct answer is (G).

17. **C** This reasoning question asks what *lines 35–38 most nearly mean*. Read a window around the line reference. The lines state that Mann's campaign was *unprecedented and daringly progressive* because it enabled *children from all social classes* to attend *the same school*. Eliminate (A) because the campaign was *unprecedented*, meaning it had not been done elsewhere. Eliminate (B) because *cautiously instated small forms, one at a time* does not match *daringly progressive*. Keep (C) because it matches the text from the passage. Eliminate (D) because neither *cost-saving measures* nor *his predecessor* are talked about in these lines. The correct answer is (C).

18. **F** This reasoning question asks how the passage's author *characterizes Mann in the U.S. Senate*. Look for the lead words *U.S. Senate* to find the window for the question. Lines 41–45 state that Mann had *similarly "radical" notions of abolition, a cause Mann would champion with equal fervor upon his election to the U.S. Senate*. Keep (F) because it matches the text from the passage. Eliminate (G) because *obsessively* would mean he focused on education only. Eliminate (H) because Mann's *voting record* is never mentioned. While Mann certainly claimed that education was the responsibility of the state, he did so as First Secretary, not as a U.S. Senator; eliminate (J). The correct answer is (F).

19. **C** This reasoning question asks how lines 72–75 support the author's earlier point. Read a window around the line reference. The passage states, *Within a year of his appointment as Secretary of the Board of Education, Mann had visited every schoolhouse in the state to assess personally the condition and quality of each*. This is an example of *how the vision of one person, pursued relentlessly and with sufficient vigor, can spark change for an entire state, a nation, and indeed the world*. There is no mention of Mann's desire to *travel* being the reason he left the state legislature; eliminate (A). There is no mention of the number of *schoolhouses* being sufficient or not; eliminate (B). Keep (C) because it matches the text from the passage. Choice (D) contradicts the passage, which describes Mann as successful primarily because of the energy and personal attention he put into his job. The correct answer is (C).

20. **G** This reasoning question asks how another *account of Mann* compares *to that of the passage's author*. Because this is a general question, it should be done after all the specific questions. Look for the Golden Thread. Both accounts use the same general criteria to praise Mann for his reforms and are not *critical* in tone—eliminate (F) and (H). Keep (G) because it matches the text from the passage. The passage's fourth paragraph recounts Mann facing criticism from various sources; eliminate (J). The correct answer is (G).

Passage III

21. **D**   This reasoning question asks about *the point of view* of the passage. Because this is a general question, it should be done after all the specific questions. Look for the Golden Thread. In the passage, the narrator fondly recalls meeting Ingrid Bergman. The narrator does indeed visit a *movie studio*, but the story's focus is on her meeting with Bergman, rather than her visit to the movie studio. Eliminate (A). The narrator never mentions wanting to become *an actress like Bergman*, so eliminate (B). There is no support for *adjusting to life* in California; the narrator merely mentions the fact that they live in California. Eliminate (C). Keep (D) because it matches the text from the passage. The correct answer is (D).

22. **F**   This reference question asks *which of the following events occurred last chronologically*. There is no good lead word for this question, so work this question later. In the final paragraph, the narrator writes, *as I read those words now...I can't help but be inspired*. She is writing about her feelings as an adult. Choices (G), (H), and (J) all occurred when she was a child, so each must have happened before her account as an adult. The correct answer is (F).

23. **C**   This reasoning question asks how the *narrator portrays Bergman* in the *description of her meeting with Bergman*. Look for the lead words *meeting with Bergman* to find the window for the question. Lines 53–66 describe the meeting as positive, and line 63 conveys Bergman's insistence on calling each other by their first names *just like friends should*. Look for an answer choice that matches this idea. Bergman's actions are not *snobbish*, so eliminate (A). The people on the movie studio lot, not Bergman, are described as *rushed* in line 41. Eliminate (B). Keep (C) because it matches the text from the passage. Eliminate (D) because it is contradicted by Bergman's quote, *I have no regrets*, in line 76. The correct answer is (C).

24. **H**   This reference question asks about the *narrator's reaction to being first addressed by Bergman*. Look for the lead words *addressed* and *Bergman* to find the window for the question. In lines 47–48, the narrator describes her initial impression of Bergman: She was *so strikingly tall and beautiful that I could barely think to say anything*. There is no evidence to show she was afraid, so eliminate (F). There is also no support that the narrator felt *envy* or *jealousy*; eliminate (G). Keep (H) because it matches the text from the passage. Eliminate (J) because the narrator describes herself and her sister as *excited* and *doubtful* in line 22, not during her meeting with Bergman. The correct answer is (H).

25. **C**   This reasoning question asks what the narrator and her sister did following *their first meeting with Bergman*. There is no good lead word for this question, so work this question later. In lines 70–73, the narrator says that she *has seen all of* Bergman's *films* and goes on to say how one film in particular *makes* her *remember that day*. Eliminate (A) because the final paragraph indicates that the narrator was too young to *really understand the magnitude of* Bergman's *accomplishments*. There is no evidence in the passage for the sisters being *too busy to think about* meeting Bergman, so eliminate (B). Keep (C) because it matches the text from the passage. Eliminate (D) because the text does not indicate that the photos were *sold*. The correct answer is (C).

26. **H** This reference question asks how *the narrator describes the building they visit at RKO*. Look for the lead word *RKO* to find the window for the question. In lines 35–38, the narrator indicates that *many of the large buildings looked nearly identical* and that the building they approached was *indistinguishable from the others*. Eliminate (F) because *riot of noise and color* refers to the movie studio lot in general, not to the buildings specifically. The narrator uses *full of spectacle and wonder* to describe her memories of the entire visit, so eliminate (G). Keep (H) because it matches the text from the passage. Eliminate (J) because it is a description of Bergman, not of the building. The correct answer is (H).

27. **A** This vocabulary in context question asks what the word *spectacle* means in line 68. Go back to the text, find the word *spectacle,* and cross it out. Carefully read the surrounding text to determine another word that would fit in the blank based on the context of the passage. In lines 68–69, the narrator compares her memories of meeting Bergman to a scene in a movie, *full of spectacle and wonder and emotion.* Therefore, spectacle should mean something like, "amazing sight." Keep (A) because *marvel* matches the text from the passage. Eliminate (B) because, while a *performance* might be an amazing sight, the narrator's memories are not likened to performances. Eliminate (C) and (D) because *demonstration* and *extravaganza* do not match "amazing sight." The correct answer is (A).

28. **G** This reasoning question asks why the *comparison* in lines 73–74 is made. Read a window around the line reference. The comparison is between the tragic character Bergman portrays in the film and *the smiling, friendly, generous woman I met.* Therefore, it emphasizes that Bergman portrayed a character very different from herself. Eliminate (F) because the comparison does not relate to Bergman's *ability to act in any kind of movie.* Keep (G) because it matches the text from the passage. Eliminate (H) because the passage never mentions Bergman's *appeal to fans of all ages.* The narrator describes Bergman as *smiling, friendly,* and *generous,* so eliminate (J). The correct answer is (G).

29. **D** This reference question asks how old the narrator was when she met Bergman. Look for the lead words *met Bergman* to find the window for the question. In line 78, the narrator states, *I was only eleven when I met Ingrid Bergman.* Eliminate (A), (B), and (C). The correct answer is (D).

30. **H** This reasoning question asks how the narrator *gains an appreciation of Bergman's accomplishments.* Look for the lead words *Bergman's accomplishments* to find the window for the question. Lines 78–82 mention the narrator's awareness of the *magnitude* of Bergman's *accomplishments,* and the narrator states, *as I read those words now...I can't help but recognize, and be inspired by, a truly independent spirit.* Eliminate (F) because the text says that the narrator's appreciation was gained as an adult. Eliminate (G) because there is no proof for the claim that the narrator's *aunt and sister* had any *influence* on the narrator's appreciation of Bergman. Keep (H) because it matches the text from the passage. There is no mention of seeing *Bergman wearing the dress Tia Elena made*; eliminate (J). The correct answer is (H).

Passage IV

31. **A**   This reference question asks what the author of Passage A believes about *efforts to define the elements* compared with *current efforts to define life*. Look for the lead words *elements* and *define life* to find the window for the question. In the opening paragraph, the author says this question is *one of the most difficult and controversial issues biologists have to contend with*. Lines 27–29 say that *scientists made monumental discoveries in physical and molecular chemistry* while making efforts to understand the *elements*. Therefore, efforts to define the elements produced more concrete results. Keep (A) because it matches the text from the passage. Eliminate (B) because it contradicts the text. Eliminate (C) because the passage does not indicate that efforts to define the elements were *more satisfying*. Eliminate (D) because the text does not indicate that the definition of the elements *required greater cooperation among scientists*. The correct answer is (A).

32. **J**   This reasoning question asks what Passage A suggests will most likely come about from *searching for a definition of "life."* Look for the lead words *definition of life* to find the window for the question. Although the author says in the third paragraph that perhaps the answer *won't be an answer at all, but a whole new series of questions,* he goes on to say that these questions could *open up new areas of study and help scientists gain a broader understanding of life*. Eliminate any answers that inconsistent with this text from the passage. Eliminate (F) because it is not consistent with the text. Eliminate (G) because the author doesn't indicate that the definition will be *impossible given the history of contention on this question*. Eliminate (H) because there is nothing about *viruses* in the text. Keep (J) because it matches the text from the passage. The correct answer is (J).

33. **C**   This reasoning question asks why *the author of Passage A describes the four elements of the universe*. Look for the lead words *four elements of the universe* to find the window for the question. After discussing the difficulties involved in defining life, the author reminds readers in the third paragraph to *remember it wasn't so very long ago that scientists considered there to be only four elements in the universe*...and then goes on to explain how efforts to define the elements led to *monumental discoveries*. The author mentions the elements to show what could be possible in the search to define life. Eliminate (A) because, although defining the elements resulted in more concrete discoveries than did current attempts to define life, the author is not arguing for one scientific pursuit over another. Eliminate (B) because the author does not attempt to *downplay* anything. Keep (C) because it matches the text from the passage. Eliminate (D) because the author does not try to establish *a precedent*. The correct answer is (C).

34. **F**   This reasoning question asks why *the author of Passage B mentions Earth and Venus in lines 54–58*. Read a window around the line reference. They are examples of planets that don't have *perfectly circular orbits*; so, they represent celestial bodies that *fall short of the clearly defined term of "planet."* Eliminate any answer choices that are inconsistent with this text from the passage. Keep (F) because it matches the text. Eliminate (G) because the author is not arguing for Earth and Venus to be *defined as planets:* they already are. The planets are mentioned as an example to support a point, not to demonstrate any *contrasts*, so eliminate (H). Eliminate (J) because it is not supported by the text: there is no evidence that Earth's status as a planet *was once debated*. The correct answer is (F).

35. **D**   This reference question asks what *claims* the *astronomers who oppose Resolution 5A* make, according to Passage B. Look for the lead words *oppose Resolution 5A* to find the window for the question. The final paragraph says that those who oppose the resolution argue that the definition *is confusing, if not misleading, and not enough astronomers were given a vote*. Eliminate any answer choices that are inconsistent with this information. Eliminate (A) because they argue that the resolution created, rather than *clarified*, confusion. Eliminate (B) because the text suggests that more members need to vote, not that the *Union* needs more *astronomers*. Eliminate (C) because there's no evidence that the resolution was *intentionally* misleading. Keep (D) because it matches the text from the passage. The correct answer is (D).

36. **J**   This reference question asks why *some scientists believe Pluto and Charon should not be defined as planet and moon*, according to Passage B. Look for the lead words *Pluto* and *Charon* to find the window for the question. The author says that some scientists *have suggested [they] be treated as a dual orbiting system of celestial bodies* because of *the gravitational forces they exert on each other*. Eliminate answers inconsistent with this text from the passage. Eliminate (F) because the issue is not about the *mass* of either of the bodies individually. Eliminate (G) because, though the text discusses the size of *Charon*, it does not say that this size prevents Charon from being *categorized as a moon*. Eliminate (H) because the passage does not indicate that the definition *requires a planet and moon to function as a dual orbiting system*; in fact, it suggests the opposite. Keep (J) because it matches the text from the passage. The correct answer is (J).

37. **A**   This reasoning question asks what the author of Passage B suggests about the *definition of "planet"* before *2006*. Look for the lead words *definition of planet* and *2006* to find the window for the question. Lines 36–42 say that in *2006*, the *IAU* passed the resolution defining "*planet*" and that the definition of "planet" had been a *fundamental assumption in the field of astronomy* until that point. Eliminate any answer choices that are inconsistent with this text from the passage. Keep (A) because it matches the text. Eliminate (B) because the IAU voted on the definition in 2006, not *before 2006*. Eliminate (C) because it's inconsistent with the chronology in the text—Pluto was stripped of its definition after the new definition was passed, not before. Eliminate (D) because the definition was a *fundamental assumption*, not a *subject of long-standing debate*. The correct answer is (A).

38. **G**   This reference question asks what both passages support about *disagreement among scientists*. Because this question asks about both passages, it should be done after the questions that ask about each passage individually. Consider the Golden Thread of both passages. Lines 33–35 in Passage A state that *the answer eventually to be found in the quest for a definition of life won't really be an answer at all, but rather a whole new series of questions* that *help scientists gain a broader understanding of life and its place in the universe*. The last paragraph of Passage B suggests that Pluto's status may have changed if *the process were opened up to more astronomers to weigh in*. Therefore, disagreement is part of the scholarly debate about scientific ideas. Look for an answer choice that matches this idea. Eliminate (F) because the passage doesn't talk about *simplistic definitions of complex concepts*. Keep (G) because it matches the text from the passage. Eliminate (H) because Passage A never mentions *rifts within scientific organizations*. Passage A never makes a distinction between disagreements in one field of science versus another, so eliminate (J). The correct answer is (G).

39. **D**   This reference question asks what *Passage A is more concerned with*, compared with Passage B. Because this question asks about both passages, it should be done after the questions that ask about each passage individually. Consider the Golden Thread of both passages. Passage A does not *criticize* controversy in the scientific community, but rather highlights the new ideas that can come from it. Eliminate (A). Eliminate (B) because Passage A focuses on the process of trying to define "life," rather than the actual outcome, which is still unknown. Eliminate (C) because Passage A does not have a *narrower historical scope* than Passage B does; in fact, the opposite is true. Keep (D) because it is true that Passage A is more concerned with *opportunities for discovery* than Passage B is. The correct answer is (D).

40. **F**   This reasoning question asks about a *main similarity in the focus of the two passages*. Because this question asks about both passages, it should be done after the questions that ask about each passage individually. Consider the Golden Thread of both passages. Both passages discuss a controversial topic in a particular field. Keep (F) because it matches this idea. Eliminate (G) because Passage A does not have any *critique of a lack of consensus*. Eliminate (H) because neither passage focuses on a definition that has been *definitively settled*. Eliminate (J) because, while both passages mention the word *earth*, neither the element earth nor the planet Earth is the focus of either passage. The correct answer is (F).

The Princeton Review®

BONUS MATERIALS

COLLEGE# ADMISSIONS# INSIDER

Admissions and Financial Aid Advice

While *ACT Prep* will prepare you for your exam, *College Admissions Insider* will help you navigate what comes next. The bonus materials included here contain invaluable information about finding your best fit college, wending your way through the financial aid process, figuring out post-college plans, and more. We wish you the best of luck with your studies and preparation for college.

Part 1

26 Tips to Help You Pay Less for College

by Kalman A. Chany, **author of**
Paying for College Without Going Broke

GETTING FINANCIAL AID

1. Learn how financial aid works. The more and the sooner you know about how need-based eligibility is determined, the better you can take steps to maximize such eligibility.

2. Apply for financial aid no matter what your circumstances. Some merit-based aid can only be awarded if the applicant has submitted financial aid application forms.

3. Don't wait until you receive an acceptance letter to apply for financial aid. Do it when applying for admission.

4. Complete all the required aid applications. All students seeking aid must submit the FAFSA (Free Application for Federal Student Aid); however, other forms may also be required. Check with each college to see what's required and when.

5. Get the best scores you can on the SAT or ACT. They are used not only in decisions for admission but they can also impact financial aid. If your scores and other stats exceed the school's admission criteria, you are likely to get a better aid package than a marginal applicant.

6. Apply strategically to colleges. Your chances of getting aid will be better at schools that have generous financial aid budgets. (Check the Financial Aid Ratings for schools on **PrincetonReview.com**.)

7. Don't rule out any school as too expensive. A generous aid award from a pricey private school can make it less costly than a public school with a lower sticker price.

8. Take advantage of education tax benefits. A dollar saved on taxes is worth the same as a dollar in scholarship aid. Look into Coverdells, 529 plans, education tax credits, and loan deductions.

SCHOLARSHIPS AND GRANTS

9. Get the best score you can on the PSAT: it is the National Merit Scholarship Qualifying Test and also used in the selection of students for other scholarships and recognition programs.

10. Check your eligibility for grants and scholarships in your state. Some (but not all) states will allow you to use such funds out of state.

11. Look for scholarships locally. Find out if your employer offers scholarships or tuition assistance plans for employees or family members. Also look into scholarships from your community groups and high school, as well as your church, temple, or mosque.

12. Look for outside scholarships realistically: they account for fewer than five percent of aid awarded. Research them at **PrincetonReview.com** or other free sites. Steer clear of scholarship search firms that charge fees and "promise" scholarships.

PAYING FOR COLLEGE

13. Start saving early. Too late? Start now. The more you save, the less you'll have to borrow.

14. Invest wisely. Considering a 529 plan? Compare your own state's plan, which may have tax benefits, with other states' programs. Get info at **SavingforCollege.com.**

15. If you have to borrow, first pursue federal education loans (Perkins, Stafford, PLUS). Avoid private loans at all costs.

16. Never put tuition on a credit card. The debt is more expensive than ever given recent changes to interest rates and other fees some card issuers are now charging.

17. Try not to take money from a retirement account or 401(k) to pay for college. In addition to likely early distribution penalties and additional income taxes, the higher income will reduce your aid eligibility.

PAYING LESS FOR COLLEGE

18. Attend a community college for two years and transfer to a pricier school to complete the degree. Plan ahead: be sure the college you plan to transfer to will accept the community college credits.

19. Look into "cooperative education" programs. Over 900 colleges allow students to combine college education with a job. It can take longer to complete a degree this way, but graduates generally owe less in student loans and have a better chance of getting hired.

20. Take as many Advanced Placement (AP) courses as possible and get high scores on AP Exams. Many colleges award course credits for high AP scores. Some students have cut a year off their college tuition this way.

21. Earn college credit via "dual enrollment" programs available at some high schools. These allow students to take college-level courses during their senior year.

22. Earn college credits by taking CLEP (College-Level Examination Program) exams. Depending on the college, a qualifying score on any of the 33 CLEP exams can earn students 3 to 12 college credits.

23. Stick to your major. Changing colleges can result in lost credits. Aid may be limited/not available for transfer students at some schools. Changing majors can mean paying for extra courses to meet requirements.

24. Finish college in three years if possible. Take the maximum number of credits every semester, attend summer sessions, and earn credits via online courses. Some colleges offer three-year programs for high-achieving students.

25. Let Uncle Sam pay for your degree. ROTC (Reserve Officer Training Corps) programs available from U.S. Armed Forces branches (except the Coast Guard) offer merit-based scholarships up to full tuition via participating colleges in exchange for military service after you graduate.

26. Better yet: attend a tuition-free college!

Part 2

7 Essential Tips for Writing Your College Essay

Most selective colleges require you to submit an essay or personal statement. It may sound daunting to represent your best self in only a few hundred words, and it will certainly take a substantial amount of work. But it's also a unique opportunity that can make a big difference at decision time. Admissions committees put the most weight on your high school grades and your test scores. However, colleges receive applications from many worthy students and use your essay (along with your letters of recommendation and extracurricular activities) to find out what sets you apart from the other talented candidates.

1. What Sets You Apart?

Your background, interests, and personality combine to make you more than just a GPA and a standardized test score. The best way to tell your story is to write a personal, thoughtful essay about something that has meaning for you. If you're honest and genuine, your unique qualities will shine through.

2. Sound Like Yourself!

Admissions counselors have to read an unbelievable number of essays. Many students try to sound smart rather than sounding like themselves. Others write about a subject they don't care about, but that they think will impress admissions departments. Don't write about the same subjects as every other applicant. You don't need to have started a company or discovered a lost Mayan temple. Colleges are simply looking for thoughtful, motivated students who will add something to first-year students.

3. Write About Something That's Important to You.

It could be an experience, a person, a book—anything that has had an impact on your life. Don't just recount—reflect! Anyone can write about how they won the big game or the time they spent in Rome. Describe what you learned from the experience and how it changed you.

4. Be Consistent and Avoid Redundancies.

What you write in your application essay or personal statement should not contradict any other part of your application, nor should it repeat it. This isn't the place to list your awards or discuss your grades or test scores. Answer the question being asked. Don't reuse an answer to a similar question from another application.

5. Use Humor with Caution!

Being funny is a challenge. A student who can make an admissions officer laugh never gets lost in the shuffle. But beware: what you think is funny and what an adult working in a college thinks is funny might be very different. We caution against one-liners, limericks, and anything off-color.

6. Start Early and Write Several Drafts.

Set the essay aside for a few days and read it again. Put yourself in the shoes of an admissions counselor: Is the essay interesting? Do the ideas flow logically? Does it reveal something about the applicant? Is it written in the applicant's own voice?

7. Ask for Feedback!

Have at least one other person edit your essay—a teacher or college counselor is best. And before you send it off, triple check to make sure your essay is free of spelling and grammar errors. We recommend asking a second person to proofread your essay, as spellcheck and grammar software won't pick up every typo. It can be tricky to spot mistakes in your own work, especially after you've spent so much time writing and rewriting.

Feel free to check out our book *Complete Guide to College Essays*.

Part 3

The Right
College
for You

By The Staff of The Princeton Review

COMMON MISTAKES TO AVOID WHILE CHOOSING A COLLEGE

The college admissions process may seem like a minefield of advice. College counselors, parents, teachers, friends, and even representatives of the colleges themselves all have admonishments to "be sure to…" and "don't ever…." Unfortunately, these tidbits, while intended to be helpful, can often contradict one another, giving students a picture of the process that looks more like a booby-trapped labyrinth than a map of a clear and straightforward path to success. In order to avoid adding to the confusion of the college selection process, here are just a few very important mistakes to avoid.

Get Started Now!

The biggest pitfall is probably the most obvious. Don't procrastinate! Getting started can be difficult, and there are plenty of places where you can get hung up or feel overwhelmed. Procrastinating can create undue stress and probably won't allow enough time to visit a campus so that you can get the most out of each college visit. And of course, there is also the ultra-last-minute procrastination of the applications themselves, which can cause you to make careless errors that could jeopardize your admissions chances. The bottom line here is that being prepared in advance for each step of the process can make the whole college admissions timeline much more manageable.

You have to take this process seriously. Which school you end up attending is the biggest factor that will shape your college experience, but many students don't put that much time or effort into this consideration. Don't make a decision without spending time researching colleges and finding out what you want. Because students don't often invest much time in exploring their options for different colleges, they can fall into the trap of assuming the best colleges are the most familiar ones. If you don't spend enough time thinking about the kind of person you are so that you can come up with a more appropriate "fit" instead of just getting in to some "brand name" institution, then you may not be able to realize your full potential, or you may just end up switching colleges after the first year because the experience wasn't what you dreamed it would be.

Schedule a College Visit

Part of taking this process seriously and doing your research properly is visiting as many colleges as you can. Often students and parents put this off, thinking it's either a waste of time or too expensive, but visiting at least a few schools is almost always worth it. Nothing can give you as much information about how a school "feels" and how you'll feel at it as actually walking around campus and getting a sense of its atmosphere. If you have the time and ability, visiting multiple schools early in your application process can help you narrow down which schools to apply to. If your candidate schools aren't local or you have limited means, it can be helpful to wait until you've received acceptances and weighed aid offers, and visit only your top two or three schools to aid in your final decision. We have multiple strategies and tips about planning an effective college visit in Part 3.

DOs	DON'Ts
Do it early, as soon as possible, or right now.	Don't procrastinate.
Do consider many schools you haven't heard of.	Don't choose a school based on name recognition alone.
Do listen to professional advice.	Don't neglect school visits.
Do it yourself!	Don't let your parents make all the decisions.
Do your research.	Don't let a school's "sticker price" scare you.

WOULD YOU RATHER?

Now that you know some of the key factors and some of the mistakes to avoid, it's time to really start figuring out what you want from colleges. Read through each question and write down your answer without thinking about it. You might be surprised what you learn about your college expectations.

Would you prefer a school that…

- is big (10,000+ undergrads), medium (4,000–10,000 undergrads), or small (fewer than 4,000 undergrads)?

- is close to home, or as far away as you can get?

- requires you to live on campus, or off?

- has an ivy-covered campus, or looks modern?

- has a set, structured list of academic requirements, or grants total academic freedom for all four years?

- is in a city, the suburbs, or a cornfield?

- is warm and sunny 340 days a year, or cold and snowy from October to April?

- has many of your high school friends as students, or is full of total strangers?

- has plenty of fraternities and sororities, or no Greek scene at all?

- has a dry campus, has somewhat of a social atmosphere, or is a party school?

- has 400 students in lecture classes, or six kids in a small class?

- is populated with liberal hipsters, or young Republicans?

- has professors who will know your name, or will refer to you by your social security number (in paperwork, since they probably won't call on you in their large classes)?

- has mostly students who live on campus all four years, or is mainly a "suitcase" school where people travel to and from campus?

- assigns lots of homework and readings, or hardly any of the same?

- is bureaucracy central, or a well-oiled machine?

- has a politically active student body, or one that never reads a newspaper?

- has tons of things to do off campus, or where the school itself is the center of all fun activities within a 20-mile radius?

- has a diverse student body, or has a fairly uniform student body?

- is very accepting of gay students, or has a "don't ask/don't tell" policy?

- is a "jock" school, or is full of students who rarely participate in sports?

- enrolls mainly pre-professional students, or kids who will "figure it out after we graduate"?

- sends almost every junior abroad for a semester or year, or where everyone stays on campus all four years?

- doesn't consider environmental issues as a top priority, or recycles everything possible?

There you have it: a few ideas about how to start your search for the college that will fit your needs.